A-Z CHELTENHAM &

C000150183

CONTENT

Key to Map Pages	2-3	Index	
Large Scale Centres	4 & 5	Village	
Map Pages	6-56	Selected Places of Interest	

REFERENCE

Motorway	**M5**	Car Park (Selected)	P
A Road	A38	Church or Chapel	†
Under Construction		Cycleway	
B Road	B4073	Fire Station	■
Dual Carriageway		Hospital	H
One-way Street	→	House Numbers Selected roads	13 8 3
Traffic flow on A Roads is also indicated by a heavy line on the driver's left.	→	Information Centre	i
Restricted Access		National Grid Reference	387
Pedestrianized Road		Park & Ride	Javelin P+
Track / Footpath		Police Station	▲
Residential Walkway		Post Office	★
		Toilet	▽
		with facilities for the Disabled	▽
Railway Level Crossing Station Tunnel Heritage Station		Viewpoint	☀
Built-up Area	BATH ST.	Educational Establishment	
		Hospital or Health Centre	
Local Authority Boundary	–·–·–	Industrial Building	
Posttown Boundary		Leisure or Recreational Facility	
Postcode Boundary within Posttown		Place of Interest	
		Public Building	
Map Continuation **28**	Large Scale Page **4**	Shopping Centre & Market	
		Other Selected Buildings	

SCALE

Map Pages 6-56	Map Pages 4 & 5
1:15840 4 inches (10.16 cm) to 1 mile, 6.31 cm to 1 km	1:7920 8 inches (20.32 cm) to 1 mile, 12.63 cm to 1 km
0 ¼ ½ Mile	0 ⅛ ¼ Mile
0 250 500 750 Metres	0 100 200 300 400 Metres

Copyright of Geographers' A-Z Map Company Limited

Fairfield Road, Borough Green, Sevenoaks, Kent TN15 8PP
Telephone: 01732 781000 (Enquiries & Trade Sales)
          01732 783422 (Retail Sales)

www.a-zmaps.co.uk

Copyright © Geographers' A-Z Map Co. Ltd.

OS Ordnance Survey® This product includes mapping data licensed from Ordnance Survey® with the permission of the Controller of Her Majesty's Stationery Office.

© Crown Copyright 2003. All rights reserved. Licence number 100017302

Edition 3 2003   Edition 3B 2006 (Part revision)

Every possible care has been taken to ensure that, to the best of our knowledge, the information contained in this atlas is accurate at the date of publication. However, we cannot warrant that our work is entirely error free and whilst we would be grateful to learn of any inaccuracies, we do not accept any responsibility for loss or damage resulting from reliance on information contained in this publication.

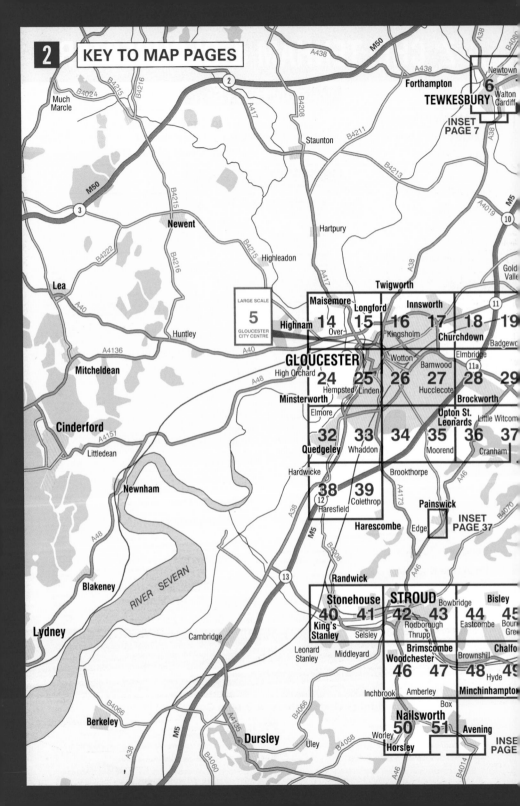

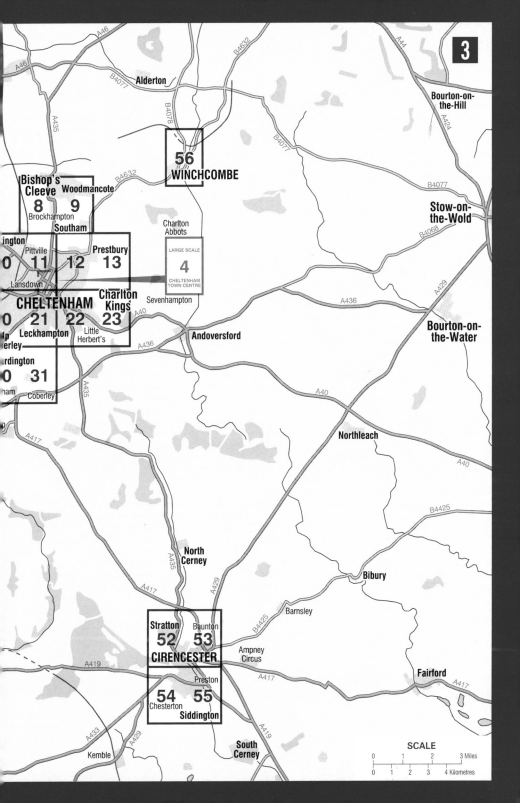

3

A46

A46

B4077

Alderton

B4077

A435

B4078

B4632

B4077

Bourton-on-the-Hill

A44

A424

A435

Bishop's Cleeve **Woodmancote**

B4632

8 **9**

Brockhampton

Southam

Charlton Abbots

Stow-on-the-Wold

B4068

ington

Pittville

Prestbury

B4077

A429

0 **11** **12** **13**

Lansdown

LARGE SCALE

4

CHELTENHAM TOWN CENTRE

Sevenhampton

A436

CHELTENHAM

Charlton Kings

Bourton-on-the-Water

0 **21** **22** **23**

A40

Leckhampton

Little Herbert's

A436

Andoversford

erley

rdington

A436

A40

0 **31**

A435

A40

Northleach

ham

Coberley

A417

A40

B4425

B4425

North Cerney

Bibury

A435

A429

Barnsley

Stratton **Baunton**

B4425

52 **53**

CIRENCESTER

Ampney Circus

Fairford

A419

Preston

A417

A417

54 **55**

Chesterton **Siddington**

A419

A433

A429

South Cerney

Kemble

SCALE

0   1   2   3 Miles

0 1 2 3   4 Kilometres

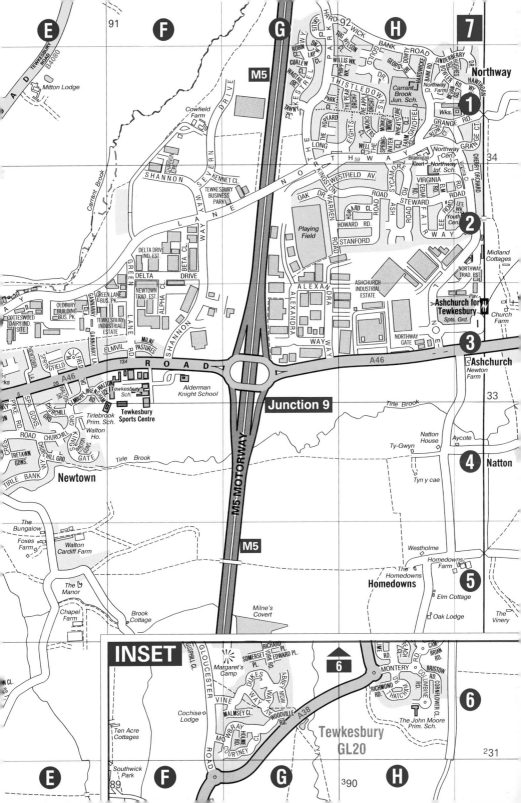

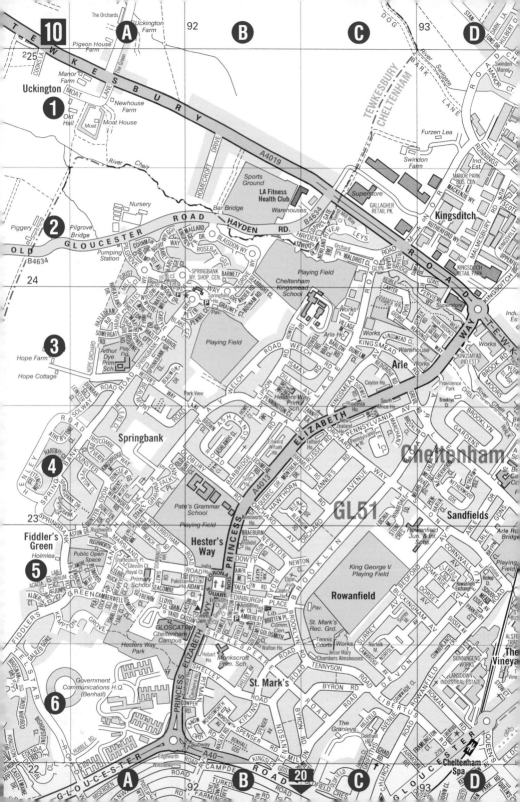

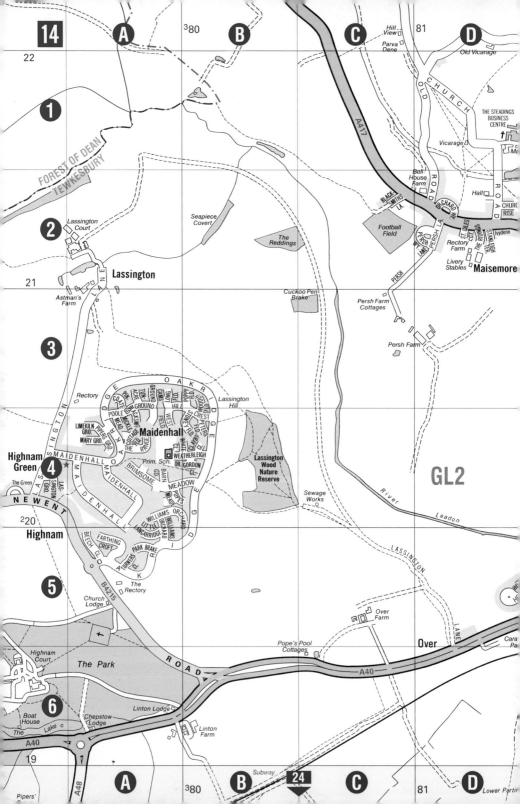

22

A   380   B   C   81   D

1

FOREST OF DEAN
TEWKESBURY

Hill View
Parva Dene
Old Vicarage

OLD CHURCH ROAD

THE STEADINGS BUSINESS CENTRE

Vicarage

2

Lassington Court

Lassington

Astman's Farm

Seapiece Covert

The Reddings

Bell House Farm

Football Field

BLACKSMITHS LA.

ORCHARD

Hall

ST. GILES

Rectory Farm

Livery Stables

Maisemore

PERSH

PERSH LA.

21

Cuckoo Pen Brake

Persh Farm Cottages

Persh Farm

3

LASSINGTON LANE

Rectory

Lassington Hill

OAKRIDGE

Maidenhall

Lassington Wood Nature Reserve

GL2

Highnam Green

4

MAIDENHALL

LAS-SINGTON GRO.

Prim. Sch.

DR. GORDON CL.

WEATHERLEIGH

MEADOW

Sewage Works

River Leadon

NEWENT

220

Highnam

WILLIAMS
LITTLE
LANGARRIDGE

ORCHARD

BRIMSOME

FARTHING CROFT

BEECH

PARK BRAKE

TURNERS

LASSINGTON LANE

5

B4215

Church Lodge

The Rectory

Over Farm

Over

CARA PA

The Green

Highnam Court

The Park

ROAD

Pope's Pool Cottages

A40

6

Boat House

The Lake

Chepstow Lodge

Linton Lodge

Linton Farm

19

A40

A48

A   380   B   C   81   D

Subway

Pipers'

Lower Partir

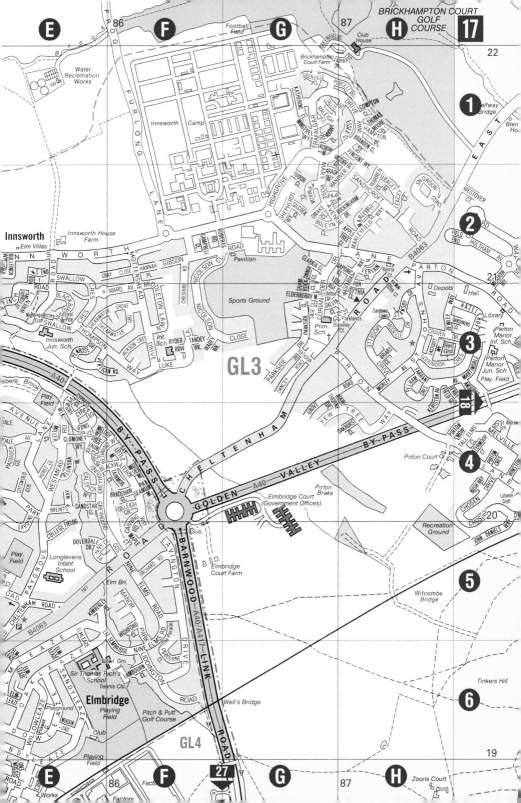

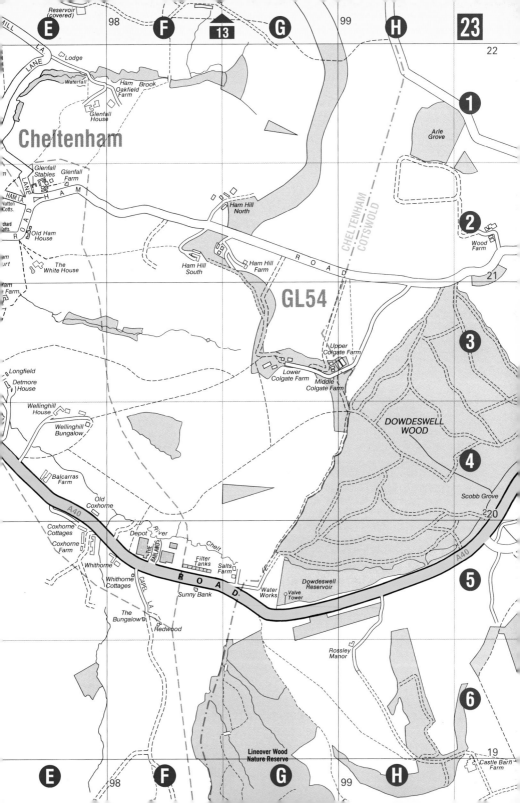

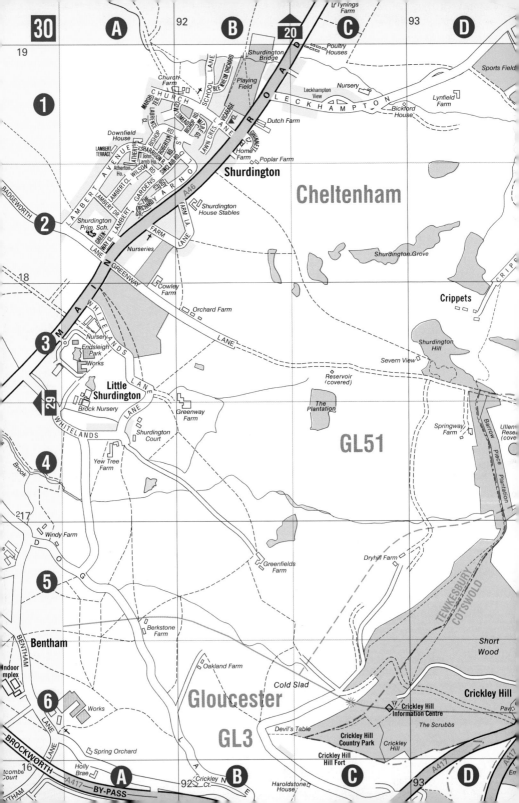

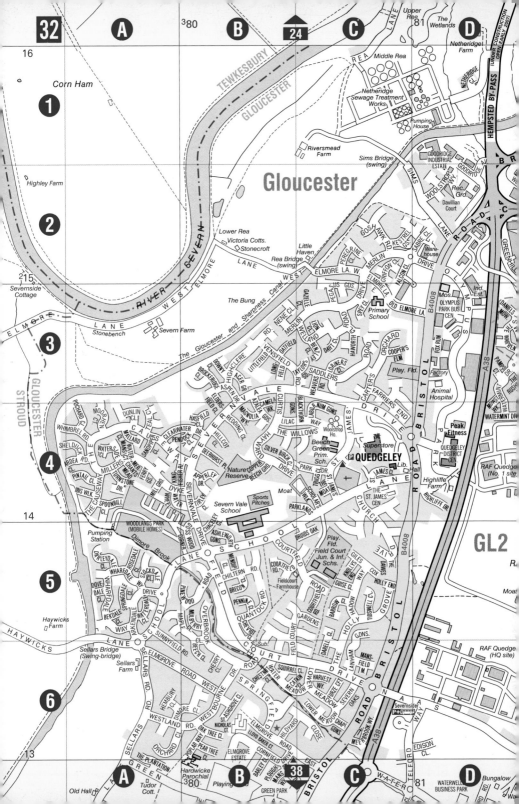

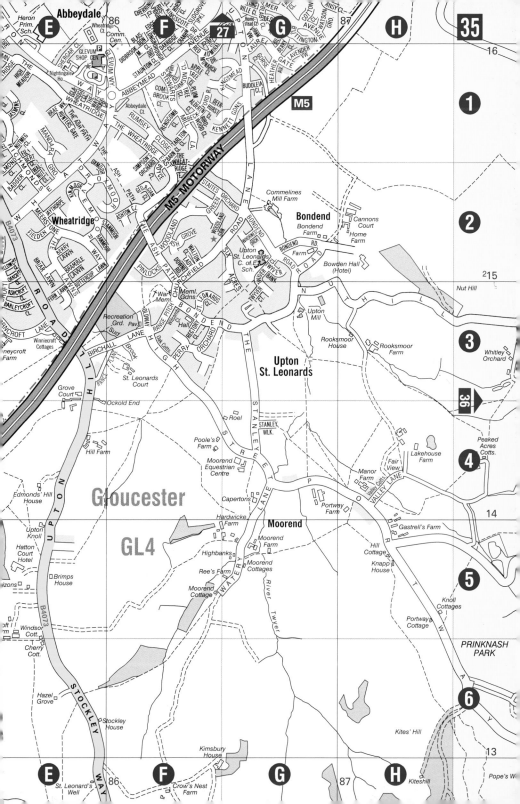

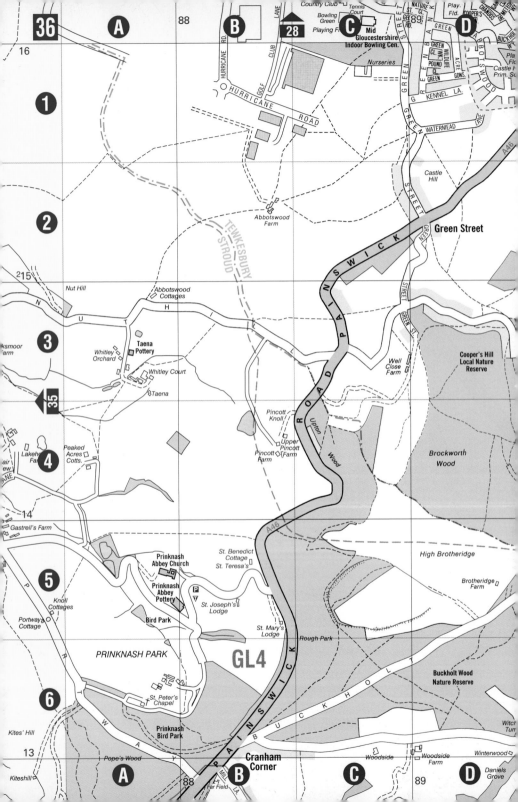

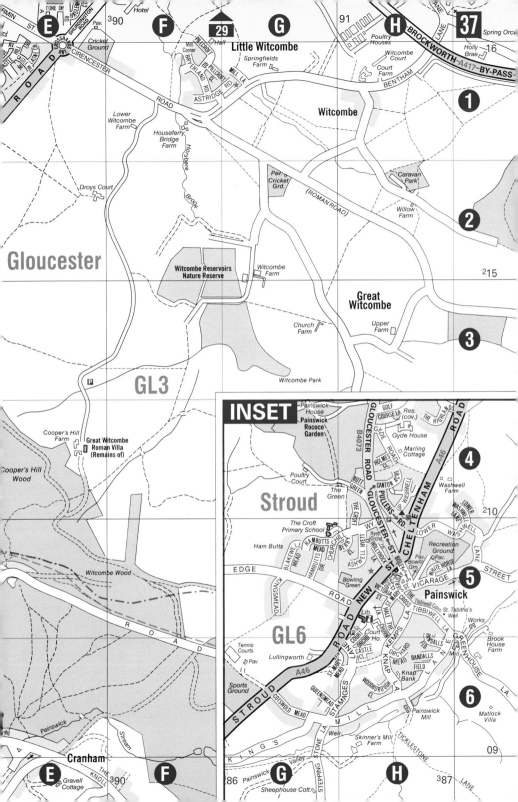

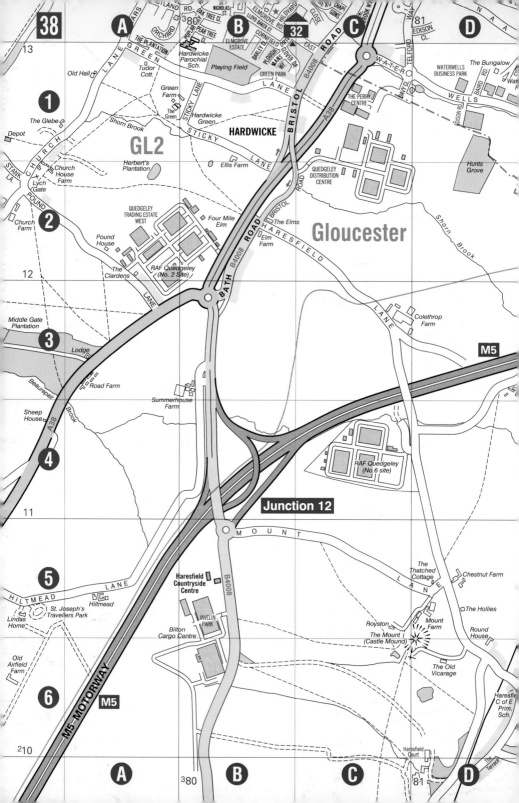

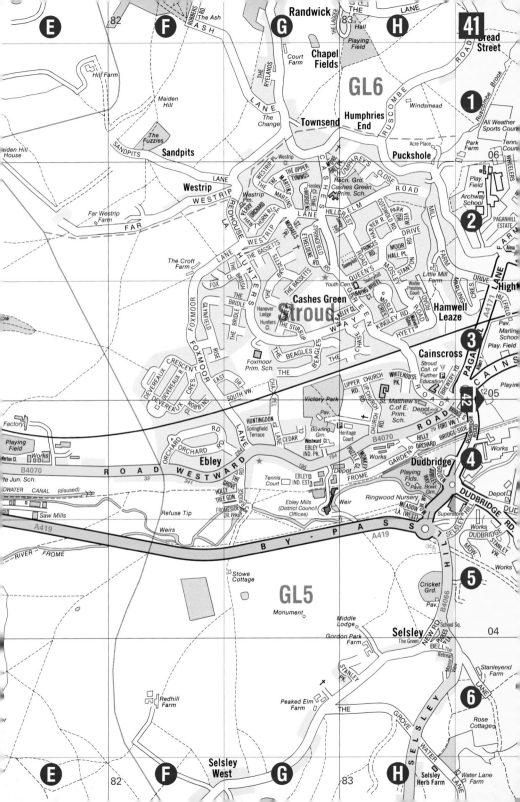

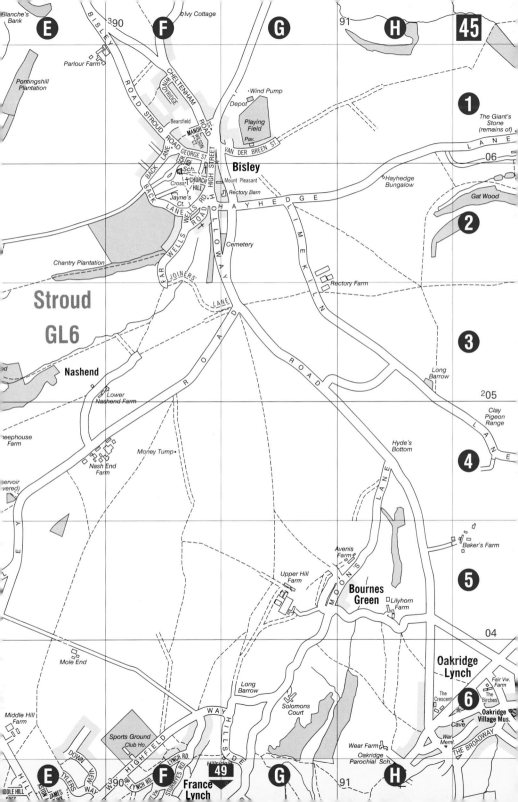

Blanche's Bank

E

BISLEY ROAD
390

F

Ivy Cottage

G

91

H

Parlour Farm

Pontinghill Plantation

CHELTENHAM
OXBRIDGE
ST
ROAD STROUD

Bearsfield

MANOR
NELSON
ST
George St
BACK LANE
HIGH STREET
Sch.
CROSS
CHURCH HILL
Jayne's Ct.
BACK LANE
WELLS ROAD
FAR WELLS ROAD
JOINERS'
LANE

Depot

Wind Pump

PLAYING FIELD
Pav.

VAN DER BREEN ST

Bisley

Mount Pleasant
Rectory Barn

HAYHEDGE

Hayhedge Bungalow

LIMEKILN

1

The Giant's Stone (remains of)

06

Gat Wood

2

Chantry Plantation

Cemetery

Rectory Farm

HOLLOWAY

ROAD

**Stroud
GL6**

Nashend

Lower Nashend Farm

ROAD

Long Barrow

3

LANE

205

Clay Pigeon Range

Sheephouse Farm

Nash End Farm

Money Tump

Hyde's Bottom

4

E

Reservoir (covered)

MOONS LANE

Baker's Farm

Avenis Farm

Upper Hill Farm

Bournes Green

Lilyhorn Farm

5

04

Mole End

Long Barrow

Solomons Court

WAY HILLSIDE

Oakridge Lynch

Fair Vw. Farm
The Birches

The Crescent

6

Cave
War Meml.

Oakridge Village Mus.

THE BROADWAY

Middle Hill Farm

Sports Ground
Club Ho.

HIGHFIELD

Wear Farm

Oakridge Parochial Sch.

DOWN VIEW WAY
TYLERS
JAMES LANK
MIDDLE HILL EDGE

E

390

STUDENTS RD
LYNCH RD
LYNCH RD

F

France Lynch

49

G

91

H

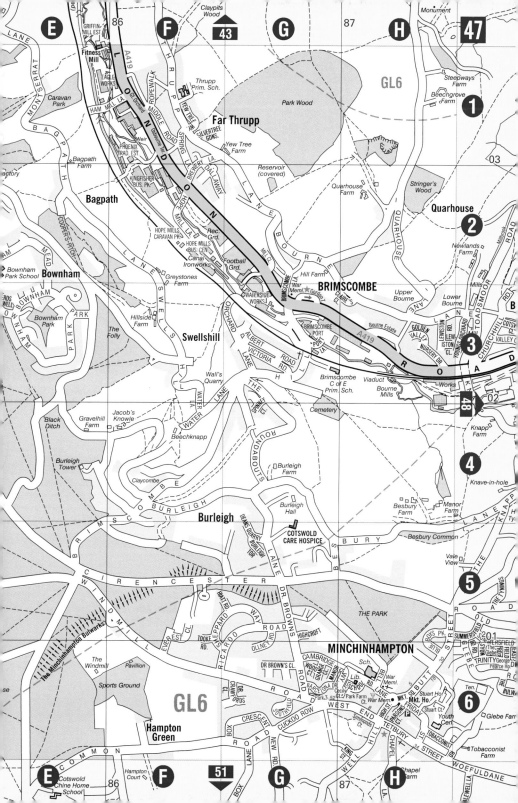

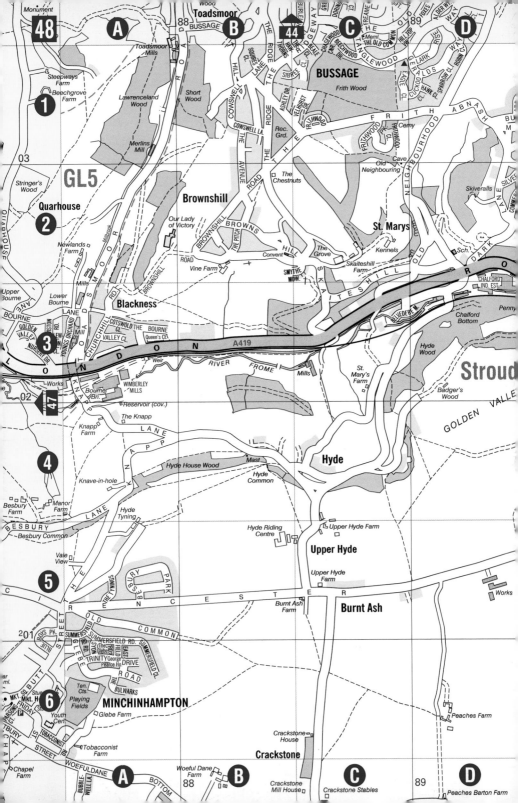

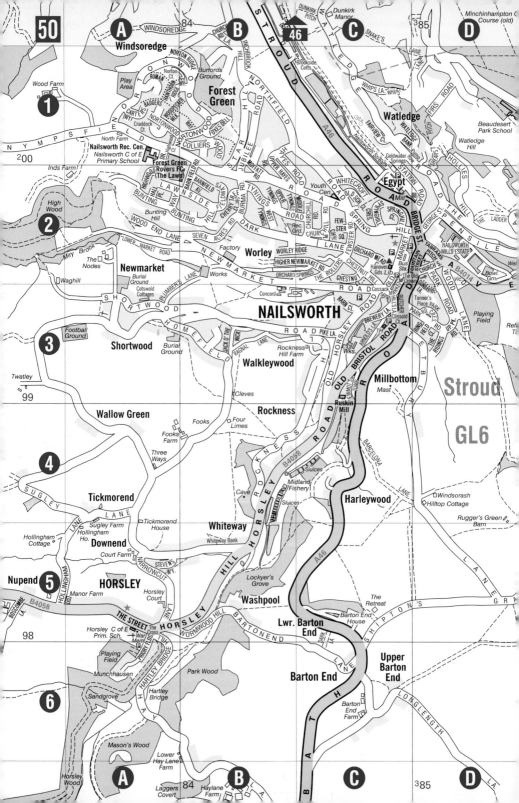

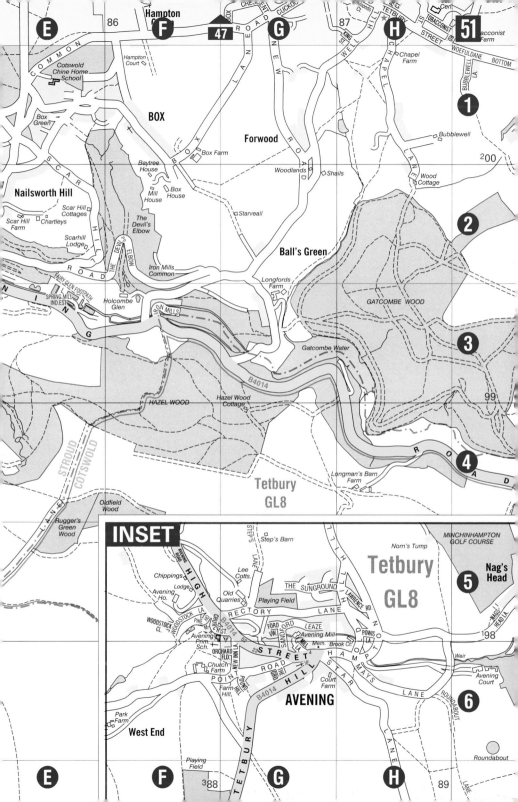

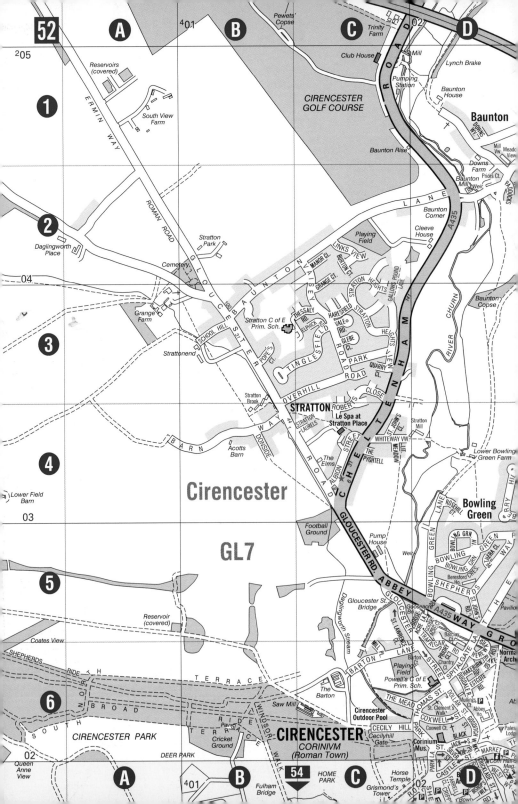

E 03 **F** Eldon Wood **G** **H** Plantation Strip **53** Wiggold

Exhibition Barn

205 Wiggold Farm

Lower Wiggold House

1

Raggedhedge Covert

Field Barn Cottage

Wiggold Cottages

New Plantation

2

Coronation Cover

04

Shooters Hill

ROMAN ROAD

FOSSE WAY

A429

Rats Castle

3

Fosse Cottage

Whiteway Farm

Dentice Bushes

Preston Field Barn

Yellow School Copse

A417

Whitelands Wood

WHITE WAY

WHITEWAY

57

Galley Hill

4

HARE BUSHES

A417

ROMAN ROAD

B4425

STREET

03

Whiteway Court

Stow Lodge

AKEMAN

Hunters Care Centre

Kennels

CHERRYTREE

ROMAN ROAD

5 Lower Norcote Cottage

Pav

Cricket Ground

Depot

Elm Tree Cottage

Norcote

FOSSE WAY

A429 ROMAN ROAD

BURFORD

LONDON ROAD

LANE

Norcote Barn

Norcote Workshops

Norcote House

6

Norcote Cottages

02

A417

KINGSHILL LANE

cester Roman Town Wall

L A N E

CORINIUM

Hill Ho.

Paget Ho.

Smythe Ho.

Orchard Ho.

market

WATERLOO

ST.

Newcombe

Arnolds Way

FOSSE

Beech Grove Court

31

19 58

WHITELANDS RD.

BEECH

GROV

QUEEN

THE GREEN

CHURCHSIDE

ST. MARY'S RD.

UPPER CHURCHILL

ARCH

CHURCHILL RD.

240

SAXON RD.

ABBOTS RD.

BLUE QUARR

PHEASANT

PARTRIDGE WAY

CENTURY

MILLBROOK

AKEMAN

PARK

BRIDGE WAY

Cirencester Kingshill School

The Beeches

55

E **F** 03 **G** 04 **H**

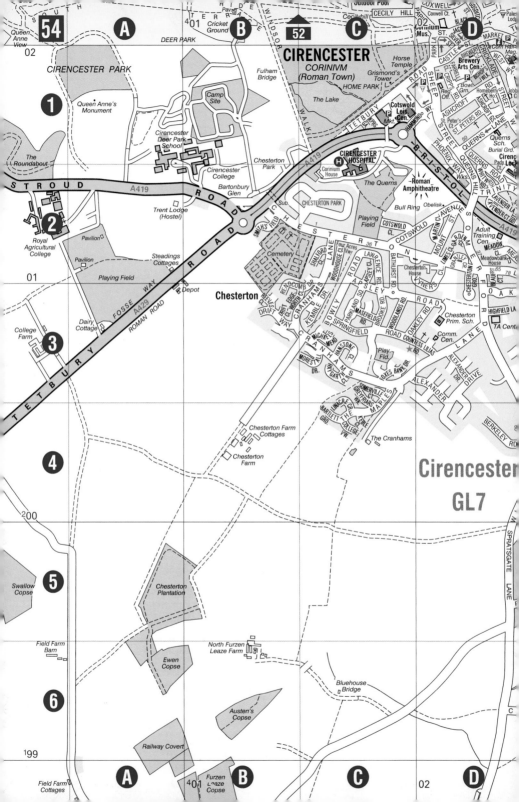

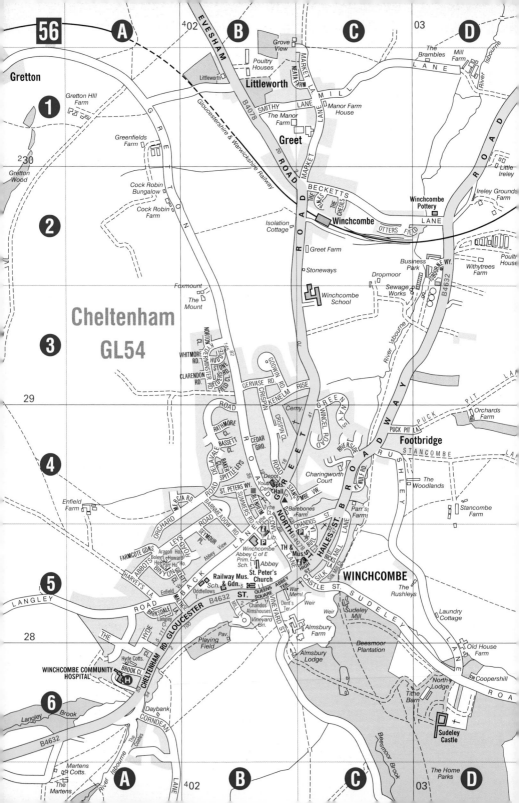

INDEX

Including Streets, Places & Areas, Hospitals & Hospices, Industrial Estates,
Selected Flats & Walkways, Junction Names, Stations and Selected Places of Interest.

HOW TO USE THIS INDEX

1. Each street name is followed by its Postcode and then by its Locality abbreviation(s) and then by its map reference; e.g. **Abbeymead Av.** GL4: A'md . . . .4E **27** is in the GL4 Postcode and the Abbeymead Locality and is to be found in square 4E on page **27**. The page number is shown in bold type.

2. A strict alphabetical order is followed in which Av., Rd., St., etc. (though abbreviated) are read in full and as part of the street name; e.g. **Ash Cl.** appears after **Ashchurch Rd.** but before **Ashcot M.**

3. Streets and a selection of flats and walkways too small to be shown on the maps, appear in the index with the thoroughfare to which it is connected shown in brackets; e.g. **Albany Ho.** GL50: Chelt . . . .1E **21** (off Lansdown Rd.)

4. Addresses that are in more than one part are referred to as not continuous.

5. Places and areas are shown in the index in BLUE TYPE and the map reference is to the actual map square in which the town centre or area is located and not to the place name shown on the map; e.g. **BATTLEDOWN**. . . .6B **12**

6. An example of a selected place of interest is Cheltenham Racecourse Mus. 1H **11**

7. Junction names are shown in the index in **BOLD CAPITAL TYPE**; e.g. **CROSSHANDS RDBT.** 1E **37**

8. An example of a station is Ashchurch for Tewkesbury Station (Rail) 3H **7**

9. An example of a hospital or hospice is CHELTENHAM AND GLOUCESTER NUFFIELD HOSPITAL 2H **19**

10. Map references for entries that appear on large scale pages **4-5** are shown first, with small scale map references shown in brackets; eg. **Academy, The.** GL50: Chelt 1B **4** (5G **11**)

GENERAL ABBREVIATIONS

All. : Alley	**Cott.** : Cottage	**Ind.** : Industrial	**Ri.** : Rise
App. : Approach	**Cotts.** : Cottages	**Info.** : Information	**Rd.** : Road
Arc. : Arcade	**Ct.** : Court	**La.** : Lane	**Rdbt.** : Roundabout
Av. : Avenue	**Cres.** : Crescent	**Lit.** : Little	**Shop.** : Shopping
Bk. : Back	**Cft.** : Croft	**Lwr.** : Lower	**Sth.** : South
Bri. : Bridge	**Dr.** : Drive	**Mnr.** : Manor	**Sq.** : Square
Bldg. : Building	**E.** : East	**Mkt.** : Market	**St.** : Street
Bldgs. : Buildings	**Est.** : Estate	**Mdw.** : Meadow	**Ter.** : Terrace
Bungs. : Bungalows	**Fld.** : Field	**M.** : Mews	**Twr.** : Tower
Bus. : Business	**Flds.** : Fields	**Mt.** : Mount	**Trad.** : Trading
Cvn. : Caravan	**Gdn.** : Garden	**Mus.** : Museum	**Up.** : Upper
C'way. : Causeway	**Gdns.** : Gardens	**Nth.** : North	**Va.** : Vale
Cen. : Centre	**Ga.** : Gate	**Pde.** : Parade	**Vw.** : View
Chu. : Church	**Gt.** : Great	**Pk.** : Park	**Vs.** : Villas
Cir. : Circus	**Grn.** : Green	**Pas.** : Passage	**Vis.** : Visitors
Cl. : Close	**Gro.** : Grove	**Pl.** : Place	**Wlk.** : Walk
Comn. : Common	**Hgts.** : Heights	**Pct.** : Precinct	**W.** : West
Cnr. : Corner	**Ho.** : House	**Res.** : Residential	**Yd.** : Yard

LOCALITY ABBREVIATIONS

A'dle : **Abbeydale**	**Ciren** : **Cirencester**	**Longl** : **Longlevens**	**Sth C** : **South Cerney**
A'md : **Abbeymead**	**Cle H** : **Cleeve Hill**	**Lypiatt** : **Lypiatt**	**Stand** : **Standish**
Amb : **Amberley**	**Cranh** : **Cranham**	**Maise** : **Maisemore**	**Stav** : **Staverton**
Ashc : **Ashchurch**	**Down H** : **Down Hatherley**	**Mats** : **Matson**	**Stok O** : **Stoke Orchard**
Aven : **Avening**	**Dudb** : **Dudbridge**	**Minch** : **Minchinhampton**	**Stone** : **Stonehouse**
Badg : **Badgeworth**	**Eastc** : **Eastcombe**	**Mins** : **Minsterworth**	**Strat** : **Stratton**
Barn : **Barnwood**	**Ebley** : **Ebley**	**More V** : **Moreton Valence**	**Stro** : **Stroud**
Baun : **Baunton**	**For G** : **Forest Green**	**Nails** : **Nailsworth**	**Swin V** : **Swindon Village**
Bent : **Bentham**	**Fram M** : **Frampton Mansell**	**Norc** : **Norcote**	**Tewk** : **Tewkesbury**
Bish C : **Bishop's Cleeve**	**Fran L** : **France Lynch**	**North** : **Northway**	**Thru** : **Thrupp**
Bis : **Bisley**	**Glou** : **Gloucester**	**Oak L** : **Oakridge Lynch**	**Tuff** : **Tuffley**
Bour G : **Bournes Green**	**Greet** : **Greet**	**Over** : **Over**	**Twig** : **Twigworth**
Box : **Box**	**Hardw** : **Hardwicke**	**Pains** : **Painswick**	**Uck** : **Uckington**
Brim : **Brimscombe**	**Hares** : **Haresfield**	**P'bury** : **Prestbury**	**Ull** : **Ullenwood**
Brock : **Brockworth**	**High** : **Highnam**	**Preston** : **Preston**	**Up H** : **Up Hatherley**
Brook : **Brookthorpe**	**Hors** : **Horsley**	**Qued** : **Quedgeley**	**Up L** : **Upton St Leonards**
Brown : **Brownshill**	**Hucc** : **Hucclecote**	**Rand** : **Randwick**	**Wal C** : **Walton Cardiff**
Burl : **Burleigh**	**Inch** : **Inchbrook**	**Rodb** : **Rodborough**	**West** : **Westrip**
Buss : **Bussage**	**Inns** : **Innsworth**	**Rodb C** : **Rodborough Common**	**Whad** : **Whaddon**
Cain : **Cainscross**	**Kings** : **Kingscourt**	**Rusc** : **Ruscombe**	**White** : **Whiteshill**
Cash G : **Cashes Green**	**King S** : **King's Stanley**	**Ryef** : **Ryeford**	**Winch** : **Winchcombe**
Chalf : **Chalford**	**Leck** : **Leckhampton**	**Sand** : **Sandhurst**	**Witc** : **Witcombe**
Chalf H : **Chalford Hill**	**Leck H** : **Leckhampton Hill**	**Sels** : **Selsley**	**Woodc** : **Woodchester**
Charl K : **Charlton Kings**	**Leo S** : **Leonard Stanley**	**Shurd** : **Shurdington**	**Woodm** : **Woodmancote**
Chelt : **Cheltenham**	**Light** : **Lightpill**	**Sidd** : **Siddington**	
Chu : **Churchdown**	**Longf** : **Longford**	**South** : **Southam**	

	ABBEYDALE 1E **35**	**Abbey Ter.** GL20: Tewk 5A **6**	**Abbots Wlk.** GL20: Tewk 5B **6**
	Abbeydale Ct. GL4: A'dle 1F **35**	GL54: Winch 5B **56**	**Abbots Way** GL10: Stone 4B **40**
125 Bus. Pk. GL2: Glou 5E **5** (2F **25**)	**Abbeyholme** GL50: Chelt 6F **11**	**Abbey Vw.** GL54: Winch 5B **56**	**Abbotswood Rd.** GL3: Brock 6D **28**
	Abbey Ho. GL7: Ciren 6D **52**	**Abbey Way** GL7: Ciren 5C **52**	**Abnash Midway** GL6: Chalf H 1D **48**
	ABBEYMEAD 6G **27**	**Abbots Cl.** GL51: Chelt 4E **21**	**Acacia Cl.** GL52: P'bury 2B **12**
	Abbeymead Av.	**Abbots Leys Rd.** GL54: Winch 5A **56**	**Acacia Ct.** GL51: Chelt 5A **10**
A	GL4: A'md 4E **27**	**Abbots M.** GL52: Bish C 3D **8**	**Acacia Pk.** GL52: Bish C 1C **8**
	Abbey Mdw. GL20: Tewk. 6G **7**	**Abbots Rd.** GL4: A'md 5F **27**	**Academy, The**
Abbenesse GL6: Chalf H 1D **48**	**Abbey Pct.** GL20: Tewk 5A **6**	GL7: Ciren 1F **55**	GL50: Chelt 1B **4** (5G **11**)
Abbey Ct. GL20: Tewk 5A **6**	**Abbey Rd.** GL2: Glou 3F **25**	**Abbots Wlk.** GL20: Tewk 6B **6**	

Acanthus Ct.—Barnwood By-Pass

Acanthus Ct. GL7: Ciren 2E **55**
Acer Gro. GL2: Qued 3B **32**
Acomb Cres. GL52: Charl K 3C **22**
Acorn Ct. GL4: A'dle 1D **34**
Acre Pl. GL5: Rusc 1H **41**
Acre St. GL5: Stro 3D **42**
Addis Rd. GL51: Chelt 4E **11**
Adelaide Gdns. GL10: Stone 1B **40**
Adelaide St. GL1: Glou 4B **26**
Admiral Cl. GL51: Chelt 5A **10**
Aerodrome, The GL52: Stok O 2A **8**
Aesops Orchard GL52: Woodm . . . 2H **9**
Aggs Hill GL54: Charl K. 6E **13**
Akeman Rd. GL7: Ciren 1F **55**
Akeman St. GL7: Ciren 5H **53**
Albany GL10: Stone. 1B **40**
Albany Ho. *GL50: Chelt. 1E 21*
(off Lansdown Rd.)
Albany M. GL50: Chelt. 1F **21**
Albany Rd. GL50: Chelt. 2E **21**
Albany St. GL1: Glou. 4A **26**
(not continuous)
Albemarle Ga. GL50: Chelt 3G **11**
Albemarle Rd. GL3: Chu. 4C **18**
Albert Dr. GL52: Chelt. 3A **12**
Albert La. GL50: Chelt 4G **11**
Albert Pl. GL52: Chelt 1D **4** (5H **11**)
Albert Rd. GL5: Brim 3G **47**
GL52: Chelt 4A **12**
Albert St. GL50: Chelt. 4G **11**
Albert Ter. GL5: Stro 3A **42**
Albert Warehouse GL1: Glou. 4F **5**
Albion Ct. GL10: Stone 3C **40**
Albion Pl. GL52: Chelt 2C **4** (5H **11**)
Albion St. GL1: Glou 5F **5** (2G **25**)
GL7: Strat 4C **52**
GL52: Chelt 2C **4** (5H **11**)
Albion Ter. GL10: Stone 4B **40**
Albion Wlk.
GL50: Chelt 2B **4** (5G **11**)
Alder Cl. GL2: Longl 5D **16**
Alder Ct. GL51: Chelt 5A **10**
Aldergate St. GL10: Stone 3C **40**
Aldergate Ter. GL10: Stone. 3C **40**
Alders, The GL53: Leck. 5E **21**
Alders Grn. GL2: Longl 4C **16**
Aldershaw Cl. GL51: Up H 3A **20**
Alderton Cl. GL4: A'md 1F **35**
Alderton Rd. GL51: Chelt 1B **20**
Alder Way GL6: Buss 6D **44**
Aldridge Cl. GL50: Chelt 4F **11**
Alexander Dr. GL7: Ciren 3D **54**
Alexandra Ho. GL1: Glou 1B **26**
Alexandra Rd. GL1: Glou 6B **16**
Alexandra St. GL50: Chelt. 2E **21**
Alexandra Wlk. *GL52: Chelt 5C 12*
(off Burma Av.)
Alexandra Way GL20: Ashc 3G **7**
Alfred St. GL1: Glou 3B **26**
Alington Cl. GL1: Glou 2B **26**
Allendale Cl. GL2: Longl 5D **16**
Allen Dr. GL5: Stro 2A **42**
Allenfield Rd. GL53: Chelt. 4F **21**
(not continuous)
All Saints' Ct. *GL52: Chelt 5A 12*
(off All Saints' Rd.)
All Saints Rd. GL1: Glou. 3A **26**
GL5: Stro. 2E **43**
GL52: Chelt 6A **12**
All Saints' Ter. GL52: Chelt. 6A **12**
All Saints' Vs. Rd. GL52: Chelt. . . 6A **12**
Alma Cl. GL51: Chelt. 2C **20**
Alma Pl. GL1: Glou. 4G **25**
(not continuous)
Alma Rd. GL51: Chelt 3C **20**
Alma Ter. GL1: Glou 4G **25**
GL5: Stro. 2A **42**
Almond Cl. GL4: A'dle 2E **35**
Almond Ct. GL51: Chelt. 5A **10**
Alney Island Nature Reserve
. . . . 3E 5 (1G 25)
Alney Ter. GL1: Glou 6F **15**
Alpha Cl. GL20: Tewk 3F **7**
Alpine Cl. GL4: A'dle. 5C **26**
ALSTONE **5E 11**
Alstone Av. GL51: Chelt. 5E **11**
Alstone Ct. GL51: Chelt. 5E **11**
Alstone Cft. GL51: Chelt 5E **11**
Alstone La. GL51: Chelt 4C **10**
Alstone La. Trad. Est.
GL51: Chelt. 5D **10**
Alstone M. GL51: Chelt 5E **11**
Althorp Cl. GL4: Tuff 3E **33**
Alverton Dr. GL52: Bish C. 3D **8**
Alvin St. GL1: Glou 2H **5** (1H **25**)
Amaranth Way GL51: Up H. 4C **20**
Amber Cl. GL4: Tuff. 2F **33**
AMBERLEY. **5D 46**
Amberley Ct. GL51: Chelt 5B **10**
Amberley Rd. GL4: Mats. 6C **26**
GL51: Chelt 5B **10**
Ambrose Pl.
GL50: Chelt 2A **4** (5G **11**)
Ambrose St.
GL50: Chelt 2A **4** (5G **11**)
Amos Cl. GL50: Chelt 5F **11**
Anapa M. GL51: Chelt. 5B **10**
Anbrook Cres. GL3: Hucc 4F **27**
Anchorage, The GL2: Glou 6E **25**
Anderson Cl. GL52: Woodm 2G **9**
Anderson Dr. GL10: Stone 3C **40**
Andorra Way GL3: Chu 3A **18**
Andover Rd. GL50: Chelt. 1E **21**
(not continuous)
Andover St. GL50: Chelt . . . 6A **4** (2F **21**)
Andover Ter. GL50: Chelt. 1F **21**
Andover Wlk. GL50: Chelt 2F **21**
Andrew's Cl. GL4: Brook. 2H **39**
Angelica Way GL4: A'md 6G **27**
Anlaby Ct. GL52: Chelt 4H **11**
Ann Edwards M. *GL4: A'dle. 1E 35*
(off The Wayridge)
Anne Goodriche Cl.
GL52: P'bury. 3D **12**
Anne Hathaway Dr. GL3: Chu 4D **18**
Ansdell Dr. GL3: Brock 5D **28**
Ansell Cl. GL51: Chelt. 3C **20**
Anson Bus. Pk. GL2: Chu 1A **18**
Apollo Cinema 3D 42
Apperley Dr. GL2: Qued 4B **32**
Apple Cl. GL52: P'bury 2B **12**
Apple Orchard GL52: P'bury 2B **12**
Apple Orchard, The
GL20: North 1H **7**
Appleton Av. GL51: Chelt 3G **19**
Appleton Way GL3: Hucc 5H **27**
Apple Tree Cl. GL3: Chu 2H **17**
GL4: A'md 1F **35**
GL52: Woodm. 3H **9**
Apsley Cl. GL7: Ciren 2C **54**
Apsley Rd. GL7: Ciren. 3C **54**
Aragon Ho. GL54: Winch 5A **56**
Aragon Way GL3: Chu. 2G **17**
Archdeacon Ct.
GL1: Glou. 2F **5** (1G **25**)
Archdeacon St.
GL1: Glou. 2F **5** (1G **25**)
Archery Rd. GL7: Ciren 1F **55**
Archibald St. GL1: Glou. . . 6H **5** (3A **26**)
Archway Gdns. GL5: Stro 2A **42**
Archway Ho. GL1: Glou. 4H **25**
Ardea Cl. GL2: Qued. 4A **32**
Arden Ho. GL2: Glou 1F **33**
Arden Rd. GL53: Chelt. 4F **21**
Ardmore Cl. GL4: Tuff. 3H **33**
Argyll M. GL53: Chelt 2H **21**
Argyll Pl. GL2: Glou 1C **26**
Argyll Rd. GL2: Glou. 1C **26**
GL53: Chelt. 1A **22**
Ariel Lodge Rd. GL52: Chelt. 5A **12**
Arkendale Dr. GL2: Hardw 5A **32**
Arkle Cl. GL50: Chelt. 2F **11**
ARLE **3C 10**
Arle Av. GL51: Chelt 5E **11**
Arle Cl. GL51: Chelt. 5E **11**
Arle Ct. GL51: Chelt 2H **19**
Arle Dr. GL51: Chelt 5D **10**
Arle Gdns. GL51: Chelt 5D **10**
Arle Rd. GL51: Chelt. 4D **10**
Arlingham GL51: Up H 4B **20**
Arlingham Rd. GL4: Tuff. 1G **33**
Arlington Rd. GL20: Wal C 6D **6**
Armada Cl. GL3: Chu 2G **17**
Armscroft Ct. GL2: Glou 2D **26**
Armscroft Cres. GL2: Glou 1C **26**
Armscroft Gdns. GL2: Glou. 2C **26**
Armscroft Pl. GL2: Glou 2C **26**
Armscroft Rd. GL2: Glou. 2D **26**
Armscroft Way GL2: Glou 2C **26**
Arnold's La. GL6: Nails 3C **50**
Arnolds Way GL7: Ciren 6F **53**
Arreton Av. GL4: Glou. 5D **26**
Arrowhead Cl. GL4: Mats 1C **34**
Arrowsmith Dr. GL10: Stone. 1C **40**
Arthur Bliss Gdns.
GL50: Chelt 3E **21**
Arthur St. GL1: Glou 5H **5** (2H **25**)
Arundel Cl. GL4: Tuff. 4F **33**
Arundel Dr. GL5: Rodb 4C **42**
Arundel Ho. GL51: Chelt 5B **10**
Arundell Mill La. GL5: Stro 4D **42**
Arundel Rd. GL20: Tewk. 2D **6**
Ascot Ct. GL1: Glou. 3B **26**
Ashbed Cl. GL4: A'md 5F **27**
ASHCHURCH **3H 7**
Ashchurch for Tewkesbury Station (Rail). **3H 7**
Ashchurch Ind. Est. GL20: Ashc. . . 2H **7**
Ashchurch Rd. GL20: Tewk 4C **6**
Ash Cl. GL53: Charl K. 5D **22**
Ashcot M. GL51: Up H 4B **20**
Ashcroft Cl. GL4: Mats 3E **35**
Ashcroft Gdns. GL7: Ciren 1D **54**
Ashcroft Ho. GL5: Stro 5E **43**
Ashcroft Rd. GL7: Ciren 1D **54**
Ashfield Cl. GL52: Bish C 2F **9**
Ashfield Ho. GL50: Chelt. 6F **11**
Ashford Rd. GL50: Chelt 2F **21**
Ash Gro. GL4: Up L 2F **35**
Ashgrove GL53: Charl K 5D **22**
Ashgrove Av. GL4: Glou 5D **26**
Ashgrove Cl. GL2: Hardw 6B **32**
Ashgrove Way GL4: Glou 4D **26**
Ashlands Cl. GL51: Chelt 4B **10**
Ashlands Rd. GL51: Chelt. 4B **10**
Ash La. GL6: Rand. 1F **41**
Ashlea Mdw. GL52: Bish C 1C **8**
Ashleigh La. GL52: Cle H 4H **9**
Ashleworth Gdns. GL2: Qued 5B **32**
Ashley Cl. GL52: Charl K. 2C **22**
Ashley Dr. GL6: Brown 1B **48**
Ashley Rd. GL52: Charl K 2C **22**
Ashmead GL2: Longl. 4C **16**
Ashmore Rd. GL4: Glou 1A **34**
Ashover La. GL50: Chelt 2F **21**
Ash Path, The GL4: A'dle, Up L. . . 1E **35**
(not continuous)
Ash Rd. GL5: Light 6B **42**
GL20: North 2H **7**
Ashton Cl. GL4: A'dle. 2F **35**
Ashton Rd. GL7: Sidd 6F **55**
Ashville Ind. Est. GL2: Glou 6F **25**
Ashville Rd. GL2: Glou 6F **25**
Ashville Trad. Est.
GL51: Chelt 1E **11**
Ashwell GL6: Pains. 5H **37**
Ashwood Way GL3: Hucc 5G **27**
Askham Ct. GL52: Chelt 5A **12**
Askwith Rd. GL4: Glou 5C **26**
Aspen Dr. GL2: Qued. 3B **32**
Asquith Rd. GL53: Chelt 3H **21**
ASTON DOWN **5H 49**
Aston Gro. GL51: Chelt 5A **10**
Aston Vw. GL6: Chalf H 1E **49**
Astor Cl. GL3: Brock 5C **28**
Astridge Rd. GL3: Witc 1F **37**
Atcombe Rd. GL5: Woodc. 4A **46**
Athelney Way GL52: Chelt 1A **22**
Atherstone Cl. GL51: Chelt 4A **10**
Atherton Cl. GL51: Shurd 1A **30**
Atherton Ho. GL51: Shurd. 2A **30**
Augustine Way GL4: A'md 5G **27**
Austin Dr. GL2: Longf 3A **16**
Austin Rd. GL7: Ciren 1F **55**
Australia Ho. GL51: Chelt 6B **10**
Autumn Ri. GL4: A'dle. 1E **35**
Avebury Cl. GL4: Tuff 3E **33**
Avenall Pde. GL53: Chelt 1A **22**
(not continuous)
AVENING **6G 51**
Avening Rd. GL4: Glou 6A **26**
GL6: Aven, Nails 2D **50**
GL8: Aven 5F **51**
AVENIS GREEN **1G 49**
Avenue, The GL2: Longl. 5D **16**
GL3: Chu. 4B **18**
GL5: Woodc 2B **46**
GL6: Brown. 1B **48**
GL7: Ciren 1E **55**
GL53: Charl K 4H **21**
Avenue Ter. GL10: Stone. 3A **40**
Avon Cres. GL3: Brock 6E **29**
Avon Rd. GL52: Chelt 5B **12**
Avon Vw. GL20: Tewk 2D **6**
Awdry Way GL4: Tuff. 3G **33**
Awebridge Way GL4: Mats 1D **34**
Aycote Cl. GL4: Glou. 6C **26**
Ayland Gdns. GL1: Glou 3B **26**
Aylton Cl. GL51: Up H. 3A **20**
Aysgarth Av. GL51: Up H. 4B **20**
Azalea Dr. GL51: Up H 4C **20**
Azalea Gdns. GL2: Qued. 4B **32**

B

Bk. Albert Pl.
GL52: Chelt 1D **4** (5H **11**)
Back La. GL6: Bis 2F **45**
GL54: Winch 5B **56**
Bk. Montpellier Ter.
GL50: Chelt. 6A **4** (1F **21**)
Back of Avon GL20: Tewk 4B **6**
Back of Mt. Pleasant
GL20: Tewk. 4C **6**
Bk. Queens Retreat
GL51: Chelt 5E 11
(off Queen's Retreat)
Bacon Theatre, The. 1C 20
BADBROOK **2D 42**
Bader Av. GL3: Chu. 4B **18**
Badger Cl. GL4: A'dle 2E **35**
Badgers Way GL6: For G. 1A **50**
Badger Va. Ct. GL2: Glou 6F **25**
BADGEWORTH **6F 19**
Badgeworth La. GL51: Badg. 6G **19**
Badgeworth Rd.
GL51: Badg, Chelt 4F **19**
Badminton Cl. GL53: Chelt 3G **21**
Badminton Rd. GL4: Mats. 6C **26**
BAFFORD **4B 22**
Bafford App. GL53: Charl K. 5A **22**
Bafford Gro. GL53: Charl K 5A **22**
Bafford La. GL53: Charl K. 4B **22**
BAGPATH **2E 47**
Bagpath La. GL5: Rodb C 1E **47**
Baird Rd. GL2: Qued. 1D **38**
Bakehouse La. GL50: Chelt. 2E **21**
Baker Ct. *GL20: Tewk 3C 6*
(off Hollams Rd.)
Baker St. GL2: Glou 6E **5** (3G **25**)
GL51: Chelt 4F **11**
Bala Rd. GL51: Chelt. 3C **20**
Balcarras GL53: Charl K 4D **22**
Balcarras Gdns. GL53: Charl K. . . 4D **22**
Balcarras Retreat
GL53: Charl K 4D **22**
Balcarras Rd. GL53: Charl K. 4D **22**
Balfour Rd. GL1: Glou. 4G **25**
Ballinode Cl. GL50: Chelt 2E **11**
Ballinska M. GL2: Longl 4E **17**
BALL'S GREEN **2G 51**
Balmoral Ct. GL53: Chelt 3A **22**
Bamfurlong La.
GL51: Stav, Chelt 1D **18**
(not continuous)
Baneberry Rd. GL4: Glou 6B **26**
Banebury Ct. GL4: Glou 1B **34**
Bank, The GL52: P'bury 3D **12**
Bank All. GL20: Tewk 4B **6**
Banyard Cl. GL51: Chelt 5A **10**
Baptist Cl. GL4: A'md 5G **27**
Barberry Cl. GL50: Chelt. 3E **21**
Barbican Rd. GL1: Glou . . . 4F **5** (1G **25**)
Barbican Way
GL1: Glou. 3F **5** (1G **25**)
Barbridge Rd. GL51: Chelt 4B **10**
Barcelona Dr. GL6: Minch 6G **47**
Barcelona La. GL6: Nails 4C **50**
Barclay Ct. GL7: Ciren 5D **52**
Barker's Leys GL52: Bish C. 1F **9**
Barksdale GL54: Winch. 5A **56**
Barlands, The GL52: Charl K. 5F **23**
Barley Cl. GL2: Hardw 1B **38**
GL51: Chelt 2A **10**
Barleycroft Cl. GL4: Mats 3E **35**
Barlow Cl. GL10: Stone. 3B **40**
Barlow Rd. GL51: Chelt. 3C **10**
Barnaby Cl. GL1: Glou 4A **26**
Barnacre Dr. GL3: Hucc 2G **27**
Barn Cl. GL4: A'dle 1F **35**
GL6: Nails 3C **50**
Barnes Wallis Way GL3: Chu 4B **18**
Barnett Cl. GL51: Chelt 2B **10**
Barnett Way GL4: Barn 2E **27**
Barnfields GL4: Glou. 6A **26**
Barn Ground GL2: High. 4A **14**
Barnhay GL3: Chu 5B **18**
Barnmeadow Rd. GL54: Winch. . . 4B **56**
Barnsfield Av. GL6: For G 2B **50**
Barnsfield Rd. GL6: For G. 2B **50**
Barn Way GL7: Strat 4B **52**
BARNWOOD **2E 27**
Barnwood Av. GL4: Barn 3E **27**
Barnwood Bus. Cen.
GL4: Barn 2E **27**
Barnwood By-Pass GL3: Hucc . . . 2G **27**

58 A-Z Cheltenham & Gloucester

Barnwood Link Rd.—Bredon Wlk.

Barnwood Link Rd.
GL3: Barn, Longl 5F **17**
Barnwood Rd. GL2: Barn, Glou . . . 1C **26**
GL3: Hucc 3F **27**
GL4: Barn, Hucc 2E **27**
Barrack Sq. GL1: Glou 3E **5** (1G **25**)
Barratts Mill La.
GL50: Chelt 4C **4** (6H **11**)
Barrett Ind. Est. GL1: Glou 5G **15**
Barrington Av. GL51: Chelt 2G **19**
Barrington Dr. GL3: Hucc 3G **27**
Barrington M. GL51: Chelt 2G **19**
Barrow Cl. GL2: Qued 5C **32**
Barrowfield Rd. GL5: Stro 1B **42**
Barrow Hill GL3: Chu 6C **18**
BARTON **2A 26**
Barton Cl. GL53: Charl K 5B **22**
Barton Ct. GL7: Ciren 6D **52**
GL20: Tewk 4C **6**
BARTON END **6C 50**
Bartonend La. GL6: Hors 5B **50**
Barton La. GL7: Ciren 6C **52**
Barton M. GL20: Tewk 4C **6**
Barton Rd. GL20: Tewk 4C **6**
Barton St. GL1: Glou 2A **26**
GL20: Tewk 4B **6**
Barton Way GL51: Up H 3B **20**
Barwick Rd. GL51: Up H 4C **20**
Base La. GL2: Sand 1G **15**
Basil Cl. GL4: A'dle 1E **35**
Bassett Cl. GL54: Winch 4B **56**
Bassetts, The GL5: Cash G 3G **41**
Bateman Cl. GL4: Tuff 4G **33**
Bathleaze GL10: King S 6D **40**
Bath M. GL53: Chelt 5C **4** (1H **21**)
Bath Pde. GL53: Chelt 4C **4** (6H **11**)
Bath Rd. GL2: Hardw 3B **38**
GL5: Inch, Woodc 1B **46**
GL5: Light, Stro, Rodb 5B **42**
GL6: Hors, Nails 6C **50**
GL10: King S, Leo S 6A **40**
GL10: Stone 3C **40**
GL53: Chelt 6B **4** (2G **21**)
Bath Rd. Trad. Est. GL5: Light . . . 5A **42**
Bath St. GL5: Stro 3D **42**
GL50: Chelt 4C **4** (6H **11**)
Bath Ter. GL50: Chelt 2G **21**
Bathurst Rd. GL1: Glou 5A **26**
GL7: Ciren 2C **54**
Bathville M.
GL53: Chelt 6B **4** (1G **21**)
BATTLEDOWN **6B 12**
Battledown App.
GL52: Charl K 1B **22**
Battledown Cl. GL52: Charl K 6B **12**
Battledown Dr. GL52: Charl K 1B **22**
Battledown Grange
GL52: Charl K 1B **22**
Battledown Mead
GL52: Charl K 6B **12**
Battledown Priors
GL52: Charl K 6B **12**
Battledown Trad. Est.
GL52: Chelt 1B **22**
Battle Rd. GL20: Tewk 6A **6**
BAUNTON **1D 52**
Baunton La. GL7: Strat 3B **52**
Baynham Way
GL50: Chelt 2B **4** (5G **11**)
BAYS HILL **4A 4** (**6F 11**)
Bayshill La. GL50: Chelt . . . 4A **4** (6F **11**)
Bayshill Rd.
GL50: Chelt 4A **4** (1F **21**)
Bay Tree Ct. GL52: P'bury 3D **12**
Bay Tree Rd. GL4: A'md 6G **27**
Bazeley Rd. GL4: Mats 3C **34**
Beacon Rd. GL4: Mats 3C **34**
Beagles, The GL5: Cash G 3G **41**
Beale Cl. GL6: Buss 1C **48**
Beale Rd. GL51: Chelt 4A **10**
Beard's La. GL5: Stro 3B **42**
(not continuous)
Bear Hill GL5: Rodb C 2B **46**
Bearland GL1: Glou 3F **5** (1G **25**)
Bearland House 3F 5
Bearsfield GL6: Bis 1F **45**
Beaufort Bldgs. GL1: Glou 6G **5**
Beaufort Ct. GL7: Ciren 2D **54**
GL50: Chelt 2F **21**
Beaufort Ho. GL1: Glou . . . 6G **5** (3H **25**)
Beaufort Pl. GL20: Tewk 6B **6**
Beaufort Rd. GL4: Glou 6A **26**
(not continuous)
GL52: Charl K 2B **22**
Beaufort Sports Cen. 3E 33
Beaumont Dr. GL51: Chelt 3A **10**
Beaumont Rd. GL2: Longl 4D **16**
GL51: Chelt 3A **10**
Becketts La. GL54: Greet 2C **56**
Beckford Rd. GL4: A'md 1F **35**
Beckside Ct. GL1: Glou 2A **26**
Bedford Av. GL51: Chelt 5C **10**
Bedford St. GL1: Glou 4H **5** (2A **26**)
GL5: Stro 3D **42**
Beech Cl. GL2: Hardw 6B **32**
GL2: High 5A **14**
GL52: P'bury 3E **13**
Beechcroft Rd. GL2: Longl 4B **16**
BEECHES, THE **1G 55**
Beeches, The GL10: King S 6D **40**
Beeches Cl. GL10: King S 6D **40**
BEECHES GREEN **3C 42**
Beeches Grn. GL5: Stro 2C **42**
Beeches Rd. GL7: Ciren 1E **55**
GL53: Charl K 5C **22**
Beech Gro. GL5: Woodc 2B **46**
GL7: Ciren 6F **53**
Beech Gro. Ct. GL7: Ciren 6F **53**
Beechmore Dr. GL51: Up H 4B **20**
Beechurst Av. GL52: Chelt 6A **12**
Beechurst Way GL52: Bish C 1C **8**
Beechwood Cl. GL52: Charl K 1C **22**
Beechwood Dr. GL6: Buss 1C **48**
Beechwood Gro. GL4: Tuff 2H **33**
Beechwood Shop. Cen.
GL52: Chelt 3C **4** (6H **11**)
Belfry Cl. GL4: Barn 3F **27**
Belgrave Rd. GL1: Glou . . . 5H **5** (2H **25**)
Belgrove Ter. GL1: Glou 4A **26**
Belland Dr. GL53: Charl K 5B **22**
Bella Vista GL52: Woodm 2G **9**
Belle Vue Cl. GL5: Stro 3D **42**
Belle Vue Rd. GL5: Stro 3D **42**
Bellflower Rd. GL20: Wal C 6D **6**
Bell La. GL1: Glou 4H **5** (2H **25**)
GL5: Sels 6H **41**
GL6: Minch 6H **47**
Bell Wlk. GL1: Glou 4G **5** (2H **25**)
Belmont Av. GL3: Hucc 5A **28**
Belmont Lodge GL52: Chelt 2D **4**
Belmont Rd. GL5: Stro 4F **43**
GL52: Chelt 2D **4** (5H **11**)
Belmore Pl.
GL53: Chelt 5B **4** (1G **21**)
Belvedere M. GL6: Chalf 3C **48**
Belworth Ct. GL51: Chelt 2D **20**
Belworth Dr. GL51: Chelt 2C **20**
Bendall Ho. GL52: Chelt 1D **4**
BENHALL **1A 20**
Benhall Av. GL51: Chelt 1A **20**
Benhall Gdns. GL51: Chelt 6B **10**
Bennington St.
GL50: Chelt 2B **4** (5G **11**)
Benson Cl. GL4: A'md 5F **27**
BENTHAM **6H 29**
Bentham Indoor Sports Complex
. . . . 6H 29
Bentham La. GL3: Witc 6H **29**
Bentley Cl. GL2: Qued 3C **32**
Bentley La. GL52: South 6H **9**
Beresford Ho. GL7: Ciren 5D **52**
Berkdale Cl. GL2: Hardw 5A **32**
Berkeley Cl. GL3: Hucc 5B **28**
GL5: Cash G 3G **41**
Berkeley Ct. GL52: Chelt 4D **4**
Berkeley Ho. *GL52: Chelt 5A 12*
(off Selkirk Cl.)
Berkeley M. GL52: Chelt 4D **4**
Berkeley Pl.
GL52: Chelt 4D **4** (6H **11**)
Berkeley Rd. GL7: Ciren 4D **54**
Berkeley St. GL1: Glou 3F **5** (1G **25**)
GL52: Chelt 4D **4** (6H **11**)
Berry Cl. GL6: Pains 5H **37**
Berryfield GL5: Woodc 2A **46**
Berryfield Glade GL3: Chu 3H **17**
Berry Hill Cres. GL7: Ciren 4D **52**
Berry Hill Rd. GL7: Ciren 5D **52**
Berry Lawn GL4: A'dle 2E **35**
Berrymore Rd. GL5: Woodc 2A **46**
Berwick Rd. GL52: Bish C 1E **9**
Besbury La. GL6: Burl, Minch 5G **47**
Besbury Pk. GL6: Minch 5A **48**
Beta Cl. GL20: Tewk 2F **7**
Bethesda St. GL50: Chelt 2G **21**
Betjeman Cl. GL2: Glou 1F **33**
Bette Vw. Ter. GL6: Chalf 2E **49**
Bettridge Ct. GL52: P'bury 3C **12**
Bevan Gdns. GL20: North 1H **7**
Beverley Cft. GL51: Chelt 5A **10**
Beverley Gdns. GL52: Woodm 2H **9**
Bewley Way GL3: Chu 3H **17**
Bibury Rd. GL4: Glou 5A **26**
GL51: Chelt 1B **20**
Bicks La. GL54: Winch 5C **56**
Bijou Ct. GL1: Glou 5A **16**
Bilberry Cl. GL4: A'md 1G **35**
Billbrook Rd. GL3: Hucc 4H **27**
Billingham Cl. GL4: Glou 5C **26**
Billings Way GL50: Chelt 3E **21**
GL51: Chelt 3E **21**
Bingham Cl. GL7: Ciren 1E **55**
Birchall Av. GL4: Mats 3D **34**
Birchall La. GL4: Up L 3E **35**
Birch Av. GL4: Glou 5C **26**
Birch Cl. GL52: Woodm 1G **9**
GL53: Charl K 5D **22**
Birches, The GL6: Oak L 6H **45**
Birches Cl. GL5: Stro 2D **42**
Birches Dr. GL5: Stro 2D **42**
Birchfield Rd. GL52: Bish C 1F **9**
Birchley Rd. GL52: Charl K 1B **22**
Birchmore Rd. GL1: Glou 3B **26**
Birch Rd. GL5: Kings 1B **46**
Birchwood Flds. GL4: Tuff 2G **33**
Bird Pk. 5A 36
Bird Rd. GL3: Hucc 5A **28**
Birds Crossing GL5: Woodc 2B **46**
Birdwood Cl. GL4: A'md 1F **35**
Bishop Ct. GL51: Chelt 5D **10**
Bishop Hooper's Monument 2F 5
Bishop Rd. GL51: Shurd 1A **30**
Bishop's Castle Way
GL1: Glou 3B **26**
BISHOP'S CLEEVE **1F 9**
Bishop's Cleeve By-Pass
GL52: Bish C 2D **8**
Bishops Cl. GL5: Stro 4E **43**
GL52: Bish C 2F **9**
Bishops Dr. GL52: Bish C 2E **9**
Bishops Mdw. GL52: Bish C 1D **8**
Bishops Rd. GL4: A'md 5F **27**
Bishopstone Cl. GL51: Chelt 6A **10**
Bishopstone Rd. GL1: Glou 3B **26**
Bishops Wlk. GL7: Ciren 1D **54**
GL20: Tewk 3B **6**
BISLEY **1F 45**
Bisley Old Rd. GL5: Stro 3E **43**
Bisley Rd. GL4: Tuff 4H **33**
GL5: Stro 3E **43**
GL6: Bis 1E **45**
GL6: Eastc 5D **44**
GL6: Lypiatt 3H **43**
GL51: Chelt 1B **20**
Bisley St. GL6: Pains 5H **37**
BISMORE **4D 44**
Bittern Av. GL4: A'dle 5D **26**
Blaby Cl. GL4: A'md 6G **27**
Blackberry Cl. GL4: A'md 1F **35**
Blackberry Fld. GL52: P'bury 4D **12**
Blackberry Gro. GL52: Bish C 1D **8**
Blackbird Av. GL3: Inns 3E **17**
Blackbird Ct. GL10: Stone 2C **40**
Black Dog Way
GL1: Glou 2H **5** (1H **25**)
Blackfriars 4F 5
Blackfriars GL1: Glou 4F **5** (2G **25**)
Black Jack M. *GL7: Ciren 6D 52*
(off Black Jack St.)
Black Jack St. GL7: Ciren 6D **52**
Blacklow Cl. GL5: Woodc 2A **46**
BLACKNESS **3A 48**
Blacksmith La. GL3: Chu 5C **18**
Blacksmiths Ground
GL2: High 4A **14**
Blacksmiths La. GL2: Maise 2C **14**
GL52: P'bury 3C **12**
Blackthorn End GL53: Leck 5D **20**
Blackthorn Gdns. GL2: Qued 3C **32**
Blackwater Way GL2: Longl 4E **17**
Blackwell Cl. GL10: Stone 2C **40**
Bladon M. GL51: Chelt 1G **19**
Blaisdon Cl. GL4: A'md 6F **27**
Blaisdon Way GL51: Chelt 2B **10**
Blake Cft. GL51: Chelt 3A **10**
Blake Hill Way GL4: A'md 5E **27**
Blakeley Ct. GL3: Chu 3H **17**
Blakeney Cl. GL4: Tuff 2G **33**
Blake Rd. GL7: Ciren 6D **52**
Blakewell Mead GL6: Pains 5G **37**
Bleasby Gdns. GL51: Chelt 1D **20**
Blenheim Ct. GL54: Winch 4B **56**
Blenheim Orchard
GL51: Shurd 1B **30**
Blenheim Rd. GL1: Glou 3A **26**
Blenheim Sq. GL51: Chelt 4B **10**
Blinkhorns Bri. La. GL2: Glou 2C **26**
Bloomfield Rd. GL1: Glou 4G **25**
Bloomfield Ter. GL1: Glou 5G **25**
Bloomsbury St. GL51: Chelt 5F **11**
Bluebell Chase GL6: Buss 6D **44**
Bluebell Cl. GL4: A'md 6E **27**
Bluebell Dr. GL7: Sidd 3F **55**
Bluebell Gro. GL51: Up H 4C **20**
Bluebell Ri. GL6: Buss 6D **44**
Blueboy Pk. GL6: Minch 6H **47**
Blue Quarry Rd. GL7: Ciren 6F **53**
Boakes Dr. GL10: Stone 3B **40**
Bodenham Fld.
GL4: A'dle, A'md 5E **27**
Bodiam Av. GL4: Tuff 3E **33**
Bodnam Rd. GL51: Chelt 3B **10**
Boleyn Cl. GL3: Chu 2G **17**
Boleyn Ho. GL54: Winch 5A **56**
BONDEND **2F 35**
Bondend Rd. GL4: Up L 3F **35**
Bonds Mill Est. GL10: Stone 3A **40**
Bootenhay Rd. GL52: Bish C 1F **9**
Borage Cl. GL4: A'md 6G **27**
Boscombe La. GL6: Hors 5A **50**
Bospin La. GL5: Woodc 3A **46**
Boulton Rd. GL50: Chelt 2G **11**
Bouncers La.
GL52: Chelt, P'bury 4C **12**
Bourne, The GL6: Brim 3A **48**
Bourne Est. GL5: Brim 3H **47**
Bourne La. GL5: Brim 2G **47**
BOURNES GREEN **5H 45**
BOURNSIDE **2D 20**
Bournside Cl. GL51: Chelt 2D **20**
Bournside Dr. GL51: Chelt 2D **20**
Bournside Rd. GL51: Chelt 2D **20**
Bournside School Sports Cen.
. . . . 3D 20
Bourton Rd. GL4: Tuff 3H **33**
Boverton Av. GL3: Brock 5C **28**
Boverton Dr. GL3: Brock 5C **28**
BOWBRIDGE **5E 43**
Bowbridge La. GL5: Stro 5E **43**
GL52: P'bury 2C **12**
Bowbridge Lock GL5: Stro 5E **43**
Bowen Cl. GL52: Chelt 4B **12**
Bowler Rd. GL20: North 1H **7**
Bowl Hill GL5: Kings 1B **46**
BOWLING GREEN **4D 52**
Bowling Grn. Av. GL7: Ciren 5D **52**
Bowling Grn. Cres. GL7: Ciren . . . 5D **52**
Bowling Grn. La. GL7: Ciren 5D **52**
Bowling Grn. Rd. GL7: Ciren 5D **52**
Bowly Cres. GL7: Sidd 5F **55**
Bowly Rd. GL1: Glou 5G **25**
GL7: Ciren 3C **54**
BOWNHAM **2E 47**
Bownham Mead GL5: Rodb C 2D **46**
Bownham Pk. GL5: Rodb C 3E **47**
BOX **1F 51**
Box Cres. GL6: Minch 6G **47**
Box La. GL6: Box, Minch 1F **51**
Boyce Cl. GL4: A'dle 2F **35**
Bracelands GL6: Eastc 5D **44**
Bradford Rd. GL2: Glou 1C **26**
Bradley Cl. GL2: Longl 5D **16**
Bradley Rd. GL53: Charl K 5B **22**
Bradshaw Cl. GL2: Longl 4F **17**
Braeburn Cl. GL2: Glou 1D **26**
GL51: Chelt 5B **10**
Brae Wlk. GL4: A'dle 1E **35**
Bramble Chase GL52: Bish C 1D **8**
Bramble La. GL10: Stone 2C **40**
Bramble Lawn GL4: A'dle 2E **35**
Bramble Ri. GL52: P'bury 4D **12**
Bramley M. GL4: A'md 5H **27**
Bramley Rd. GL20: Tewk 3C **6**
GL51: Chelt 4B **10**
Branch Hill Ri. GL53: Charl K 5B **22**
Branch Rd. GL51: Chelt 2F **19**
(not continuous)
Brandon Cl. GL3: Chu 1H **17**
Brandon Pl. GL50: Chelt 3F **21**
Brannigan Ct. GL20: North 1H **7**
Brantwood Rd. GL6: Chalf H 1E **49**
Bravender Ct. GL7: Ciren 1E **55**
BREAD STREET **1A 42**
Brecon Cl. GL2: Qued 5B **32**
Bredon Rd. GL20: Tewk 3C **6**
Bredon Wlk. GL52: Chelt 4C **12**

A-Z Cheltenham & Gloucester 59

Bregawn Cl. GL52: Bish C 3D 8
Breinton Way GL2: Longl 4E 17
Brensham Rd. GL20: Tewk 3E 7
Brevel Ter. GL53: Charl K 4C 22
Brewery Arts Cen. 1D 54
Brewery Cl. GL7: Ciren 1D 54
Brewery Wlk. GL5: Thru 2F 47
　　GL6: Nails 3C 50
Brewery Yd. GL5: Cain 3H 41
Briarbank Ri. GL52: Charl K 2D 22
Briar Cl. GL5: Stro. 1E 43
Briarfields Camping Site
　　GL51: Chelt. 1G 19
Briar Lawn GL4: A'dle 2E 35
Briars Cl. GL3: Chu. 3H 17
Briar Wlk. GL52: P'bury 4D 12
Brickfield Ter. GL5: Rodb 4B 42
Brickrow GL5: Stro 3D 42
Bridge Cl. GL2: Glou 5E 25
　　GL7: Ciren 3E 55
Bridge End GL7: Ciren. 2E 55
Bridge Farm GL2: Maise 2E 15
BRIDGEND 4B 40
Bridgend Ct. GL10: Stone 4B 40
Bridgend Rd. GL51: Chelt. 2H 19
Bridgend Works GL10: Stone 4B 40
Bridge Rd. GL5: Ebley. 4G 41
　　GL7: Ciren 3E 55
　　　　　　(not continuous)
Bridgeside GL5: Cain 4H 41
Bridge St. GL5: Cain 4H 41
　　GL6: Nails 2D 50
　　GL51: Chelt 3E 11
Bridle, The GL5: Cash G 3G 41
Brierley Cl. GL4: A'md 6F 27
Brighouse Ct. GL4: Barn 2F 27
Brighton Rd. GL52: Chelt 6A 12
Brimley GL10: Leo S. 6C 40
BRIMSCOMBE 3G 47
Brimscombe La. GL5: Brim 3G 47
Brimscote Port GL5: Brim. 3G 47
Brimsome Mdw. GL2: High. 4A 14
Brindle Cl. GL4: Mats 1D 34
Brionne Way GL2: Longl 4C 16
Brisbane GL10: Stone 1B 40
Bristol Rd. GL1: Glou 6F 5 (5F 25)
　　GL2: Glou, Qued 6C 32
　　　　　　(not continuous)
　　GL2: Hardw 2B 38
　　GL7: Ciren 1D 54
　　GL10: Stone 3A 40
Bristow Rd. GL20: Wal C 6H 7
Britannia Way GL52: Woodm 2G 9
Britten Pl. GL51: Chelt. 5B 10
Brizen La. GL53: Leck. 5D 20
Broad Leys Rd. GL4: Barn 4E 27
Broad Oak Way GL51: Chelt 3B 20
Broad Ride GL7: Ciren 6A 52
Broadstone Cl. GL4: Barn 3F 27
Broad St. GL10: King S 6D 40
Broad Wlk., The
　　GL50: Chelt 5A 4 (1G 21)
Broadway GL2: Glou 6A 26
Broadway, The GL6: Oak L. 6H 45
Broadway GL7: P'bury 2B 12
Broadway Rd. GL54: Winch 4C 56
Broadwell Cl. GL4: A'md 6F 27
Brock Cl. GL51: Chelt 3G 19
Brockeridge Cl. GL2: Qued 3B 32
BROCKHAMPTON 4B 8
Brockhampton La. GL50: P'bury . . 4B 8
　　GL51: Swin V 6A 8
Brockley Acres GL6: Eastc 5D 44
Brockley Rd.
　　GL10: King S, Leo S 6C 40
BROCKWORTH 5D 28
Brockworth By-Pass
　　GL3: Brock, Hucc 3A 28
Brockworth Rd.
　　GL3: Brock, Chu 6C 18
Brockworth Sports Cen. 5E 29
Brome Rd. GL4: A'md 6G 27
Bronte Cl. GL51: Chelt 2C 20
Brookbank Cl. GL50: Chelt 5F 11
Brook Cl. GL54: Winch 6A 56
Brook Ct. GL20: Tewk 2D 6
　　GL50: Chelt 3E 21
Brooke Rd. GL7: Ciren 3C 54
Brookfield La. GL3: Chu 4D 18
Brookfield Rd. GL3: Chu 5C 18
　　GL3: Hucc 4F 27
　　GL51: Badg 5C 18
Brook Ho. GL51: Chelt. 2C 20

Brooklands Pk. GL2: Longl 4D 16
Brooklyn Cl. GL51: Chelt. 4C 10
Brooklyn Ct. GL51: Chelt. 3D 10
Brooklyn Gdns. GL51: Chelt 4D 10
Brooklyn Rd. GL51: Chelt 5B 10
Brook Rd. GL51: Chelt 3D 10
Brooksdale La. GL53: Chelt. 3F 21
Brookside GL20: Tewk 2D 6
Brookside Cl. GL3: Hucc. 4H 27
Brookside Cotts. GL6: Inch 1C 50
Brookside Vs. GL2: Glou. 1C 26
Brook St. GL1: Glou 3H 25
　　　　　　(not continuous)
BROOKTHORPE 2H 39
Brookthorpe Cl. GL4: Tuff 2G 33
Brook Va. GL52: Charl K 2B 22
Brookway Dr. GL53: Charl K 3B 22
Brookway Rd. GL53: Charl K. 3B 22
Broom Bungs. GL4: Glou 6B 26
Brosnan Dr. GL51: Chelt 6A 10
Brown Cl. GL51: Chelt 4B 10
Browning M. GL51: Chelt 2C 20
BROWNSHILL 2B 48
Browns Hill GL6: Brown 2B 48
Brownshill Rd. GL6: Brown 3A 48
Brown's La. GL10: Stone 4D 40
Brunel Cl. GL2: Glou 1E 39
Brunel Mall Shop. Cen., The
　　GL5: Stro 4D 42
Brunel Way GL10: Stone. 1A 40
Brunswest Ct. GL1: Glou. 5G 5
Brunswick Rd.
　　GL1: Glou 6G 5 (2H 25)
Brunswick Sq.
　　GL1: Glou 5G 5 (2H 25)
Brunswick St.
　　GL50: Chelt 1A 4 (5G 11)
Brush, The GL5: Cash G 2C 42
Bruton Way GL1: Glou 3H 5 (1A 26)
Bryaston Cl. GL51: Chelt. 5D 10
Bryerland Rd. GL3: Witc 1F 37
Brymore Av. GL52: P'bury 3B 12
Brymore Cl. GL52: P'bury. 2B 12
Bryony Bank GL53: Leck 5E 21
Bubblewell La. GL6: Minch 6A 48
Buckholt Cl. GL4: Cranh. 6B 36
Buckholt Rd. GL3: Brock. 6D 28
Buckholt Wood Nature Reserve
　　. 6D 36
Buckingham Av. GL51: Chelt 5C 10
Buckingham Cl. GL20: Wal C 6D 6
Buckingham Ct. GL50: Chelt. 4B 4
Buckingham Dr. GL3: Chu 2H 17
Buckland Cl. GL52: Bish C 1E 9
Bucklehaven GL53: Charl K. 4A 22
Buckles Cl. GL3: Charl K. 4C 22
Budding, The GL5: Stro. 1F 43
Buddleia Cl. GL4: A'md 1G 35
Buddleia Ct. GL3: Chu 2H 17
　　　　　　(off Wisteria Way)
Bullfinch Rd. GL4: A'dle 5D 26
Bullfinch Way GL3: Inns 2E 17
Bull La. GL1: Glou 3G 5 (1H 25)
Bulwarks, The GL6: Minch 6A 48
Bunting Hill GL6: For G 2A 50
Bunting Way GL6: For G 2A 50
Burcombe Cl. GL6: Chalf H 1D 48
Burcombe Way GL6: Chalf H 1E 49
Burdett Cl. GL10: Stone 3C 40
Burdett Rd. GL10: Stone 3D 40
Burford M. GL1: Glou 5B 26
Burford Rd. GL7: Ciren 6F 53
Burgage, The GL52: P'bury 2C 12
Burge Ct. GL7: Ciren 2E 55
BURLEIGH 4G 47
Burleigh Cl. GL5: Burl 4F 47
Burleigh Cft. GL3: Hucc 3G 27
Burleigh Tor GL5: Burl 5G 47
Burleigh Vw. GL6: Buss 6C 44
Burma Av. GL52: Chelt 5C 12
Burma Rd. GL6: For G 2B 50
Burnet Cl. GL4: Glou 1B 34
Burnet Cl. GL4: Glou 1F 33
BURNT ASH 5C 48
Burton St. GL50: Chelt . . . 1A 4 (5F 11)
Buscombe Gdns. GL3: Hucc 4A 28
Bushcombe Cl. GL52: Woodm 1H 9
Bushcombe La.
　　GL52: Woodm. 1H 9
Bush Cl. GL52: P'bury. 4C 12
Bush Hay GL3: Chu 4A 18

Bushy Way GL51: Chelt. 2A 10
BUSSAGE 6C 44
Bussage Hill GL6: Buss 6B 44
Butcher Hill's La. GL6: Nails. 3C 50
Buttercross La. GL52: P'bury 4E 13
Buttercup Lawn GL4: A'dle 2E 35
Buttermere Cl. GL51: Chelt. 3B 20
Buttermilk La. GL3: Chu 3A 18
Butterow Hill
　　GL5: Rodb C, Stro. 6D 42
Butterow La. GL5: Rodb C 6E 43
Butterow W. GL5: Rodb 5C 42
BUTTERROW 5E 43
Butt Grn. GL6: Pains 4H 37
Buttington GL4: A'md 6G 27
Button Mills Est. GL10: Stone. 4B 40
BUTTS, THE 5C 42
Butts, The GL4: Glou 1B 34
Butt's La. GL52: Woodm 1H 9
Butt St. GL6: Minch. 6H 47
Butts Wlk. GL51: Chelt. 2H 19
Byard Rd. GL2: Glou 6E 25
Bybrook Gdns. GL4: Tuff 4G 33
Bybrook Rd. GL4: Tuff 4G 33
Byfield Cl. GL52: Woodm 3H 9
Byron Av. GL52: Chelt 5C 12
Byron Cl. GL20: Wal C 5D 6
Byron Ct. GL52: Chelt 5A 12
Byron Rd. GL5: Stro 2A 42
　　GL51: Chelt 6B 10

C

Cadbury Cl. GL3: Hucc 5A 28
Cadogan Ho. GL52: Chelt 5A 12
Caernarvon Cl. GL51: Chelt 3B 20
Caernarvon Cl. GL51: Chelt 3A 20
Caernarvon Rd.
　　GL51: Chelt, Up H 3A 20
Caesar Rd. GL2: Glou 6F 25
CAINSCROSS 3H 41
Cainscross Rd. GL5: Stro 3A 42
Cakebridge Pl. GL52: Chelt. 4A 12
Cakebridge Rd. GL52: Chelt 3A 12
Calderdale GL4: A'md 6G 27
Calderwood Ct.
　　GL50: Chelt 6A 4 (1G 21)
Caledonian Rd. GL4: Mats 3D 34
CALLOWELL 1B 42
Calspick Way GL2: Longl 4E 17
Calton Rd. GL1: Glou 6H 25
Calverley M. GL51: Up H 4B 20
Camberley Cl. GL3: Hucc. 4H 27
Camberwell Rd. GL51: Chelt 5A 10
Cambray Ct.
　　GL50: Chelt 4B 4 (6G 11)
Cambray M. GL50: Chelt. . 4C 4 (6G 11)
Cambray Pl.
　　GL50: Chelt 4B 4 (6G 11)
Cambrian Rd.
　　GL20: Wal C . . . . 6D 6 & 6H 7
Cambridge Av. GL51: Chelt 6C 10
Cambridge Way GL6: Minch. 6G 47
Cambry Cl. GL7: Ciren 1E 55
Camellia Ct. GL51: Up H 4D 20
Camellia Wlk. GL2: Qued 4B 32
Camomile Cl. GL4: A'md 6G 27
Campbell Cl. GL3: Inns 2F 17
Campden Rd. GL4: Tuff 2H 33
Campion Cl. GL4: Glou 1B 34
Campion Pk. GL51: Up H 5C 20
Camp Rd. GL52: Charl K 6C 12
Cam Rd. GL52: Chelt. 4C 12
Cams Ground GL2: High 3A 14
Canada Wharf GL2: Glou. 5F 25
Canal Way GL2: Over 5E 15
Canberra GL10: Stone. 1B 40
Canberra Ho. GL51: Chelt 6B 10
Cane Sq. GL51: Chelt 6A 10
Canning Rd. GL2: Longl 5F 17
Canterbury Leys GL20: Tewk 3D 6
Canterbury Wlk. GL51: Chelt 3D 20
Canton Acre GL6: Pains 4H 37
Cantors Ct. GL52: Bish C 3E 9
Cantors Dr. GL52: Bish C 3D 8
Capel Ct. GL5: Stro 2E 43
　　GL52: P'bury. 3C 12
Capel La. GL52: Charl K 5F 23
Capel Rd. GL4: Mats 3D 34
Capitol Pk. GL2: Glou 1E 33
Captain Barton Cl. GL5: Stro. 2F 43
Cardinal Dr. GL2: Qued 4D 32

Cares Cl. GL52: Bish C 1F 9
Carisbrooke Dr. GL52: Charl K . . 3D 22
Carisbrooke Rd. GL3: Hucc 5H 27
Carlton Gdns. GL5: Stro 3D 42
Carlton Pl. GL50: Chelt 4F 11
Carlton St. GL51: Chelt 6A 12
Carlyle Gro. GL51: Chelt 3A 10
Carmarthen Rd.
　　GL1: Glou 3A 20
Carmarthen St. GL1: Glou. 4A 26
Carne Pl. GL4: Glou 2D 26
Carpenters La. GL7: Ciren. 1E 55
Carrant Rd. GL20: Tewk 3C 6
Carrol Gro. GL51: Chelt 3A 10
Carter Rd. GL51: Chelt 3C 10
Carter's Orchard GL2: Qued 3C 32
Carters Way GL6: For G 1A 50
Carwardine Fld. GL4: A'md. 5F 27
Cascades Leisure Cen. 4C 6
Casey Cl. GL1: Glou 2C 26
CASHES GREEN 2G 41
Cashes Grn. Rd. GL5: Cash G . . . 2G 41
Casino Pl. GL50: Chelt 2F 21
Cassin Dr. GL51: Chelt 5B 10
Castanum Ct. GL51: Chelt. 2D 20
Castle, The GL5: Stro 4D 42
Castle Cl. GL6: Pains 6H 37
Castle Cotts. GL3: Hucc 3G 27
Castlefields Av. GL52: Charl K . . . 3D 22
Castlefields Dr. GL52: Charl K . . . 3D 22
Castlefields Rd. GL52: Charl K. . . . 3D 22
Castle Hill Dr. GL3: Brock. 1E 37
Castlemaine Dr. GL51: Chelt 1H 19
Castlemead Rd. GL5: Rodb 4C 42
Castle Meads Way
　　GL1: Glou 3E 5 (2F 25)
Castle Pitch GL5: Stro 4D 42
Castle Ri. GL5: Stro 4D 42
Castle St. GL5: Stro 3D 42
　　GL7: Ciren 1D 54
　　GL54: Winch 5C 56
Castleton Rd. GL4: Barn 3E 27
Catherine Ct. GL1: Glou 4H 25
Catherine's Cl. GL5: Stro 3F 43
Catkin Cl. GL2: Qued. 6B 32
Catswood Cl. GL5: Stro. 1F 43
Causeway, The GL2: Qued 4A 32
Cavendish Av. GL3: Chu 4C 18
Cecil Rd. GL1: Glou. 4F 25
Cecily Cl. GL6: Minch 6G 47
Cecily Hill GL7: Ciren 6C 52
Cedar Cl. GL5: Ebley. 4G 41
　　GL53: Charl K 4C 22
Cedar Ct. GL53: Chelt 5B 4
Cedar Ct. Rd.
　　GL53: Chelt 5B 4 (1G 21)
Cedar Gdns. GL10: Stone 2C 40
Cedar Gro. GL54: Winch 4B 56
Cedar Rd. GL3: Brock 4C 28
　　GL20: North 2H 7
Cedars, The GL3: Hucc. 3H 27
Cedarwood Dr. GL4: Tuff 2H 33
Celandine Bank GL52: Woodm. . . . 1G 9
Cemetery Rd. GL4: Glou. 5B 26
Central Cross Dr. GL50: Chelt. 4H 11
　　GL52: Chelt 4H 11
Central Rd. GL1: Glou. 5A 26
　　GL5: Stro. 3A 42
Central Trad. Est. GL2: Glou 2E 33
Centre Severn GL4: Barn 1F 27
Centre Way GL51: Chelt. 5E 11
Centurion Cl. GL4: A'md 5F 27
Century Cl. GL7: Ciren 6G 53
Century Ct. GL50: Chelt . . . 6B 4 (1G 21)
Ceylon Ho. GL51: Chelt. 3C 10
Chaceley Cl. GL2: Qued 5B 32
　　GL4: A'md 6F 27
Chadbournes GL3: Chu 3H 17
Chad Rd. GL51: Chelt 6C 10
Chadwick Cl. GL4: Tuff 3G 33
Chaffinch Cl. GL3: Inns 2E 17
Chaffinch Cl. GL10: Stone. 2C 40
CHALFORD 2E 49
Chalford Av. GL51: Chelt. 2G 19
CHALFORD HILL 1E 49
Chalford Ind. Est. GL6: Chalf 2D 48
Chalford Rd. GL4: Tuff 4H 33
Chamwells Av. GL2: Longl 5C 16
Chamwells Wlk. GL2: Longl 5C 16
　　　　　　(not continuous)
Chancel Cl. GL4: Glou. 2C 26
Chancel Pk. GL53: Charl K 3A 22
Chancel St. GL53: Charl K 3B 22

Chance St. GL20: Tewk 4C 6
Chandler Rd. GL52: Bish C 3E 9
Chandler's Ct. GL20: Tewk 4A 6
(off Church St.)
Chandos Almshouses
GL54: Winch 5B 56
Chandos Dr. GL3: Brock 6D 28
Chandos Rd. GL5: Rodb 6B 42
Chandos St. GL54: Winch 4C 56
Chantry Cl. GL7: Ciren 6D 52
Chantry Ga. GL52: Bish C 3D 8
CHAPEL FIELDS 1G 41
Chapel Gdns. GL2: Qued 6C 32
Chapel Hay Cl. GL3: Chu 5B 18
Chapel Hay La. GL3: Chu 5C 18
Chapel Ho. GL20: Tewk 4B 6
Chapel La. GL5: Ebley 3G 41
GL6: Minch 6H 47
GL50: Chelt 2G 21
GL52: Woodm 2G 9
Chapel Row GL10: Stone 3C 40
Chapel St. GL5: Stro 3E 43
GL50: Chelt 2A 4 (5G 11)
Chapel Wlk.
GL50: Chelt 4A 4 (6G 11)
Chapman Way GL51: Chelt 2C 20
CHARGROVE 6C 20
Chargrove La.
GL51: Shurd, Up H 4A 20
Charlecote Av. GL4: Tuff 5F 33
Charlecote Cnr. GL52: Bish C . . . 2D 8
Charles Cl. GL20: Wal C 6E 7
Charles St. GL1: Glou 2A 26
GL51: Chelt 4F 11
Charleswood All. GL20: Tewk 4B 6
(off East St.)
Charlie's Way GL3: Hucc 3A 28
Charlock Cl. GL4: Glou 1B 34
Charlotte Rose Ho.
GL50: Chelt 6E 11
Charlton Av. GL53: Charl K 4A 22
Charlton Cl. GL1: Glou 1A 26
Charlton Ct. Rd.
GL52: Charl K 2B 22
Charlton Dr. GL53: Charl K 2A 22
CHARLTON KINGS 4B 22
Charlton Kings Ind. Est.
GL53: Chelt 5B 22
Charlton La. GL53: Chelt 4G 21
Charlton Lawn GL53: Charl K . . . 3B 22
CHARLTON PARK 2A 22
Charlton Pk. Dr. GL53: Chelt . . . 2H 21
Charlton Pk. Ga. GL53: Chelt . . . 3H 21
Charlton Way GL2: Longl 4D 16
Charnwood Cl. GL53: Chelt 4G 21
Charnwood Rd. GL53: Chelt 4G 21
Charter Cl. GL1: Glou 3A 26
Chartwell Cl. GL2: Glou 5D 24
Chase, The GL3: Chu 5C 18
GL4: A'dle 6E 27
GL5: Cash G 3G 41
Chase Av. GL52: Charl K 3D 22
Chase La. GL4: Glou 4C 26
Chase La. Ind. Est. GL4: Glou . . . 4C 26
Chasely Cres. GL51: Up H 4B 20
Chasewood Cnr. GL6: Buss 6C 44
Chatcombe Cl. GL53: Charl K . . . 5C 22
Chatcombe Rd. GL4: Mats 6C 26
Chatsworth Av. GL4: Tuff 4F 33
Chatsworth Dr. GL53: Chelt 5G 21
Chaucer Cl. GL1: Glou 6G 25
Cheapside GL5: Stro 3C 42
Chedworth Rd. GL4: Tuff 2G 33
Chedworth Way GL51: Chelt 1B 20
Chelbury M. GL52: Chelt 4B 12
Chelmsford Av. GL51: Chelt 4D 20
Chelsea Cl. GL53: Chelt 2A 22
Chelsea Cl. GL1: Glou 4G 5 (2H 25)
CHELTENHAM 2B 4 (6G 11)
CHELTENHAM AND GLOUCESTER
NUFFIELD HOSPITAL 2H 19
Cheltenham Art Gallery & Mus.
. . . . 2A 4 (6G 11)
Cheltenham Cemetery & Crematorium
GL52: Chelt 4D 12
Cheltenham Croquet Club 3H 21
CHELTENHAM GENERAL HOSPITAL
. . . . 6C 4 (1H 21)
Cheltenham Ladies' College
Sports Cen. 6E 11
Cheltenham Racecourse 1A 12
Cheltenham Racecourse
Gloucestershire &
Warwickshire Railway 6D 8

Cheltenham Racecourse Cvn. Club Site
GL52: P'bury 2A 12
Cheltenham Racecourse Mus.
. . . . 1H 11
Cheltenham Recreation Cen. 3G 11
Cheltenham Recreation Cen.
Swimming Pool 3G 11
Cheltenham Rd.
GL2: Glou, Longl 6C 16
GL6: Bis 1F 45
GL6: Nails 2C 50
GL7: Ciren 6F 53
GL7: Baun, Strat 4C 52
GL52: Bish C 5E 9
GL54: Winch 6A 56
Cheltenham Rd. E. GL2: Chu 4F 17
GL3: Chu 4F 17
Cheltenham Spa Station (Rail)
. . . . 6D 10
Cheltenham Town FC 4A 12
Cheltenham Trade Pk.
GL51: Chelt 4E 11
Chelt Rd. GL52: Chelt 4C 12
Chelt Wlk. GL51: Chelt 3D 10
Chequers Rd. GL4: Glou 4B 26
Cheriton Cl. GL51: Up H 4C 20
Cherrington Dr. GL4: A'md 6F 27
Cherry Av. GL53: Charl K 5D 22
Cherry Blossom Cl.
GL52: Bish C 1D 8
Cherry Cl. GL2: Hardw 6B 32
Cherry Gdns. GL3: Hucc 3H 27
Cherry Orchard GL20: North 2H 7
Cherry Tree Cl. GL6: For G 2B 50
Cherry Tree Dr. GL7: Ciren 3F 55
Cherrytree La.
GL7: Ciren, Norc 5G 53
Cherrywood Gdns. GL4: Tuff 2H 33
Cherston Cl. GL4: Barn 3F 27
Chervil Cl. GL4: Glou 1C 34
Chesford Dr. GL3: Chu 4B 18
Cheshire Rd. GL3: Inns 3F 17
Chesils, The GL54: Greet 2C 56
Chesmann Ct. GL1: Glou 5A 16
Chester Cres. GL7: Ciren 1E 55
Chester M. GL7: Ciren 1E 55
Chester Rd. GL4: Glou 3D 26
Chester St. GL7: Ciren 1E 55
Chester Wlk.
GL50: Chelt 2A 4 (5G 11)
Chesterton Av. GL10: Stone 2C 40
Chesterton Cl. GL2: Qued 6B 32
Chestnut Cl. GL20: Tewk 2C 50
Chestnut Hill GL6: Nails 2C 50
Chestnut La. GL5: Stro 3A 42
Chestnut Pl. GL53: Leck 5E 21
Chestnut Rd. GL4: A'md 6F 27
Chestnuts, The
GL1: Glou 6F 5 (3G 25)
Chestnut Ter. GL53: Charl K 4B 22
Chestnut Wlk. GL53: Charl K 4B 22
Cheviot Cl. GL2: Qued 6B 32
Cheviot Rd. GL52: P'bury 3C 12
Cheyney Cl. GL4: Glou 5C 26
Chillingworth M.
GL1: Glou 5G 5 (2H 25)
Chiltern Av. GL52: Bish C 1D 8
Chiltern Rd. GL2: Qued 5B 32
Chislet Way GL4: Tuff 4G 33
Choirs Cl. GL4: A'md 5F 27
Chosen Dr. GL3: Chu 4A 18
Chosen Vw. Rd. GL51: Chelt 2E 11
Chosen Way GL3: Hucc 3G 27
Christchurch Ct. GL50: Chelt . . . 1E 21
Christ Church Rd. GL50: Chelt . . . 1E 21
Christ Chu. Ter. GL50: Chelt . . . 5E 11
Christowe Cl. GL53: Chelt 2H 21
Christowe La. GL53: Chelt 2H 21
Church App. GL52: Bish C 1E 9
Church Av. GL7: Sidd 4F 55
CHURCHDOWN 4B 18
Churchdown La. GL3: Hucc 4A 28
Churchdown Sports Cen. 3A 18
Church Dr. GL2: Qued 4C 32
Church Farm Bus. Cen.
GL51: Leck 6E 21
Churchfield Rd. GL4: Up L 3F 35
GL5: Stro 4E 43

Churchfields GL52: Bish C 1F 9
Church Hill GL6: Bis 2F 45
Churchill Dr. GL52: Charl K 2B 22
Churchill Gro. GL20: Tewk 4E 7
Churchill Ind. Est.
GL53: Chelt 3G 21
Churchill Pl. GL6: Nails 2C 50
Churchill Rd. GL1: Glou 4G 25
GL6: Brim 3A 48
GL7: Ciren 6F 53
GL53: Chelt 3G 21
Churchill Way GL6: Pains 5G 37
Church La. GL2: Hardw 2A 38
GL4: Barn 3E 27
GL4: Whad 5H 33
GL5: Woodc 2A 46
GL10: Stone 3A 40
GL51: Shurd 1A 30
GL52: P'bury 3C 12
Church Piece GL53: Charl K 4B 22
Church Rd. GL5: Rodb 5B 42
Church Ri. GL2: Maise 2D 14
Church Rd. GL2: Longl 5D 16
GL2: Maise 1D 14
GL3: Chu 5B 18
GL4: Cain 4H 41
GL5: Woodc 2A 46
GL6: For G 6B 46
GL10: Leo S 6B 40
GL51: Chelt 1C 20
GL51: Leck 6E 21
GL51: Swin V 1D 10
GL52: Bish C 1E 9
GL53: Leck 6E 21
Church St. GL2: Glou 5F 5 (3G 25)
GL5: Stro 3D 42
GL6: Nails 2D 50
GL7: Ciren 2E 55
GL8: Aven 5F 51
GL10: King S 6D 40
GL20: Tewk 4B 6
GL50: Chelt 2B 4 (5G 11)
GL53: Charl K 4B 22
Churchview GL4: Barn 3E 27
Church Wlk. GL53: Charl K 3B 22
Church Way GL4: Glou 5D 26
Churn, The GL6: Pains 5H 37
Churn Av. GL52: Chelt 5B 12
Cineworld Cinema 6E 5 (3F 25)
Circle, The GL5: Stro 2D 42
CIRENCESTER 6D 52
Cirencester Bus. Est.
GL7: Ciren 3E 55
Cirencester Bus. Pk.
GL7: Ciren 3E 55
CIRENCESTER HOSPITAL 1C 54
Cirencester Lock-up 1D 54
Cirencester Outdoor Pool 6C 52
Cirencester Pk. 1A 54
Cirencester Rd. GL3: Brock 1E 37
GL5: Minch 5E 47
GL6: Chalf, Minch 5A 48
GL7: Preston 4H 55
GL53: Charl K 2B 22
Cirencester Roman Town Wall
. . . . 6E 53
Cirencester Town FC 2G 55
City Bank Rd. GL7: Ciren 2E 55
City Bank Vw. GL7: Ciren 2F 55
City Bus. Cen. GL2: Glou 3H 47
Claire's Ct. GL5: Brim 3H 47
Clapham Ct. GL1: Glou . . . 1H 5 (6A 16)
Clare Ct. GL5: Stro 3F 43
Claremont Cl. GL52: Chelt 5A 12
Claremont Ct. GL1: Glou 1A 26
Claremont Rd. GL1: Glou 1A 26
Clarence Cl. GL52: Chelt 1C 4
Clarence Pde.
GL50: Chelt 3B 4 (6G 11)
Clarence Rd. GL20: Tewk 6B 6
GL52: Chelt 1C 4 (5H 11)
Clarence Row
GL1: Glou 2H 5 (1H 25)
Clarence Sq.
GL50: Chelt 1C 4 (4H 11)
Clarence St. GL1: Glou . . . 4H 5 (2H 25)
GL50: Chelt 2A 4 (5G 11)
Clarence Wlk.
GL1: Glou 2H 5 (2H 25)
GL50: Chelt 3A 4 (6G 11)
Clarendon Cl. GL5: Stro 3D 42
Clarendon Rd. GL54: Winch 3B 56
Clare Pl. GL53: Chelt 2G 21

Clare St. GL1: Glou 2F 5 (1G 25)
GL53: Chelt 2G 21
Claridge Cl. GL4: A'dle 1E 35
Clarington M.
GL50: Chelt 1C 4 (4H 11)
Clarke Way GL50: Chelt 4G 11
Clarkia Cl. GL3: Chu 2G 17
Clark's All. GL20: Tewk 3B 6
Clark's La. GL7: Sidd 6D 54
Claudians Cl. GL4: A'md 4F 27
Clayburn Cl. GL2: High 4B 14
Claypits La. GL6: Lypiatt 6F 43
Claypits Path GL53: Chelt 3H 21
Clearwater Dr. GL2: Qued 4A 32
Clee Ho. GL20: Tewk 5B 6
Cleeve Bus. Pk. GL52: Bish C . . 4D 8
Cleeve Cl. GL52: Bish C 2E 9
Cleeve Cloud La. GL52: P'bury . . 4E 13
Cleevecroft Av. GL52: Bish C . . . 2F 9
CLEEVE HILL 3H 9
Cleeve Lake Ct. GL52: Bish C . . 1D 8
Cleevelands Av. GL50: Chelt . . . 2G 11
Cleevelands Cl. GL50: Chelt . . . 2H 11
Cleevelands Dr. GL50: Chelt . . . 2H 11
Cleeveland St. GL51: Chelt 4F 11
Cleevemont GL52: Chelt 2H 11
Cleevemount Cl. GL52: Chelt . . . 4A 12
Cleevemount Rd. GL52: Chelt . . . 4A 12
Cleeve Rd. GL4: Mats 1D 34
Cleeve Sports Cen. 3F 9
Cleeve Vw. Rd. GL52: Chelt . . . 5B 12
Clegram Rd. GL1: Glou 4G 25
Clematis Ct. GL52: Bish C 2D 8
Clement St. GL1: Glou 3B 26
Clent Ct. GL52: Chelt 6A 12
Clevedon Rd. GL1: Glou 5A 26
Clevedon Sq. GL51: Chelt 5D 10
Clifford Av. GL20: Wal C 6H 5
Clifton Rd. GL1: Glou 3G 25
Clinton Ho. GL7: Ciren 6E 53
Clissold Ct. GL6: Nails 3C 50
Cloisters, The GL52: Bish C . . . 1D 8
Clomoney Way GL52: Longl 4E 17
Close, The GL7: Sidd 5F 55
GL52: South 5H 9
GL53: Leck 5G 21
Clover Dr. GL2: Hardw 1B 38
Clover Piece GL4: A'md 5E 27
Clyde Cres. GL52: Chelt 5B 12
Clyde Rd. GL3: Brock 6D 28
Coach Ho. M. GL7: Ciren 1E 55
Coal Wharf GL2: Maise 2E 15
Coates, The GL54: Winch 6A 56
Coates Gdns. GL10: Stone 2C 40
Coates Ho. GL51: Chelt 5B 10
Coberley Rd. GL4: Tuff 1H 33
GL51: Chelt 1A 20
Cobham Ct. GL51: Chelt 4E 11
Cobham Rd. GL51: Chelt 4E 11
Coburn Gdns. GL51: Chelt 6A 10
Cochran Cl. GL3: Chu 4B 18
Cockerell Rd. GL2: Qued 1E 39
Cold Pool La.
GL51: Badg, Up H 6F 19
Coldray Cl. GL1: Glou 4A 4
Cole Av. GL2: Glou 2D 32
Colebridge Av. GL2: Glou 6D 16
Colerne Dr. GL3: Hucc 4A 28
Colesbourne Rd. GL51: Chelt . . . 2A 20
COLETHROP 5F 39
Colin Rd. GL4: Barn 2E 27
College Baths Rd.
GL53: Chelt 6D 4 (1H 21)
College Cl. GL1: Glou . . . 3G 5 (1H 25)
College Flds. GL2: Longl 5E 17
College Ga.
GL53: Chelt 6D 4 (1H 21)
College Grn. GL1: Glou . . 2F 5 (1H 25)
College Lawn GL53: Chelt 2H 21
College Pl. GL50: Chelt 4A 4
(off Royal Well Pl.)
College Rd. GL5: Stro 2B 42
GL53: Chelt 6C 4 (1H 21)
College Vw. GL7: Ciren 4C 54
GL10: Stone 3C 40
College Yd. GL1: Glou 3G 5
(off College St.)
Colletts Dr. GL51: Chelt 4E 11
Colliers Wood GL6: For G 1B 50
Collingbourne Rd. GL4: Glou . . . 4B 26
Collins Ct. GL20: Tewk 4B 6
(off Back of Avon)
Collum End Ri. GL53: Leck 5F 21

Colne Av.—Dorset Ho.

Colne Av. GL52: Chelt 5B 12
Coltham Cl. GL52: Chelt 1A 22
COLTHAM FIELDS 1A 22
Coltham Flds. GL52: Chelt 1A 22
Coltham Rd. GL52: Chelt 2A 22
Coltman Cl. GL1: Glou 2C 26
Columbia Cl. GL1: Glou 2H 5 (1A 26)
Columbia St.
GL52: Chelt 2D 4 (5H 11)
Columbine Rd. GL20: Wal C 6H 7
Colville Ho. GL7: Ciren 6D 52
Colwell Av. GL3: Hucc 2H 27
Colwell School Cl. GL1: Glou 2B 26
Colwyn Dr. GL51: Chelt 3B 20
Combrook Cl. GL4: A'md 1F 35
Commercial Rd.
GL1: Glou 4F 5 (2G 25)
GL6: Chalf 2D 48
Commercial St. GL50: Chelt 2G 21
Common, The GL7: Sidd 5G 55
Common Rd. GL6: Box 1E 51
Compton Cl. GL2: Chu 1H 17
Compton Rd. GL51: Chelt 3E 11
Compton's All. *GL20: Tewk 4B 6*
(off Barton St.)
Concord GL6: Nails 3B 50
Concorde Way GL4: Glou 4C 26
Conduit St. GL1: Glou 6H 5 (4H 25)
CONEY HILL 4C 26
Coney Hill Pde. GL4: Glou 4D 26
Coney Hill Rd. GL4: Glou 4C 26
Conifers, The GL1: Glou 4B 26
GL52: Chelt 4B 12
Conigree La. GL20: Tewk 6B 6
Coniston Rd. GL2: Longl 5D 16
GL51: Chelt 2B 20
Constance Cl. GL5: Light 5A 42
Constitution Wlk.
GL1: Glou 4G 5 (2H 25)
Convent La. GL5: Woodc 4A 46
Conway Rd. GL3: Hucc 3H 27
Cooks La. GL51: Uck 1A 10
Cooks Orchard GL1: Glou 5A 16
Coombe Glen La.
GL51: Chelt, Up H 3A 20
Coombe Meade GL52: Woodm 2G 9
Coopers Ct. GL3: Brock 6D 28
GL53: Charl K 4C 22
Cooper's Elm GL2: Qued 3C 32
Cooper's Hill Local Nature Reserve
3D 36
Cooper's Pitch GL5: Rodb C 2E 47
Cooper's Vw. GL3: Brock 6D 28
Copper Beech Gro. GL2: Qued 4B 32
Copperfield Cl. GL4: Mats 1C 34
Coppice Ga. GL51: Chelt 2C 10
Coppice Hill GL6: Chalf 1F 49
Copse, The GL4: Barn 4F 27
Copt Elm Cl. GL53: Charl K 3B 22
Copt Elm Rd. GL53: Charl K 3B 22
Coral Cl. GL4: Tuff 2E 33
Cordingley Cl. GL3: Chu 5B 18
Corfe Cl. GL52: P'bury 4D 12
Coriander Dr. GL3: Chu 3G 17
Corinium Av. GL4: Barn 1E 27
Corinium Cen. 4E 55
Corinium Ga. GL7: Ciren 6E 53
Corinium Ho. GL7: Ciren 2C 54
Corinium Mus. 6D 52
Corinium Stadium 2G 55
Cormorant Av. GL20: Wal C 6D 6
Corncroft La. GL4: Mats 3E 35
Corndean La. GL54: Winch 6A 56
Cornfield Dr. GL2: Hardw 6B 32
GL52: Bish C 1D 8
Cornfields, The GL52: Bish C 1D 8
Cornflower Cl. GL20: Wal C 6H 7
Cornflower Rd. GL4: A'md 6F 27
Cornhill GL5: Stro 3D 42
Cornhill Shop. Cen. *GL5: Stro 3D 42*
(off Cornhill)
Cornmeadow Dr. GL51: Chelt 2A 10
Cornwall Av. GL51: Chelt 5D 10
Corolin Rd. GL2: Glou 1E 33
Coronation Flats GL52: Charl K 2B 22
Coronation Gro. GL2: Glou 1C 26
Coronation Rd. GL5: Rodb 4C 42
GL52: P'bury 3C 12
Coronation Sq. GL51: Chelt 5B 10
Corpus St. GL52: Chelt 5D 4 (1H 21)
Cossack Sq. GL6: Nails 3C 50
Cotswold Av. GL7: Ciren 2C 54
Cotswold Bowl 2E 11
COTSWOLD CARE HOSPICE 5G 47
Cotswold Cl. GL6: Brim 3A 48
GL7: Ciren 2C 54
Cotswold Cotts. GL6: Nails 3A 50
Cotswold Edge Bus. Cen.
GL2: Glou 3F 25
Cotswold Gdns. GL2: Longl 4E 17
GL20: Tewk 3C 6
Cotswold Grn. GL10: Stone 2C 40
Cotswold Indoor Bowls Club *3D 42*
(off Merrywalks)
Cotswold Leisure Cen. 1C 54
Cotswold Lodge GL52: Chelt 5A 12
Cotswold Mead GL6: Pains 6G 37
Cotswold Mill GL7: Ciren 1D 54
Cotswold Pl. GL20: Tewk 3C 6
Cotswold Playhouse 3E 43
Cotswold Rd. GL5: Cash G 2H 41
GL52: Chelt 4B 12
Cotswold Vw. GL52: Woodm 2G 9
Cottage Fld. GL2: High 4A 14
Cott. Rake Av. GL50: Chelt 2F 11
Cotteswold Dairy Ind. Site
GL20: Tewk 3E 7
Cotteswold Ri. GL5: Stro 3E 43
Cotteswold Rd. GL4: Glou 5B 26
GL20: Tewk 3C 6
Cotton Cl. GL4: A'md 6G 27
Countess Lilias Rd. GL7: Ciren 3C 54
County Ct. Rd.
GL50: Chelt 3B 4 (6G 11)
County Cres. GL1: Glou 2B 26
Courtenay St. GL50: Chelt 4G 11
Courtenay Vs. GL50: Chelt 4G 11
Court Farm M. GL10: Stone 3A 40
Courtfield Dr. GL52: Charl K 3C 22
Courtfield Rd. GL2: Qued 5B 32
Court Gdns. GL2: Glou 5E 25
Courtiers Dr. GL52: Bish C 2F 9
Court M. GL52: Charl K 2B 22
Courtney Cl. GL20: Tewk 6G 7
Court Orchard GL6: Pains 6H 37
Court Pl. GL4: Glou 5E 27
Court Rd. GL3: Brock 6D 28
GL52: P'bury 3D 12
Court Vw. GL6: Fran L 1F 49
GL10: Stone 3A 40
Court Way GL5: Rodb 5B 42
Courtyard, The GL1: Glou 1B 26
GL50: Chelt 5A 4 (1F 21)
Cousley Cl. GL3: Hucc 4H 27
Coventry Cl. GL20: Tewk 6C 6
Cowcombe Hill GL6: Chalf 3E 49
Cowcombe La.
GL6: Chalf, Fram M 4H 49
Cow La. GL5: Inch 6B 46
Cowle Rd. GL5: Stro 4E 43
Cowley Cl. GL51: Chelt 2B 20
Cowley Rd. GL4: Tuff 2H 33
Cowl La. GL54: Winch 5B 56
Cowlsmead GL51: Shurd 1B 30
Cowper Rd. GL51: Chelt 6B 10
Cowslip Mdw. GL52: Woodm 2G 9
Cowswell La.
GL6: Brown, Buss 1B 48
Coxmore Cl. GL3: Hucc 4H 27
Cox's Way GL4: A'md 5H 27
Coxwell Ct. GL7: Ciren 6D 52
Coxwell St. GL7: Ciren 6D 52
CRAB END 4C 22
Crabtree La. GL7: Ciren 1G 55
Crab Tree Pl. GL50: Chelt 4F 11
CRACKSTONE 6B 48
Craddock Ct. GL6: For G 1A 50
Cranford Cl. GL52: Woodm 2H 9
CRANHAM 6E 37
Cranham Cl. GL4: A'md 6F 27
CRANHAM CORNER 6B 36
Cranham La. GL3: Chu 6C 18
Cranham Rd. GL52: Chelt 6A 12
Cranhams La. GL7: Ciren 3B 54
Cranwell Cl. GL4: Mats 1D 34
Craven Dr. GL3: Chu 3H 17
Credon Rd. GL3: Hucc 2F 27
Crescent, The GL1: Glou 1B 26
GL3: Brock 5C 28
GL6: Oak L 6H 45
GL50: Chelt 6D 10
Crescent Cl. GL10: Stone 4B 40
Crescentdale GL2: Longf 3B 16
Crescent Pl.
GL50: Chelt 3A 4 (6G 11)
Crescent Rd. GL10: Stone 4B 40
Crescent Ter.
GL50: Chelt 3A 4 (6G 11)
Crest Way GL4: Barn 2G 27
Cricklade Rd.
GL7: Ciren, Preston 3F 55
Cricklade St. GL7: Ciren 1D 54
CRICKLEY HILL 6D 30
Crickley Hill Country Pk. 6C 30
Crickley Hill Hill Fort
GL3: Witc 6C 30
Crickley Hill Info. Cen. 6D 30
Criftycraft La. GL3: Chu 6B 18
CRIPPETS 3D 30
Crippetts La. GL51: Leck 6E 21
Crippetts Rd. GL51: Leck 2D 30
Cripps Rd. GL7: Ciren 1D 54
Crispin Cl. GL2: Longl 4D 16
GL54: Winch 4B 56
Crispin Rd. GL54: Winch 3B 56
Crock Mead GL4: A'md 5F 27
Croft, The GL6: Pains 4H 37
Croft Av. GL53: Charl K 4B 22
Croft Cl. GL3: Chu 5C 18
Croft Dr. GL53: Charl K 4B 22
Croft Gdns. GL53: Charl K 5C 22
Croft La. GL53: Chelt 3G 21
Croft Pde. GL53: Charl K 4C 22
Croft Rd. GL53: Charl K 4B 22
Croft St. GL53: Chelt 3F 21
Cft. Thorne Cl. GL51: Up H 4C 20
Cromers Cl. GL20: North 1H 7
Cromwell Rd. GL52: Chelt 4A 12
Cromwell St.
GL1: Glou 5H 5 (2H 25)
Crooks Ind. Est. GL53: Chelt 3G 21
Crosby Cl. GL3: Hucc 5A 28
Cross, The GL6: Hors 5A 50
GL6: Pains 5H 37
CROSSHANDS RDBT. 1E 37
Cross Keys La.
GL1: Glou 3G 5 (1H 25)
Crouch Ct. GL20: Tewk 5B 6
Crowfield GL52: Woodm 1G 9
Crown Cl. GL52: Bish C 2E 9
Crown Ct. GL10: King S 6D 40
Crown Dr. GL52: Bish C 2E 9
Crummock Wlk. GL51: Chelt 3C 20
Crypt Ct. GL4: Tuff 2F 33
Crythan Wlk. GL51: Up H 4C 20
Cuckoo Cl. GL6: Buss 1D 48
Cuckoo Row GL6: Minch 6G 47
CUDNALL 3B 22
Cudnall St. GL53: Charl K 2B 22
Culross Cl. GL50: Chelt 3H 11
Culver Hill GL5: Amb 4B 46
Cumberland Cres. GL51: Chelt 6D 10
Cumming Ct. GL52: P'bury 3B 12
Curlew Cl. GL20: North 1G 7
Curlew Rd. GL4: A'dle 5D 26
Curtis Haywood Dr. GL2: Qued 3B 32
Cutler Rd. GL5: Stro 2E 43
Cutsdean Cl. GL52: Bish C 1C 8
Cypress Gdns. GL2: Longl 4E 17
Cypress Rd. GL20: Wal C 6D 6

D

Daffodil Cl. GL4: A'md 6F 27
Daffodil St. GL50: Chelt 6A 4 (1G 21)
Dagmar Rd. GL50: Chelt 2F 21
Dainty St. GL1: Glou 4A 26
Daisy Bank GL5: Stro 4F 43
Daisybank Rd. GL53: Leck H 1G 31
Dale Cl. GL4: Glou 6A 26
Dale Wlk. GL52: Bish C 2F 9
Dallaway GL5: Thru 2F 47
Damson Cl. GL4: A'md 1F 35
Dancers Hill GL4: A'md 5F 27
Dancey Rd. GL3: Chu 3G 17
Dane Cl. GL2: Longl 4D 16
Daniels Ind. Est. GL5: Light 5A 42
Daniels Mdw. GL2: Qued 3D 32
Daniels Rd. GL5: Stro 3G 43
Darell Cl. GL2: Qued 6C 32
Dark La. GL5: Rodb 5C 42
GL6: Chalf 2D 48
GL6: Hors 5C 50
GL6: Nails 2B 50
(not continuous)
GL51: Swin V 6A 8
Darleydale Cl. GL2: Hardw 5A 32
Dart Cl. GL2: Qued 3C 32
Dart Rd. GL52: Chelt 4C 12
Darwin Cl. GL51: Chelt 1H 19
Darwin Rd. GL4: Glou 6A 26
Davallia Dr. GL51: Up H 4C 20
Daventry Ter. GL1: Glou 3A 26
David French Ct. GL51: Chelt 4D 20
Davillian Ct. GL2: Qued 2D 32
Davis All. *GL20: Tewk 4B 6*
(off Barton St.)
Davy Cl. GL2: Qued 1C 38
Dawes, The GL2: Qued 5C 32
Daw's La. GL6: Lypiatt 1B 44
Daylesford Cl. GL51: Chelt 1A 20
Deacon Cl. GL51: Chelt 2C 20
Deacons Pl. GL52: Bish C 3E 9
Deakin Cl. GL51: Swin V 6A 8
Deans Ct. GL51: Chelt 2C 20
Deans Quarry GL5: Burl 5G 47
Deans Row GL1: Glou 5H 15
Dean's Ter. GL1: Glou 6H 15
Dean's Wlk. GL1: Glou 1G 5 (6H 15)
(not continuous)
Dean's Way GL1: Glou 1G 5 (6H 15)
GL52: Bish C 2E 9
Deep St. GL52: P'bury 3C 12
Deerhurst Cl. GL4: A'md 1F 35
Deerhurst Pl. GL2: Qued 4B 32
Deer Pk. Rd. GL3: Hucc 2H 27
De Ferriers Wlk. GL51: Chelt 5A 10
Delabere Rd. GL52: Bish C 3F 9
DELANCEY HOSPITAL 4H 21
Delavale Rd. GL54: Winch 4B 56
Dell, The GL4: Barn 4F 27
Delmont Gro. GL5: Stro 2D 42
Delphinium Dr. GL52: Bish C 2D 8
Delta Dr. GL20: Tewk 2F 7
Delta Dr. Ind. Est. GL20: Tewk 2F 7
Delta Way GL3: Brock 5A 28
Denbigh Rd. GL51: Chelt 3B 20
Denham Cl. GL4: Tuff 4F 33
GL52: Woodm 2H 9
Denley Cl. GL52: Bish C 3E 9
Denmark Ct. GL1: Glou 6B 16
Denmark Rd. GL1: Glou 6A 16
DENMARK ROAD DAY HOSPITAL
6B 16
Denning Ct. *GL50: Chelt 2F 21*
(off Painswick Rd.)
Dent's Ter. GL54: Winch 5B 56
Derby Ct. GL1: Glou 2B 26
Derby Rd. GL1: Glou 3B 26
Derwent Cl. GL3: Brock 6D 28
Derwent Dr. GL20: Tewk 2D 6
Derwent Wlk. GL51: Chelt 2C 20
Desford Cl. GL4: A'md 6G 27
Despenser Rd. GL20: Tewk 6B 6
Detmore Cl. GL52: Charl K 4E 23
Devereaux Cres. GL5: Ebley 3F 41
Devereaux Rd. GL5: Ebley 3F 41
Devil's Chimney 2G 31
Devil's Elbow, The GL6: Minch 2F 51
Devon Av. GL51: Chelt 6C 10
Devonshire Ho. GL50: Chelt 1A 4
Devonshire Pl. GL20: Tewk 6C 6
Devonshire St.
GL50: Chelt 2A 4 (5F 11)
Dewey Cl. GL52: Woodm 2G 9
Dianas Cl. GL4: A'md 5G 27
Dickens Cl. GL4: Glou 6A 26
Dickens M. GL4: Glou 6A 26
Didbrook M. GL4: A'md 1F 35
Digby Dr. GL20: Tewk 3C 6
Dill Av. GL51: Chelt 3B 10
Dimore Cl. GL2: Hardw 6A 32
Dinas Cl. GL51: Chelt 3C 20
Dinas Rd. GL51: Chelt 3C 20
Dinely St. GL1: Glou 6H 5 (3A 26)
Dinglewell GL3: Hucc 3G 27
Discovery Rd. GL4: A'md 5G 27
Distel Cl. GL50: Chelt 2F 11
Docks, The 4E 5 (2G 25)
Dodington Cl. GL4: Barn 4E 27
Dog Bark La. GL51: Swin V 1D 10
Dog La. GL3: Witc 5H 29
GL51: Bent 5H 29
Dollar St. GL7: Ciren 6D 52
Dombey Bungs. GL2: Glou 1F 33
Donside GL7: Strat 4B 52
Dora Wlk. GL1: Glou 4A 26
Dorchester Ct. GL50: Chelt 3F 21
Dorington Ct. GL6: Buss 6C 44
Dormer Rd. GL51: Chelt 3C 10
Dorney Rd. GL1: Glou 4G 25
Dorrington Wlk. GL51: Chelt 5A 10
Dorrit Cl. GL1: Glou 5A 26
Dorset Av. GL51: Chelt 5D 10
Dorset Ho. GL50: Chelt 2A 4

62 A-Z Cheltenham & Gloucester

Double Reynolds Warehouse
GL1: Glou 4E 5
Douro Rd. GL50: Chelt 6E 11
Dovedale Cl. GL2: Hardw 5A 32
Doverdale Dr. GL2: Longl 5E 17
Doverhay GL51: Up H 3C 20
Dowding Way GL3: Chu 4B 18
DOWNEND 5A 50
Downfield GL5: Stro 2A 42
Downfield Rd. GL5: Stro 3A 42
Down Hatherley La. GL2: Chu . . 1A 18
Downs Mill GL6: Fram M 4H 49
Downs GL7: Baun 1D 52
Downton Rd. GL10: Stone 4B 40
Down Vw. GL6: Chalf H 6E 45
Downy Cl. GL2: Qued 3B 32
Dowty Rd. GL51: Chelt 5B 10
Dozule Cl. GL10: Leo S 6C 40
Drake Cl. GL3: Chu 2G 17
Drakes Pl. GL50: Chelt 6E 11
Drapers Ct. GL52: Woodm 2G 9
Draycott Cl. GL51: Chelt 1B 20
Drayton Cl. GL51: Swin V 2E 11
Drayton Way GL4: Mats 6D 26
Dr Brown's Cl. GL6: Minch 6G 47
Dr Brown's Rd. GL6: Minch 5G 47
Dr Crawfords Cl. GL6: Minch . . . 6G 47
Dr Crouch's Rd. GL6: Eastc 5C 44
Drews Cl. GL3: Chu 5B 18
Drews Ct. GL3: Chu 5B 18
Drift Cl. GL7: Ciren 3B 54
Drift Way GL7: Ciren 3B 54
Drivemoor GL4: A'dle 2E 35
Dr Middletons Rd.
GL6: Chalf H 2E 49
Druids La. GL4: Glou 4D 26
Druids Oak GL2: Qued 5C 32
Dryland M. GL3: Hucc 5A 28
Dry Mdw. La. GL3: Inns 2D 16
Ducie St. GL1: Glou 4A 26
Duckworth Cl. GL53: Chelt 4G 21
DUDBRIDGE 4A 42
Dudbridge Hill
GL5: Dudb, Rodb 4A 42
Dudbridge Mdw. GL5: Dudb . . 5A 42
Dudbridge Rd.
GL5: Dudb, Light 4A 42
Duderstadt Cl. GL5: Stro 2A 42
Dugdale Rd. GL7: Ciren 6D 52
Duke of Beaufort Ct.
GL1: Glou 6G 25
Dukeries, The GL1: Glou . . 2F 5 (1G 25)
Duke St. GL1: Glou 6A 12
Dukes Way GL20: Tewk 6G 7
Dulverton Cl. GL51: Chelt 4A 10
Dumbleton Gro. GL51: Chelt . . . 3G 19
Dunalley Ct. GL50: Chelt 1B 4
Dunalley Pde. GL50: Chelt 4G 11
(not continuous)
Dunalley St.
GL50: Chelt 1B 4 (5G 11)
Dunbar Cl. GL51: Chelt 3A 10
Duncroft Rd. GL3: Hucc 2G 27
Dunelm Cl. GL51: Chelt 3C 10
Dunkirk Pitch GL5: Amb 6C 46
Dunlin Cl. GL2: Qued 4A 32
Dunstan Glen GL3: Chu 5C 18
Dunster Cl. GL4: Tuff 4E 33
GL51: Chelt 4A 10
Dunster Gdns. GL51: Chelt 4A 10
Dunster Gro. GL51: Chelt 4A 10
Dunster Rd. GL51: Chelt 4A 10
Durand Cl. GL2: Longl 3D 16
Durham Cl. GL51: Chelt 4D 20
Durham Rd. GL4: Glou 5A 26
Dyer St. GL7: Ciren 1E 55
Dynevor Cl. GL1: Glou 4A 26

E

Eagle Cl. GL6: Buss 1C 48
Eagle Mill Cl. GL5: Stro 5E 43
Eagles All. GL20: Tewk 4B 6
Eagle Way GL4: A'dle 6D 26
Eagle Works GL5: Thru 1E 47
Eardisland Rd. GL4: Tuff 3H 33
E. Approach Dr. GL52: Chelt . . . 3A 12
Eastbrook Rd. GL4: Glou 3D 26
Eastbrook Rd. Trad. Est.
GL4: Glou 3D 26
EASTCOMBE 5D 44
Eastcott Way GL3: Chu 3H 17
E. Court M. GL53: Charl K 4C 22

East Dr. GL5: Ebley 3F 41
EAST END 4D 22
East End Flats GL52: Charl K . . . 4D 22
East End Rd. GL53: Charl K 4C 22
Eastern Av. GL4: Glou 5B 26
Eastern Av. Retail Pk.
GL4: Glou 3C 26
Eastern Av. Trad. Est.
GL4: Glou 3C 26
Eastfield M. GL4: Glou 6A 26
Eastfield Rd. GL6: Minch 6A 48
East Gables GL52: Woodm 2G 9
Eastgate Mkt. GL1: Glou 4G 5
(off The Forum)
East Gate Shop. Cen.
GL1: Glou 4G 5 (2H 25)
Eastgate St. GL1: Glou . . 3G 5 (1H 25)
East Gloucestershire Tennis, Squash &
Hockey Club 3H 21
Eastholm Lawns GL3: Chu 4B 18
East St. GL20: Tewk 4B 6
Eastville Cl. GL4: Glou 3C 26
Eaton Pl. GL53: Chelt . . . 5B 4 (1G 21)
EBLEY 4G 41
Ebley By-Pass GL5: Ebley 4D 40
GL10: Ryef 4D 40
Ebley Ind. Est. GL5: Ebley 4G 41
Ebley Ind. Pk. GL5: Ebley 4G 41
Ebley Rd. GL10: Ryef 4D 40
Ebor Rd. GL2: Glou 2D 26
Ebrington Cl. GL4: Barn 3F 27
Edendale App. GL51: Chelt 1H 19
Edendale Rd. GL51: Chelt 6A 10
Edge Rd. GL6: Pains 5G 37
Edgeworth Cl. GL51: Chelt 6A 10
Edgeworth Cl. GL4: A'md 6F 27
GL7: Ciren 3B 54
Edinburgh Pl. GL51: Chelt 5B 10
Edison Cl. GL2: Qued 6D 32
Edison Rd. GL2: Qued 1D 38
Edward Massey Gdns.
GL4: Mats 2D 34
Edward Pl. GL20: Tewk 6G 7
Edward St. GL50: Chelt 2F 21
Edward Wilson Ho.
GL51: Chelt 4B 10
Edward Wilson Vs.
GL50: Chelt 3E 21
Edwy Pde. GL1: Glou 6H 15
EGYPT 2C 50
Elderberry M. GL3: Chu 3G 17
Eldersfield Cl. GL2: Qued 3B 32
GL54: Winch 3B 56
Elderwood Way GL4: Tuff 2F 33
Eldon Av. GL52: Chelt 6B 12
Eldon Rd. GL52: Chelt 6A 12
Eldorado Cres. GL50: Chelt 6E 11
Eldorado Rd. GL50: Chelt 6D 10
Elgar Ho. GL51: Chelt 5B 10
Elgin Mall GL10: Stone 3C 40
Eliot Cl. GL2: Glou 1F 33
Elizabeth Way GL7: Sidd 5F 55
Ellenborough Rd. GL52: Bish C . . 3F 9
Ellesmere Cl. GL3: Hucc 3G 27
Ellesmere Gro. GL50: Chelt 3E 21
Elliott Pl. GL51: Chelt 2C 20
Elliott Rd. GL7: Ciren 3E 55
Ellison Cl. GL4: A'md 5H 27
Ellison Rd. GL51: Chelt 5B 10
ELMBRIDGE 6E 17
Elmbridge Rd. GL2: Glou 1D 26
Elmbury Dr. GL20: Tewk 3E 7
Elm Cl. GL10: King S 6D 40
GL51: Chelt 4E 11
GL52: P'bury 2B 12
Elm Ct. GL52: Chelt 3A 12
Elm Dr. GL3: Brock 5C 28
Elmfield GL50: Chelt 6F 11
Elmfield Av. GL51: Chelt 3F 11
Elmfield Rd. GL51: Chelt 3F 11
Elm Gdn. Dr. GL51: Chelt 2F 19
Elmgrove Est. GL2: Hardw 6B 32
Elmgrove Rd. GL3: Hucc 4H 27
Elmgrove Rd. E. GL2: Hardw . . . 6B 32
Elmgrove Rd. W. GL2: Hardw . . . 6A 32
Elmira Rd. GL4: Glou 1A 34
Elmlea Rd. GL10: King S 6D 40
Elmleaze GL2: Glou 2C 26
Elmore La. E. GL2: Qued 2C 32
Elmore La. W.
GL2: Mins, Qued 3A 32
Elm Rd. GL5: Cash G 2H 41
GL20: Tewk 2H 7
Elms, The GL10: Stone 2B 40

Elms Rd. GL10: Stone 2B 40
Elmstone St.
GL50: Chelt 1A 4 (5F 11)
Elm St. GL51: Chelt 4E 11
Elmvil Rd. GL20: Tewk 3F 7
Elphick Rd. GL7: Strat 3C 52
Eltham Lawn GL50: Chelt 1E 21
Emerald Cl. GL4: Tuff 2F 33
Emine Pde. GL3: Brock 5C 28
Emmanuel Gdns. GL53: Chelt . . . 3G 21
Emmots Tump GL6: Nails 3C 50
Emperor Cl. GL51: Chelt 5A 10
Emperor Ct. GL50: Chelt 5F 11
Empire Way GL2: Glou 6E 25
Enborne Cl. GL4: Tuff 4G 33
Enfield Vs. GL51: Chelt 5A 56
Ennerdale Av. GL2: Longl 4E 17
Ennerdale Rd. GL51: Chelt 2B 20
Enstone Cvn. Pk. GL51: Chelt . . . 2H 19
Enterprise Way GL51: Chelt 4E 11
Epney Rd. GL4: Tuff 2F 33
Erin Pk. GL5: Light 5B 42
Ermin Cl. GL3: Brock 5C 28
Ermin Pl. GL7: Ciren 3F 55
Erminster Dr. GL3: Hucc 4H 27
Ermin St. GL3: Brock 5B 28
Ermin St. GL5: Light 5B 42
Esland Pl. GL7: Ciren 3E 55
Esporta Health & Fitness
(Gloucester) 1F 27
Essex Av. GL51: Chelt 5D 10
Essex Cl. GL3: Chu 1H 17
Estcote Rd. GL7: Ciren 6D 52
Estcourt Cl. GL1: Glou 5B 16
Estcourt Rd. GL1: Glou 5A 16
Etheldene Rd. GL5: Cash G 2G 41
Etheridge Pl. GL1: Glou 2C 26
Ettington Cl. GL51: Chelt 4A 10
Evelyn Cl. GL53: Charl K 4H 21
Evelyn Ct. GL50: Chelt 1F 21
Evenlode Av. GL52: Chelt 5B 12
Everest Cl. GL4: Tuff 4G 33
Everest Cl. GL6: Minch 6F 47
Everest Rd. GL53: Chelt 5H 21
Evergreen Wlk. GL2: Longl 3E 17
Everyman Theatre 3B 4 (6G 11)
Evesham Rd. GL1: Glou 3A 26
Evesham Rd. GL52: P'bury 2H 11
GL52: Bish C 1E 9
GL52: Chelt 1C 4 (5H 11)
GL54: Greet 1B 56
Evington Rd. GL51: Chelt 5B 10
Ewens Rd. GL52: Charl K 1B 22
Ewlyn Rd. GL53: Chelt 3G 21
Ewlyn Ter. GL53: Chelt 3G 21
Exmouth Cl. GL53: Chelt 2G 21
Exmouth St. GL53: Chelt 2G 21
Eynon Cl. GL53: Chelt 4F 21

F

Fairfax Cl. GL7: Ciren 2E 55
Fairfax Rd. GL7: Ciren 2E 55
Fairfield Av. GL53: Chelt 3G 21
Fairfield Pde. GL53: Chelt 3G 21
Fairfield Pk. Rd. GL53: Chelt . . . 3G 21
Fairfield Rd. GL53: Chelt 3G 21
Fairfield St. GL53: Chelt 3G 21
Fairfield Wlk. GL53: Chelt 3G 21
Fairford Way GL4: Glou 4C 26
Fairhaven Av. GL3: Brock 5D 28
Fairhaven Cvn. Pk.
GL51: Chelt 3G 19
Fairhaven Rd. GL53: Chelt 3G 21
Fairhavens Ct. GL52: Chelt 5A 12
(off Pittville Cir. Rd.)
Fairharm Rd. GL53: Chelt 3G 21
Fairmile Gdns. GL2: Longl 4A 16
Fairmount Rd. GL51: Chelt 6C 10
FAIRVIEW. 6A 12
Fair Vw. Cvn. Pk. GL1: Glou 6F 15
Fairview Cl. GL6: Nails 1C 50
GL52: Chelt 3D 4 (6H 11)
Fairview Ct.
GL52: Chelt 3D 4 (6A 12)
Fairview Rd.
GL52: Chelt 2C 4 (5H 11)
Fairview St.
GL52: Chelt 2D 4 (5H 11)
Fairwater Pk. GL4: Barn 2E 27
Fairway GL20: North 2H 7
Fairways Dr. GL2: Chu 1H 17

Fairy Glen Footpath GL6: Nails . . 2E 51
Falcon Cl. GL2: Qued 2C 32
GL3: Inns 3D 16
Faldo Cl. GL4: A'md 6G 27
Falfield Rd. GL4: Tuff 2G 33
Falkland Pl. GL51: Chelt 4A 10
Falkner St. GL1: Glou 6H 5 (3H 25)
(not continuous)
Faraday Cl. GL1: Glou 4A 26
Faringdon Rd. GL51: Chelt 2A 20
Far Leazes GL5: Stro 3E 43
Farleigh Cl. GL52: Charl K 3D 22
Farm Cl. GL20: North 1H 7
GL51: Chelt 4B 10
Farmcote Cl. GL6: Buss 6C 44
Farmcote Gdns. GL50: Chelt 3A 12
Farmfield Rd. GL51: Chelt 3C 20
Farmhill Cres. GL5: Stro 1A 42
Farmhill La. GL5: Stro 2A 42
Farmington Cl. GL4: A'md 6F 27
Farmington Rd. GL51: Chelt 1B 20
Farm La. GL51: Leck 5E 21
GL51: Shurd 2A 30
GL53: Leck 5E 21
Farm M. GL1: Glou 3H 25
Farm St. GL1: Glou 3H 25
Farrant Av. GL3: Chu 3H 17
Farrell Cl. GL7: Ciren 1D 54
Farriers Cl. GL51: Chelt 4F 11
Farriers Cft. GL6: Buss 6C 44
Farriers End GL2: Qued 3C 32
Farriers Reach GL52: Bish C 1C 8
Farr's La. GL5: Stro 3D 42
Far Sandfield GL3: Chu 4B 18
Farthing Cft. GL2: High 5A 14
FAR THRUPP 1F 47
Far Wells Rd. GL6: Bis 2F 45
Far Westrip GL5: West 2F 41
Fauconberg Rd.
GL50: Chelt 4A 4 (6F 11)
Fawkes Pl. GL5: Stro 3D 42
Fawley Dr. GL52: P'bury 3D 12
Fennel Cl. GL4: A'dle 1E 35
Fennells Vw. GL5: Stro 1F 43
Ferndale Cl. GL2: Longl 4C 16
Ferndales Cl. GL51: Up H 4C 20
Fern Lawn GL4: A'dle 3E 35
Fernleigh Cres. GL51: Up H 3B 20
Ferris Ct. Vw. GL6: Buss 6C 44
Ferry Gdns. GL2: Qued 4A 32
Festival Ho. GL52: Chelt 4D 4
Festival Rd. GL10: Stone 3B 40
Fewster Rd. GL6: Nails 2C 50
Fewster Sq. GL6: Nails 2C 50
FIDDLER'S GREEN 5A 10
Fiddler's Grn. La. GL51: Chelt . . 5A 10
Fidges La. GL6: Eastc 5D 44
Fieldcote Dr. GL3: Hucc 4H 27
Field Ct. Dr. GL2: Qued 5B 32
Fieldcourt Farmhouse
GL2: Qued 5B 32
Field Ct. Gdns. GL2: Qued 6B 32
Fielden GL4: A'dle 2E 35
Field End GL3: Chu 2A 18
Fieldfare GL4: A'dle 6F 27
Fieldgate Rd. GL52: Bish C 1F 9
Fieldhouse Gdns. GL5: Stro 4E 43
Field Rd. GL5: Rodb 4B 42
GL5: Stro 4D 42
Field Ter. GL5: Rodb 4C 42
Fieldways GL6: For G 2B 50
Filbert Cl. GL4: A'dle 1E 35
Filton Way GL4: Glou 4C 26
Finchcroft Ct. GL52: P'bury 3E 13
Finchcroft La. GL52: P'bury 4D 12
Finchmoor M. GL2: Longl 4A 16
Finch Rd. GL3: Inns 3E 17
Finlay Pl. GL4: Glou 6A 26
Finlay Rd. GL4: Glou 1H 33
Finsbury Ho. GL1: Glou 1B 26
Finstock Cl. GL51: Chelt 1C 20
Fircroft Cl. GL3: Hucc 3G 27
Fircroft Rd. GL51: Chelt 3A 16
Firethorne Cl. GL51: Longl 4C 16
Firgrove Wlk. GL51: Chelt 2H 19
Firs, The GL1: Glou 6A 16
GL51: Swin V 6A 8
Firs Rd. GL6: Amb 1D 50
Fir Tree Cl. GL52: P'bury 3B 12
Firwood Dr. GL4: Tuff 2H 33
Fish All. GL20: Tewk 4B 6
(off Barton St.)
Fishers La. GL52: Chelt . . . 2C 4 (5H 11)
Fishers Way GL5: Kings 6B 42

Fisher Wlk. GL51: Chelt.......3C 10
Fitness Mill..........1E 47
Flaxley Rd. GL4: Tuff.......2G 33
Flecker's Dr. GL51: Chelt.....2C 20
Fleming Cl. GL2: Longl.......3D 16
Fletcher's All. GL20: Tewk......4B 6
(off Barton St.)
Flint Rd. GL51: Chelt.......3B 20
Florida Dr. GL2: P'bury.......3D 12
Flower Way GL2: Longl.......5C 16
Foley Cl. GL4: Tuff.......3G 33
Folk Mus. 2F 5 (1G 25)
Folland Av. GL3: Hucc.......5A 28
Folly Cl. GL5: Stro.......1E 43
Folly La. GL5: Stro.......3D 42
  GL6: Stro.......1E 43
  GL50: Chelt.......3G 11
Folly Ri. GL5: Stro.......1E 43
FOOTBRIDGE.......4C 56
Forbes Cl. GL4: A'md.......5G 27
Foresters Rd. GL20: Tewk.......6B 6
FOREST GREEN.......1B 50
Forest Green Rovers FC.......1A 50
Forest Vw. Rd. GL4: Tuff.......3H 33
Forsythe Way GL4: Glou.......4C 26
Forsythia Cl. GL3: Chu.......3H 17
Fortina Cl. GL50: Chelt.......2F 11
Fort Vw. Ter. GL5: Cain.......4H 41
Forty Acre La. GL6: Lypiatt.......3H 43
Forum, The GL1: Glou.......4G 5
(off Market Way)
  GL7: Ciren.......1E 55
FORWOOD.......1G 51
Fosse Cl. GL4: A'md.......5F 27
  GL7: Ciren.......6F 53
Foster Cl. GL52: Bish C.......1F 9
Fountain Sq. GL1: Glou....2F 5 (1G 25)
Fountain St. GL6: Nails.......2D 50
Four Acres Vw. GL7: Ciren.......2C 54
Fox Cl. GL4: A'md.......6G 27
  GL5: Cash G.......3F 41
Foxcote GL2: Longl.......4C 16
Fox Elms Rd. GL4: Tuff.......3H 33
Foxes Bank Dr. GL7: Ciren.......3C 54
Foxes Cl. GL6: Buss.......6D 44
Foxes Dell GL6: For G.......1B 50
Foxglove Cl. GL4: A'md.......6F 27
  GL7: Sidd.......3F 55
Foxgrove Cl. GL52: Chelt.......6B 12
Foxleigh Cres. GL2: Longl.......4F 17
Foxmoor Cl. GL52: Bish C.......1D 8
Foxmoor La. GL5: Ebley.......3F 41
Foxrun GL2: Qued.......3D 32
Foxtail Cl. GL4: Glou.......6B 26
Foxwell Dr. GL3: Hucc.......3G 27
Framlington Cl. GL51: Chelt.......6D 10
Frampton M. GL51: Chelt.......2G 19
Frampton Rd. GL1: Glou.......4G 25
FRANCE LYNCH.......1F 49
Frances Cl. GL52: Chelt.......6A 12
Francis St. GL53: Chelt.......2G 21
Francis Woodcock Trad. Est.
  GL1: Glou.......3B 26
Frank Brookes Rd.
  GL51: Chelt.......3D 10
Franklyn Cl. GL51: Chelt.......5B 10
Frazier's Folly GL7: Sidd.......5F 55
Freame Cl. GL6: Buss.......6C 44
Freedom Camping & Cvn. Pk.
  GL51: Chelt.......1F 19
Fretherne Rd. GL4: Tuff.......2G 33
Frewin Cl. GL51: Chelt.......5A 10
Friars Cl. GL51: Chelt.......4E 21
Friary Rd. GL4: A'md.......5F 27
Friday St. GL6: Minch.......6H 47
  GL6: Pains.......5H 37
Frith, The GL6: Brown.......1B 48
Frithwood Cl. GL6: Brown.......1C 48
Frithwood Cl. GL6: Brown....1C 48
Frithwood Pk. GL6: Brown.......1C 48
Frobisher M. GL3: Chu.......1G 17
Frog Furlong La. GL2: Down H....1F 17
  GL3: Inns.......1F 17
Frogmarsh La. GL5: Woodc.......4A 46
Frome Av. GL5: Rodb.......4B 42
Frome Gdns. GL5: Cain.......4H 41
Frome Hall La. GL5: Rodb.......4B 42
Frome Pk. Rd. GL5: Rodb.......4B 42
Fromeside GL5: Stro.......4C 42
Fromeside Cl. GL5: Ebley.......4G 41
Fromeside Ind. Est. GL5: Stro....4C 42
Frying Pan Alley Footpath
  GL6: Nails.......2C 50
(off Fewster Rd.)

Fulbrook Cl. GL51: Chelt.......2A 10
Fullers Ct. GL1: Glou.....2F 5 (1G 25)
Furlong La. GL52: Bish C.......2A 8
Furlong Rd. GL1: Glou.......4H 25
Furze, The GL4: Glou.......1B 34
Furze Cft. GL2: Qued.......6C 32

G

Gable Point GL52: Woodm.......2G 9
Gadshill Rd. GL53: Charl K.......6C 22
Gadwell Rd. GL20: Wal C.......5D 6
Gainsborough Dr. GL4: Tuff.......3F 33
Galileo Cl. GL51: Chelt.......6A 10
Gallagher Retail Pk.
  GL51: Chelt.......2C 10
Gallops, The GL4: Glou.......4E 25
Gallops La. GL52: P'bury.......4E 13
Gallops Soren GL2: Glou.......5E 25
Gallows Pound La. GL7: Strat....3C 52
Gambier Parry Gdns.
  GL2: Longl.......5A 16
Gambles La. GL52: Woodm.......3H 9
Gannaway La. GL20: Tewk.......3E 7
(not continuous)
Gannet Cl. GL3: Brock.......6D 28
Gannicox Rd. GL5: Stro.......3B 42
Gara Cl. GL51: Chelt.......2C 10
Garden, The GL5: Woodc.......2B 46
Gardeners Way GL10: King S....6D 40
Gardenia Gro. GL51: Up H.......4C 20
Garden Rd. GL53: Charl K.......5C 22
Gardens, The GL52: Chelt.......3H 11
Garden Way GL2: Longl.......5C 16
Gardiner Cl. GL8: Buss.......6D 44
Gardiners Cl. GL3: Chu.......3A 18
Gardner Ct. GL7: Ciren.......2E 55
Gardner's La. GL51: Chelt.......3F 11
Garland Ct. GL7: Ciren.......2D 54
(off Meadow Rd.)
Garlandstone Wlk. GL2: Glou....5F 25
Garnalls Rd. GL4: Mats.......1D 34
Gatcombe Cl. GL52: Bish C.......2D 8
Gatmeres Rd. GL4: Mats.......2D 34
Gatton Way GL3: Hucc.......6G 27
Gazelle Cl. GL2: Qued.......3C 32
Genista Way GL51: Up H.......4C 20
George Cl. GL6: Pains.......5H 37
  GL10: Stone.......2C 40
George Dowty Dr. GL20: North....1H 7
George Maisey Ho.
  GL52: Chelt.......4B 12
George Pearce Ho.
  GL6: Minch.......6A 48
George Readings Way
  GL51: Chelt.......1C 20
  GL5: Stro.......3D 42
  GL6: Bis.......1F 45
  GL6: Nails.......2D 50
George Whitefield Cl.
  GL4: Mats.......1D 34
Georgian Cl. GL4: A'dle.......3A 18
Geralds Way GL6: Buss.......1D 48
Gere Cl. GL4: Tuff.......4G 33
Gervase Rd. GL54: Winch.......3B 56
Gibson Cl. GL5: Stro.......3G 43
Gibson Ct. GL7: Ciren.......2D 54
Gibson Rd. GL3: Inns.......2F 17
Giddynap La. GL5: Amb, Inch....5B 46
Giffard Way GL53: Leck.......5G 21
Gifford Cl. GL2: Longl.......4D 16
Gilbert Rd. GL2: Longl.......4D 16
Gilberts La. GL4: Whad.......6A 34
Gilbert Ward Ct. GL53: Charl K....4B 22
Gilder Rd. GL52: Bish C.......3F 9
Gilders Paddock GL52: Bish C....1E 9
Giles Cox GL2: Qued.......5C 32
Gillett Cl. GL54: Winch.......5A 56
Gilpin Av. GL3: Hucc.......2G 27
Gimson Cl. GL4: Tuff.......3G 33
Gipsy La. GL6: Chalf.......3G 49
GL1 Gloucester Leisure Cen....2A 26
Glade, The GL7: Sidd.......3F 55
Gladiator Cl. GL3: Brock.......6D 28
Gladstone Rd. GL1: Glou.......5F 25
  GL53: Charl K.......4B 22
Glamorgan Rd. GL51: Chelt....3B 20
Glass Ho., The GL50: Chelt......6F 11
Glebe, The GL6: Minch.......6A 48
Glebe Rd. GL7: Strat.......3C 52

Glebe Farm Ct. GL51: Up H.......4C 20
Glebe Rd. GL6: Minch.......6A 48
Glebe Sq. GL7: P'bury.......3C 12
Glencairn Av. GL4: Tuff.......4F 33
Glencairn Ct. GL50: Chelt.......1D 20
Glencairn Pk. Rd. GL50: Chelt....1D 20
Glen Cl. GL10: Stone.......2C 40
Glendower Cl. GL3: Chu.......1G 17
Glenfall St. GL52: Chelt....1D 4 (5H 11)
Glenfall Way GL52: Charl K.......3C 22
Glenlea Gro. GL51: Up H.......4C 20
Glen Pk. Cres. GL5: Kings.......6B 42
Glensanda Ct.
  GL50: Chelt.......5A 4 (1G 21)
Glenthorne Cl. GL10: Stone....1C 40
Glenville Pde GL3: Hucc.......4H 27
Glevum Cl. GL2: Longl.......5C 16
Glevum Ct. GL51: Chelt.......5A 10
Glevum Shop. Cen. GL4: A'dle....1E 35
Glevum Way GL4: A'dle.......1F 35
Glevum Works Trad. Est.
  GL1: Glou.......4B 26
GLOUCESTER.......3H 5 (2H 25)
Gloucester Bus. Pk.
  GL3: Brock.......5A 28
Gloucester Cathedral....2G 5 (1H 25)
Gloucester City Mus. & Art Gallery
  ....4G 5 (2H 25)
Gloucester Crematorium
  GL4: Glou.......4D 26
Gloucester Grn. GL4: Barn.......1E 27
Gloucester Greyfriars.......4G 5
Gloucester Northern By-Pass
  GL2: Glou.......5F 15
  GL2: Longf, Longl.......4A 16
  GL3: Longl.......4A 16
Gloucester Pl.
  GL52: Chelt.......3C 4 (6H 11)
Gloucester Retail Pk.
  GL4: Glou.......3D 26
Gloucester Rd. GL5: Pains.......4H 37
  GL7: Ciren, Strat.......2B 52
  GL10: Stand, Stone.......1C 40
  GL20: Tewk.......5A 6 & 6F 7
  GL51: Chelt.......1H 19
Gloucester RUFC.......1H 5 (6H 15)
Gloucester St Margarets Church
  ....1B 26
GLOUCESTERSHIRE AIRPORT....1B 18
Gloucestershire &
  Warwickshire Railway
  Cheltenham Racecourse....6D 8
GLOUCESTERSHIRE ROYAL HOSPITAL
  ....1B 26
Gloucester Ski & Snowboard Cen.
  ....2C 34
Gloucester Station (Rail)
  ....3H 5 (1A 26)
Gloucester St. GL5: Stro.......3D 42
  GL6: Pains.......4H 37
  GL7: Ciren.......5C 52
  GL54: Winch.......5A 56
Gloucester Trad. Est.
  GL3: Hucc.......6A 28
Glynbridge Ct. GL1: Glou.......4A 26
Glynbridge Gdns. GL51: Chelt....2C 10
Glyndthorpe Gro. GL51: Up H....4B 20
Glynfield Ri. GL5: Ebley.......3F 41
Glynrosa Rd. GL53: Charl K.......4C 22
Goddard Way GL4: Tuff.......3G 33
Godfrey Cl. GL51: Chelt.......2D 20
Godwin Cl. GL52: Chelt.......5A 12
Godwin Rd. GL54: Winch.......3B 56
Goldcrest Cl. GL10: Stone.......2C 40
Golden Cl. GL4: Tuff.......3F 33
Golden Farm Rd. GL7: Ciren....1F 55
Golden Jubilee Way
  GL5: Dudb.......4H 41
Golden Miller Rd. GL50: Chelt....2F 11
Golden Va. GL3: Chu.......3A 18
Golden Valley GL5: Brim.......3H 47
Golden Valley By-Pass
  GL3: Chu.......4G 17
  GL51: Badg, Chelt.......4G 17
GOLDEN VALLEY INTERCHANGE
  ....2E 19
Goldfoot Ho. GL51: Chelt.......6C 10
Goldsborough Cl. GL4: Glou....4C 26
Goldsmith Cl. GL51: Chelt.......5B 10
Goldsmith Rd. GL51: Chelt.......5B 10
Goldwater Springs GL6: Nails....1C 50
Golf Club La. GL3: Brock.......1B 36
Golf Course Rd. GL6: Pains.......4H 37
Goodmoor Cres. GL3: Chu.......3H 17

Goodridge Av. GL2: Glou.......2D 32
Goodridge Ind. Est. GL2: Glou....1D 32
Goodwin Cl. GL1: Glou.......4H 25
Goodyere St. GL1: Glou.....6H 5 (3A 26)
  (not continuous)
Gooseacre Ct. GL7: Ciren.......5D 52
Gooseacre La. GL7: Ciren.......5D 52
Gordon Cl. GL2: High.......4B 14
Gordon Rd. GL53: Chelt.......4F 21
Gordon Ter. GL5: Brim.......3G 47
Gorse Cl. GL4: A'md.......1G 35
Gosditch St. GL7: Ciren.......6D 52
Goshawk Rd. GL2: Qued.......2C 32
Goswood Cnr. GL2: Qued.......5B 32
Gotherington La. GL52: Bish C....1F 9
Gothic Cotts. GL1: Glou.......2A 26
(off Barton St.)
Gouda Way GL1: Glou.....1G 5 (6H 15)
Goulds Gro. GL20: North.......1H 7
Grace Gdns. GL51: Chelt.......2A 20
Grafton Cl. GL50: Chelt.......2F 21
(off Norwood Rd.)
Grafton Rd. GL2: Glou.......6C 16
  GL50: Chelt.......2F 21
Graham Ct. GL20: Tewk.......3C 6
Graham Gdns. GL1: Glou.......4H 25
Graham Pl. GL51: Chelt.......4A 10
Grange Cl. GL6: Minch.......6G 47
Grange Ct. GL7: Strat.......3C 52
  GL20: North.......1H 7
Grange Dr. GL52: Bish C.......2E 9
Grangefield App. GL52: Bish C....2D 8
Grange Orchard Cvn. Pk.
  GL51: Chelt.......2G 19
Grange Rd. GL4: Tuff.......2F 33
  GL20: North.......1H 7
Grange Vw. GL5: Stro.......2D 42
Grange Wlk. GL53: Charl K.......4C 22
  (not continuous)
Granley Cl. GL51: Chelt.......1C 20
Granley Dr. GL51: Chelt.......1C 20
Granley Gdns. GL51: Chelt.......1C 20
Granley M. GL51: Chelt.......1C 20
Gransmoor Grange GL3: Hucc....4A 28
Grantley Cres. GL7: Ciren.......2D 54
Granville St. GL1: Glou.......4F 25
  GL50: Chelt.......1A 4 (5F 11)
Grasby Cl. GL4: Barn.......4F 27
Grasmere Rd. GL2: Longl.......5D 16
  GL51: Chelt.......2C 20
Gratton Rd. GL50: Chelt.......2F 21
Gratton St. GL50: Chelt.......2G 21
Gravel Pit La. GL52: P'bury.......2D 12
Gravel Wlk. GL20: Tewk.......3C 6
  GL52: South.......5H 9
Gravney Cl. GL51: Chelt.......3B 10
Gray Cl. GL3: Inns.......2F 17
Grayling Cl. GL4: A'md.......6F 27
Grayson Cl. GL20: Tewk.......2D 6
Greatfield Dr. GL53: Charl K.......4A 22
Greatfield La. GL51: Up H.......3A 20
  (not continuous)
Great Gro. GL4: A'md.......4E 27
Gt. Norwood St. GL50: Chelt....2F 21
Gt. Orchard GL5: Thru.......1F 47
Gt. Western Ct. GL1: Glou.......2B 26
Gt. Western Rd. GL1: Glou.......1A 26
  GL50: Chelt.......5F 11
Gt. Western Ter. GL50: Chelt....5F 11
GREAT WITCOMBE.......3H 37
Great Witcombe Roman Villa
  (remains of).......4E 37
Grebe Cl. GL4: A'dle.......6D 26
Green, The GL2: Hardw.......1A 38
  GL2: High.......4A 14
  GL3: Chu.......6B 18
  GL5: Sels.......6H 41
  GL7: Ciren.......6F 53
  GL10: King S.......6D 40
  GL51: Uck.......1A 10
  GL52: Bish C.......2E 9
Green Acre GL3: Brock.......6D 28
Green Bank GL3: Brock.......1D 36
Green Cl. GL3: Brock.......1D 36
Greenfields GL2: Chu.......1G 17
Green Gdns. GL3: Brock.......1D 36
Greenhill Cl. GL4: Tuff.......2E 33
Greenhill Dr. GL2: Glou.......2D 32
Greenhills Cl. GL53: Chelt.......4H 21
Greenhills Rd. GL53: Charl K....4A 22
Greenhouse La. GL6: Pains.....6H 37

Greenings, The GL51: Up H 4C **20**
Green La. GL2: Hardw 1A **38**
GL3: Brock. 4F **29**
(not continuous)
GL3: Chu. 5B **18**
GL3: Hucc. 5H **27**
GL20: Tewk 2F **7**
Green La. Bus. Pk. GL20: Tewk . . 3E **7**
Green Mdw. Bank GL52: Bish C . . 2D **8**
Greenmeadows Cvn. Pk.
GL51: Stav. 1E **19**
Greenmead Pk. Cvn. Site
GL51: Up H 4A **20**
Green Pk. GL2: Hardw 1B **38**
Green Pippin Cl. GL2: Glou 1D **26**
GREEN STREET. 2D **36**
Green St. GL3: Brock 1C **36**
GL10: Stone 2C **40**
Green Way GL3: Brock 6D **28**
Greenway GL52: Woodm 2G **9**
Greenway, The GL1: Glou. 6G **25**
Greenway Cl. GL51: Shurd 2A **30**
Greenway La. GL51: Shurd. 2A **30**
GL51: Ull 4E **31**
GL52: Charl K 2B **22**
GL53: Ull 4E **31**
Greenways GL54: Winch. 3C **56**
Greenwood Cl. GL3: Hucc. 5A **28**
GREET 1B **56**
Greet Rd. GL54: Winch 4B **56**
Grenadier Cl. GL4: A'md. 5G **27**
Grenadier Rd. GL51: Chelt 3B **10**
Grenville Cl. GL3: Chu 1G **17**
Gresham Ct. GL51: Chelt 5B **10**
GRETTON 1A **56**
Gretton Rd. GL54: Winch 1A **56**
Greville Cl. GL2: Glou. 5H **15**
Greville Ct. GL51: Chelt 1C **20**
Grevil Rd. GL51: Chelt 3C **10**
Greyfriars GL1: Glou 4G **5** (2H **25**)
Greyfriars Wlk. GL7: Ciren 3C **54**
Greyhound Gdns. GL2: Longl . . . 4E **17**
Greylag Cres. GL20: Wal C 5D **6**
Greys Cl. GL6: Buss 6C **44**
Greystone Lodge GL3: Hucc 4A **28**
Grierson Cl. GL3: Hucc 5A **28**
Griffin Mill Est. GL5: Thru. 6E **43**
Griffiths Av. GL51: Chelt 1C **20**
Griffon Cl. GL2: Quod 2C **32**
Grimwade Cl. GL51: Chelt 6C **10**
Grisedale Cl. GL2: Longl. 4E **17**
Grist Mill Cl. GL51: Chelt 2A **20**
Grosvenor Ho.
GL1: Glou 3H **5** (1H **25**)
GL52: Chelt 1D **4**
Grosvenor Pl. Sth.
GL52: Chelt 3C **4** (6H **11**)
Grosvenor Rd. GL2: Glou 1C **26**
GL10: Stone 5A **40**
Grosvenor St.
GL52: Chelt 4C **4** (6H **11**)
Grosvenor Ter.
GL52: Chelt 3C **4** (6H **11**)
Grove, The GL5: Ebley 4G **41**
GL5: Sels 6H **41**
GL8: Aven 6G **51**
GL10: Stone 4D **40**
GL50: Chelt 1E **21**
GL52: Chelt 6B **12**
Grove Cres. GL4: Barn 2D **35**
Grovefield Way
GL51: Badg, Chelt. 2G **19**
Grovelands GL4: Barn 3F **27**
Grovelands Cl. GL3: Charl K . . . 3B **22**
Grove La. GL7: Ciren 5D **52**
Grove Pk. Rd. GL5: Stro 2D **42**
Grove Rd. GL3: Chu 4G **17**
Grove St. GL1: Glou 3A **26**
GL50: Chelt. 2A **4** (5F **11**)
Guardian Cl. GL53: Charl K 3A **22**
Guestriss Cotts. GL50: Chelt . . . 2F **11**
Guildhall Arts Cen. 4H **5** (1H **25**)
Guildings Way GL10: King S 1B **48**
Guinea St. GL1: Glou. . . . 1H **5** (6A **16**)
Guise Av. GL3: Brock 1E **37**
Guise Cl. GL2: Quod 5C **32**
Gunbarrel La. GL6: Nails 3D **50**
Gunhouse La. GL5: Stro 5E **43**
Gurney Av. GL4: Tuff 3G **33**
Gusphill Cl. GL20: Tewk 4B **6**
Gwernant Rd. GL51: Chelt 3C **20**
Gwinnett Ct. GL51: Shurd 1B **30**
Gyde Rd. GL6: Pains. 4H **37**
Gypsy Pk. GL4: Brook 2F **39**

H

Hadow Way GL2: Qued 5C **32**
Hadrians Way GL4: A'md 4F **27**
Hailes Rd. GL4: Glou 4E **27**
Hailes St. GL54: Winch. 5C **56**
Hakeburn Rd. GL7: Ciren 6D **52**
Hale La. GL6: Pains 5H **37**
Hales Cl. GL52: Chelt 6B **12**
Hale's Rd. GL52: Chelt 1A **22**
Halford Ho. GL2: Glou 1F **33**
Halland Rd. GL53: Chelt. 4G **21**
Hallmead Cl. GL51: Chelt 2A **10**
Hall of Fame (Cheltenham Racecourse)
. . . . 1H **11**
Hall Rd. GL53: Leck 5G **21**
HAM 2D **22**
Hambledon Cl. GL7: Sth C 6H **55**
Hambrook St. GL2: Charl K. . . . 2C **22**
Hambrook Ter. GL52: Charl K . . . 3C **22**
Hambutts Dr. GL6: Pains 5G **37**
Hambutts Mead GL6: Pains 5G **37**
Ham Cl. GL2: Charl K 2D **22**
Hamer St. GL1: Glou 2C **26**
Hamilton St. GL53: Charl K. . . . 2B **22**
Hamlet Cl. GL4: Charl K 2E **23**
Hamlet Cl. GL51: Chelt. 5B **10**
Ham Mill La. GL5: Thru 1E **47**
Hammond Cl. GL4: Barn. 2E **27**
GL53: Chelt. 2H **21**
Hammond Way GL4: Barn. 2E **27**
GL7: Ciren 1C **54**
Hampden Way
GL1: Glou 4H **5** (2H **25**)
Hampton Cl. GL3: Hucc 4A **28**
GL51: Chelt. 4D **20**
HAMPTON GREEN 6F **47**
Hampton Hill GL8: Aven 6H **51**
Hampton Pl. GL3: Chu 1H **17**
Ham Rd. GL52: Charl K. 2D **22**
GL54: Charl K 2E **23**
Ham Sq. GL2: Charl K 2D **22**
Hanman Rd. GL1: Glou 4A **26**
Hanna Ct. GL50: Chelt. . . . 2A **4** (5G **11**)
Hannah Pl. GL3: Inns 2F **17**
Hannam Ct. GL53: Chelt 5G **21**
Hanover Ct. GL7: Ciren 1E **55**
GL20: Tewk. 4B **6**
GL51: Chelt 1E **21**
Hanover Gdns. GL6: Nails. 2C **50**
Hanover Ho. GL51: Chelt 1E **21**
Hanover Lodge GL5: Cash G . . . 3G **41**
Hanover Pde. GL50: Chelt 4G **11**
Hanover St. GL50: Chelt 4G **11**
Hanover Way GL3: Chu. 2G **17**
Hanson Gdns. GL52: Bish C . . . 1C **8**
Hanstone Cl. GL7: Ciren 3C **54**
Harbourside GL20: Tewk 3C **6**
Harbour Vw. GL20: Tewk. 3C **6**
Harbury M. GL1: Glou 3B **26**
Hardwick Bank Rd. GL20: North. . 1G **7**
HARDWICKE 6B **32**
Hardwicke Bank Rd.
GL20: North. 1H **7**
Hardy Rd. GL52: Bish C 1E **9**
Harebell Rd. GL4: A'md. 6F **27**
Harefield Gro. GL50: Chelt 3F **21**
Hare La. GL1: Glou 3H **5** (1H **25**)
(not continuous)
HARESCOMBE 6H **39**
Harescombe Dr. GL1: Glou 2B **26**
HARESFIELD 6E **39**
Haresfield GL7: Strat 3C **52**
Haresfield Countryside Cen. 5B **38**
Haresfield La. GL10: Hares 6C **38**
GL7: Ciren 2B **38**
GL4: Brook 4H **39**
GL10: Hares 2B **38**
Haresfield Lodge GL4: Mats 1C **34**
Harewood Cl. GL4: Tuff 4F **33**
Harleys Fld. GL4: A'md. 4E **27**
HARLEYWOOD 4C **50**
Harness Cl. GL2: Glou. 5E **25**
Harper Rd. GL5: Cash G 2H **41**
Harpfield Cl. GL52: Bish C 2E **9**
Harpfield Rd. GL52: Bish C 2E **9**
Harp Hill GL52: Charl K. 6B **12**
Harrington Dr. GL51: Chelt 2B **20**
Harris Cl. GL3: Chu. 4B **18**
Harrison Rd. GL51: Shurd 1A **30**
Harry Yates Way GL51: Chelt . . . 3A **10**

Hartbury Cl. GL51: Chelt 4A **10**
Harthurstfield Pk. GL51: Chelt . . 1G **19**
Hartington Rd. GL1: Glou 5F **25**
Hartland Rd. GL1: Glou. 5A **26**
Hartlebury Way GL52: Charl K . . 3D **22**
Hartley Av. GL4: A'md 4F **27**
Hartley Cl. GL53: Charl K 5A **22**
Hartley Ct. GL52: Chelt 5B **12**
Hartley La. GL53: Leck H 3F **31**
Harvesters Vw. GL52: Bish C . . . 1C **8**
Harvest Gro. GL51: Chelt 2A **10**
Harvest Way GL2: Qued 6C **32**
Harvey Cl. GL2: Glou 6F **25**
Harvey's La. GL54: Winch 5A **56**
Harwell Cl. GL4: Tuff 4G **33**
Hasfield Cl. GL2: Qued 4B **32**
Haslemere Ct. GL3: Brock 6E **29**
Haslette Way GL1: Up H 4B **20**
Hastings Pl. GL20: Tewk. 6B **6**
Hatfield Rd. GL1: Glou 4B **26**
Hathaway Cl. GL2: Glou. 1F **33**
HATHERLEY 2B **20**
Hatherley Brake GL51: Chelt. . . . 2B **20**
Hatherley Ct. GL51: Chelt 2E **21**
Hatherley Ct. Rd. GL51: Chelt . . 2E **21**
Hatherley Ga. GL51: Chelt 2E **21**
Hatherley Hall GL51: Chelt. 2D **20**
Hatherley La. GL51: Chelt 1H **19**
Hatherley M. GL51: Chelt 2E **21**
Hatherley Rd. GL1: Glou 4A **26**
GL51: Chelt. 3A **20**
Hatherley St. GL50: Chelt 2E **21**
Hathorn Rd. GL3: Hucc 5A **28**
Havelock Rd. GL3: Hucc. 3H **27**
Haven Av. GL10: Stone 4B **40**
Haven Ct. GL2: Glou 6D **16**
Haven Pk. Mobile Home Site
GL51: Up H 4H **19**
Haver, The GL57: Charl K 2C **22**
Hawcombe M. GL51: Up H 3C **20**
Haweswater Rd. GL51: Chelt . . . 5E **27**
Hawk Cl. GL4: A'dle 5E **27**
GL6: Buss 1D **48**
Hawkmoth Cl. GL20: Wal C 6D **6**
Hawkswood Rd. GL51: Chelt . . . 4E **21**
Haworth Cl. GL2: Qued 3C **32**
Hawthorn Dr. GL52: Woodm. . . . 2G **9**
Hawthorne Av. GL4: A'dle 6D **26**
Hawthorne Dr. GL3: Chu. 3H **17**
Hawthornes, The GL51: Up H . . . 3A **20**
Hawthorn Ri. GL5: Cash G 2G **41**
Hawthorn Ridge GL6: For G 1A **50**
Hawthorn Rd. GL51: Chelt 4B **10**
Hawthorns, The GL6: Buss 5A **44**
Hawthorn Way GL20: North 1H **7**
Haycroft Cl. GL52: Bish C 1D **8**
Haycroft Dr. GL4: Mats 3E **35**
Haydale Gdns. GL2: Longl 4D **17**
Hayden Rd. GL51: Chelt 2B **10**
(not continuous)
Hayes Ct. GL2: Longl 3A **16**
GL52: Chelt 5B **12**
Hayes Rd. GL6: For G 1B **50**
GL52: Chelt 5A **12**
Hayfield Way GL52: Bish C 1C **8**
Haygarth Pl. GL7: Ciren 3C **54**
Hayhedge La. GL6: Bis 2G **45**
Hay La. GL6: Hors. 6A **50**
Haylea Rd. GL52: Bish C 1C **8**
Haymes Dr. GL52: Cle H 4H **9**
Haymes Rd. GL52: Cle H 4H **9**
Hay's Cotts. GL53: Chelt 3H **21**
Hayward Cl. GL4: A'md 4E **27**
Haywards La. GL52: Charl K . . . 1B **22**
Hayward's Rd.
GL52: Charl K, Chelt 5A **12**
Haywicks La. GL2: Hardw 5A **32**
Hazebrouck Cl. GL51: Chelt . . . 2B **20**
Hazel Cl. GL2: Longl 4C **16**
Hazel Ct. GL4: Barn 2E **27**
Hazelcroft GL3: Chu 4B **18**
Hazelhurst GL50: Chelt 6D **10**
Hazels, The GL4: A'md 4F **27**
Hazelton Cl. GL4: Glou 5A **26**
Hazledean Rd. GL51: Chelt 4E **21**
Hazlewood Cl. GL51: Chelt 4E **21**
Hazlitt Cft. GL51: Chelt 3A **10**
Headlam Cl. GL4: Tuff 4G **33**
Headlands, The GL5: Woodc . . . 2A **46**
Healey M. GL1: Glou 1B **26**
Heapey Cl. GL52: Bish C 5A **10**
Hearne Cl. GL53: Charl K 3C **22**
Hearne Rd. GL53: Charl K 3C **22**
Heathdean Rd. GL3: Chu 3G **17**

Heather Av. GL4: A'md 1G **35**
Heather Cl. GL5: Rodb 6B **42**
Heathfield Rd. GL5: Stro 1B **42**
Heath Lodge GL52: Chelt 5A **12**
Heathville Rd. GL1: Glou 1A **26**
Heazle Pl. GL5: Stro 2D **42**
Hedgerow, The GL2: Longl 5C **16**
Helens Cl. GL51: Chelt 4A **10**
Hembury Cl. GL2: Hardw 6A **32**
Hemmingsdale Rd. GL2: Glou . . 2F **25**
Hemming Way GL52: Bish C . . . 2E **9**
HEMPSTED 5E **25**
Hempsted La. GL2: Glou. 5E **25**
Hendingham Cl. GL4: Tuff. 3E **33**
Hendre M. GL50: Chelt 6F **11**
HENLEY 6F **29**
Henley Bank La. GL3: Brock . . . 5F **29**
Henley Cl. GL5: Cash G 2G **41**
Henley Pl. GL1: Glou 6G **25**
Henley Rd. GL51: Chelt. 4A **10**
Henley Vs. GL5: Stro 2D **42**
Henrietta St.
GL50: Chelt 2B **4** (5G **11**)
Henry Rd. GL1: Glou. 1A **26**
Henry Ryder Cl. GL4: A'md 5G **27**
Henry St. GL1: Glou 1A **26**
Herbert Stark Cl. GL7: Ciren . . . 1F **55**
(off Queen Elizabeth Rd.)
Herbert St. GL1: Glou. 3B **26**
Hereford Cl. GL50: Chelt. 1A **4**
Hereford Pl.
GL50: Chelt. 1A **4** (5F **11**)
Hereward Rd. GL7: Ciren 6D **52**
Heritage Pk. GL5: Cain 4H **41**
Hermitage St. GL53: Chelt 2G **21**
Heron Cl. GL2: Glou 2B **20**
Heron Way GL4: A'dle 6D **26**
Hertford Rd. GL52: Bish C 1E **9**
HESTER'S WAY 5B **10**
Hester's Way La. GL51: Chelt. . . 3A **10**
Hester's Way Rd. GL51: Chelt . . 4A **10**
Hethersett Rd. GL1: Glou 3B **26**
Hetton Gdns. GL53: Charl K . . . 3B **22**
Hever Cl. GL20: Wal C 6D **6**
Hewlett Pl. GL52: Chelt 4D **4** (6H **11**)
Hewlett Rd.
GL52: Chelt 4D **4** (6H **11**)
Hiatt Rd. GL6: Minch 5G **47**
Hickley Gdns. GL3: Brock 5D **28**
Hicks Beach Rd. GL51: Chelt . . . 4A **10**
Hidcote Av. GL51: Up H 4D **20**
Hidcote Cl. GL6: Buss. 6C **44**
Highbank Pk. GL2: Longl 5A **16**
Highbury La.
GL52: Chelt 4C **4** (6H **11**)
Highbury M. GL52: Chelt 5D **4**
Highclere Rd. GL2: Qued 3B **32**
Highcroft GL6: Minch 5G **47**
Higher Newmarket Rd.
GL6: Nails 3A **42**
HIGHFIELD 3A **42**
Highfield La. GL7: Ciren 3D **54**
Highfield Pl. GL4: Glou 4C **26**
Highfield Rd. GL4: Glou 4C **26**
GL5: Stro 4F **43**
Highfield Way GL6: Fran L 1F **49**
Highgrove, The GL52: Bish C . . . 2D **8**
Highgrove Way GL3: Chu 2G **17**
Highland Rd. GL53: Chelt. 5H **21**
Highlands, The GL6: Pains 4H **37**
Highliffe Dr. GL2: Longl 4D **32**
High Mdw. GL4: A'dle 1E **35**
HIGHNAM 5A **14**
HIGHNAM GREEN 4A **14**
HIGH ORCHARD 6F **5** (3G **25**)
GL2: Glou. 6E **5** (3G **25**)
High St. GL1: Glou 4A **26**
GL4: Up L 3F **35**
GL5: Stro 3D **42**
GL5: Woodc 3A **46**
GL6: Bis. 2F **45**
GL6: Chalf 2E **49**
GL6: Minch 6H **47**
GL8: Aven 5F **51**
GL10: King S 6D **40**
GL10: Stone 2C **40**
GL20: Tewk 4B **6**
GL50: Chelt. 1A **4** (5F **11**)
GL51: Chelt. 4F **11**
GL52: P'bury. 3D **12**
GL54: Winch 5C **56**
High Vw. GL2: Glou 5D **24**

High Vw. Lodge—Kings Barton St.

High Vw. Lodge *GL5: Stro 3D 42*
(off Wesley Ct.)
Highwood Av. GL53: Chelt 3F **21**
Highwood Ct. GL6: For G 1A **50**
Highwood Dr. GL6: For G 2A **50**
Highworth Rd. GL1: Glou 5A **26**
Hildyard Cl. GL2: Hardw 6B **32**
Hill, The GL5: Stro 3C **42**
Hillands Dr. GL53: Chelt 5G **21**
Hillary Rd. GL53: Chelt 5H **21**
Hillborough Rd. GL4: Tuff 2H **33**
Hillclose Est. GL5: Light 6B **42**
Hillcot Cl. GL2: Qued 4B **32**
Hill Cotts. GL1: Glou 6A **16**
Hill Ct. GL52: Chelt 2H **11**
Hill Ct. Rd. GL52: Chelt 3H **11**
Hill Crest GL2: High 3A **14**
Hillcrest Rd. GL5: Cash G 2G **41**
Hillfield GL5: Stro 3A **42**
GL51: Chelt 6C **10**
Hillfield Ct. GL1: Glou 1B **26**
Hillfield Ct. Rd. GL1: Glou 6B **16**
Hill Hay Rd. GL4: Mats 2D **34**
Hill Ho. GL7: Ciren 6E **53**
Hillier Cl. GL5: Stro 1E **43**
Hillier Dr. GL51: Up H 4D **20**
Hill Mead GL4: Brook 2H **39**
Hill Rd. GL4: Glou 1A **34**
Hillside GL6: Fran L 6G **45**
Hillside Cl. GL51: Chelt 2D **20**
GL52: Woodm 2H **9**
Hillside Gdns. GL52: Woodm 2H **9**
Hill Top Cl. GL5: Stro 3F **43**
Hill Top Rd. GL50: Chelt 2G **11**
Hill Top Vw. GL6: Buss 6C **44**
Hillview Av. GL3: Brock 5C **28**
Hill Vw. Cotts. GL4: Tuff 3H **33**
Hillview Dr. GL3: Hucc 3G **27**
Hillview Rd. GL3: Hucc 3G **27**
GL52: Chelt 5C **12**
Hilly Orchard GL5: Cain 4H **41**
Hiltmead La. GL2: More V 5A **38**
Hilton Cl. GL2: Glou 5E **25**
Hine Gdns. GL52: Chelt 4A **12**
Hinton Rd. GL1: Glou 5A **16**
Hisnams Fld. GL52: Bish C 2E **9**
Hithe, The GL5: Rodb C 1C **46**
Hobart Ho. GL51: Chelt 6B **10**
Hobby Cl. GL53: Chelt 4F **21**
Holder Rd. GL52: Bish C 3E **9**
Hollams Rd. GL20: Tewk 3C **6**
Holland Ct. *GL1: Glou 6B 16*
(off Denmark Rd.)
Hollies Hill GL6: Nails 1D **50**
Hollingham La. GL6: Hors 5A **50**
Hollis Gdns. GL51: Chelt 3A **20**
Hollis Rd. GL51: Chelt 3A **20**
Holloway Rd. GL6: Bis 2F **45**
Hollow La. GL5: Stro 3E **43**
Holly End GL2: Qued 5C **32**
Holly Gro., The GL2: Qued 6C **32**
Hollyhock La. GL6: Pains 5H **37**
HOLLY HOUSE (HOSPITAL) 5E **27**
Holly Tree Gdn. GL5: Ebley 4F **41**
Holmer Cres. GL51: Up H 3A **20**
Holme Rd. GL20: Tewk 6G **7**
Holmleigh Pde. GL4: Tuff 3F **33**
Holmleigh Rd. GL4: Tuff 2F **33**
Holmoak Cl. GL20: Wal C 6D **6**
Holmwood Cl. GL4: Tuff 3G **33**
Holmwood Dr. GL4: Tuff 3F **33**
Holst Birthplace Mus. 1C **4** (5H **11**)
Holst Way GL4: Tuff 3G **33**
Holt, The GL4: Barn 4F **27**
GL52: Bish C 3D **8**
Holtham Av. GL3: Chu 2A **18**
Homeabbey Ho. GL20: Tewk 3B **6**
Homeberry Ho. GL7: Ciren 1D **54**
Home Cl. GL51: Chelt 4B **10**
Homecroft Dr. GL51: Uck 2B **10**
HOMEDOWNS 5H **7**
Home Farm Ct. GL52: Charl K 2B **22**
Homefield GL6: Nails 3A **50**
Home Ground GL4: A'md 5F **27**
Homespa Ho. GL50: Chelt 6E **11**
Homespring Ho. GL52: Chelt 5B **12**
Homestead Ct. GL4: A'md 6G **27**
Hone Ct. GL20: Tewk 4B **6**
Honeybourne Dr. GL51: Chelt 3A **10**
Honeybourne Rd. GL51: Chelt 3A **10**
Honeybourne Way GL50: Chelt 5F **11**
Honeysuckle Cl. GL52: P'bury 4D **12**
Honeysuckle Dr. GL4: A'md 6F **27**
Honeysuckle Way GL52: Bish C 1E **9**
Honeythorne Cl. GL2: Glou 4E **25**
Honyatt Rd. GL1: Glou 6A **16**
Hooper Cl. GL4: Glou 5C **26**
Hope Mill La. GL5: Brim 2F **47**
Hope Mills Bus. Cen.
GL5: Brim 2F **47**
Hope Mills Cvn. Pk.
GL5: Brim 2F **47**
Hope Orchard GL51: Chelt 3A **10**
Hope St. GL51: Chelt 4E **11**
Hopewell St. GL1: Glou 3A **26**
Hopton Ct. *GL20: Tewk 4B 6*
(off Barton St.)
Hopwood Gro. GL52: Chelt 6B **12**
Hopyard, The GL20: North 1G **7**
Hornbeam M. GL2: Longl 4C **16**
Horns Rd. GL5: Stro 4E **43**
Horsbere Rd. GL3: Hucc 3H **27**
Horsefair Cl. GL53: Charl K 4B **22**
Horsefair St. GL53: Charl K 3B **22**
Horseshoe Dr. GL2: Over 5D **14**
Horseshoe Way GL2: Glou 5E **25**
HORSETROUGH RDBT. 4C **40**
HORSLEY 5A **50**
Horsley Cl. GL4: A'md 6F **27**
Horsley Hill GL6: Hors 5A **50**
Horsley Rd. GL6: Hors, Nails 5B **50**
Horton Rd. GL1: Glou 2B **26**
HOUNDSCROFT 3D **46**
House of the Tailor of Gloucester Mus.
3G **5** (1H **25**)
Howard Cl. GL20: North 2H **7**
Howard Ho. GL54: Winch 5A **56**
Howard Pl. GL3: Hucc 4H **27**
Howard Rd. GL20: North 2H **7**
Howard St. GL1: Glou 3H **25**
Howcroft GL3: Chu 5B **18**
Howell Rd. GL51: Chelt 3B **10**
(not continuous)
Howells Rd. GL20: Tewk 4B **6**
Howgate Cl. GL4: A'md 5G **27**
Hubble Rd. GL51: Chelt 6A **10**
HUCCLECOTE 3G **27**
HUCCLECOTE GREEN 5H **27**
Hucclecote La. GL3: Hucc 1C **28**
Hucclecote Lodge GL3: Hucc 4A **28**
Hucclecote M. GL3: Hucc 4G **27**
Hucclecote Rd. GL3: Hucc 3G **27**
Huddlestone Rd. GL54: Winch 3B **56**
Hudson St. GL50: Chelt 4G **11**
Hughes All. *GL20: Tewk 4B 6*
(off Saffron Rd.)
Hughes Cl. GL20: North 1H **7**
Hulbert Cl. GL51: Swin V 6A **8**
Hulbert Cres. GL51: Up H 4C **20**
Humber Pl. GL3: Brock 6E **29**
Humber Rd. GL52: Chelt 5B **12**
Humphreys Cl. GL5: Cash G 2H **41**
HUMPHRIES END 1H **41**
Hungerford St. GL50: Chelt 4G **11**
Hunters Cl. GL5: Cash G 3G **41**
Hunters Ga. GL4: A'dle 1E **35**
Hunters Rd. GL52: Bish C 1D **8**
Hunters Way GL5: Cash G 2G **41**
Huntingdon Cl. GL5: Ebley 4G **41**
Huntley Cl. GL4: A'md 6F **27**
Huntscote Rd. GL51: Chelt 2D **10**
Huntsfield Cl. GL50: Chelt 3H **11**
Hunts Gro. Vw. GL2: Qued 6E **33**
Huntsmans Cl. GL52: Bish C 1F **9**
Hurcombe Way GL3: Brock 5D **28**
Hurricane Rd. GL3: Brock 1B **36**
Hurst Cl. GL2: Longl 4E **17**
Huxley Rd. GL1: Glou 4A **26**
Huxley Way GL52: Bish C 1C **8**
Hyatts Way GL52: Bish C 2F **9**
HYDE 4C **48**
Hyde, The GL54: Winch 5A **56**
Hyde Cl. GL1: Glou 1B **26**
Hyde Cotts. GL54: Winch 6A **56**
Hyde La. GL1: Glou 1B **26**
GL50: P'bury 6C **8**
Hyde Rd. GL51: Swin V 1E **11**
Hyett Cl. GL6: Pains 5H **37**
Hyett Orchard GL6: Pains 5H **37**
Hyett Rd. GL5: Cash G 3H **41**

I

Ibis Wlk. GL2: Qued 4A **32**
Icombe Cl. GL52: Bish C 2E **9**
Idsall Dr. GL52: P'bury 3D **12**
Imjin Rd. GL52: Chelt 5C **12**
Imperial Cir.
GL50: Chelt 3B **4** (6G **11**)
Imperial Ct. GL50: Chelt 4B **4**
Imperial Ga. GL50: Chelt 4B **4**
Imperial La.
GL50: Chelt 4A **4** (6G **11**)
Imperial Sq.
GL50: Chelt 4A **4** (6G **11**)
Ince Castle Way GL1: Glou 3B **26**
INCHBROOK 6B **46**
Inchbrook Hill GL6: Inch 6B **46**
Inchbrook Trad. Est.
GL5: Woodc 5B **46**
India Ho. GL51: Chelt 5B **10**
India Rd. GL1: Glou 3B **26**
(not continuous)
Inglecote Cl. GL52: Charl K 3C **22**
Inkerman La. GL50: Chelt 2E **21**
INNSWORTH 3E **17**
Innsworth La. GL2: Longl 4D **16**
GL3: Inns 2D **16**
GL3: Longl 4D **16**
Innsworth Technology Pk.
GL3: Inns 2D **16**
Insley Gdns. GL3: Hucc 3G **27**
Iron Mills GL6: Minch 3F **51**
Irving Ct. GL52: Chelt 4D **4**
Irving Ho. *GL52: Chelt 5A 12*
(off Pittville Cir. Rd.)
Isbourne Rd. GL52: Chelt 5C **12**
Isbourne Way GL54: Winch 2D **56**
Ismay Rd. GL51: Chelt 3B **10**
Iston Cl. GL5: Brim 3H **47**
Ivanhoe Ho. GL2: Glou 1F **33**
Ivory Cl. GL4: Tuff 3F **33**
Ivy Bank GL52: P'bury 4D **12**
Ivydene GL2: Maise 2D **14**
Ivy M. GL1: Glou 6A **26**

J

Jack o' the Nick GL6: Nails 3B **50**
Jackson Cres. GL3: Inns 3F **17**
Jacob's Ladder GL52: Charl K 1C **22**
James Ct. GL51: Chelt 1C **20**
James Donovan Ct.
GL52: Chelt 5B **12**
James Drove GL53: Charl K 5C **22**
James Grieve Rd. GL4: A'md 6G **27**
James Way GL3: Hucc 5B **28**
Japonica Cl. GL3: Chu 2H **17**
Japonica Dr. GL51: Up H 4D **20**
Jardine Dr. GL52: Bish C 1D **8**
Jasmine Cl. GL4: A'dle 1E **35**
Jasmin Way GL51: Up H 5C **20**
Javelin Cl. GL3: Brock 6E **29**
Javelin Pk. GL10: Hares 5B **38**
Jaythorpe GL4: A'dle 2E **35**
Jeffries Ct. GL7: Ciren 1E **55**
Jenner Cl. GL3: Hucc 3G **27**
Jenner Gdns.
GL50: Chelt 2A **4** (5G **11**)
Jenner Wlk.
GL50: Chelt 2A **4** (5G **11**)
Jennings Wlk.
GL1: Glou 4H **5** (2H **25**)
Jersey Av. GL52: Chelt 6A **12**
Jersey Rd. GL1: Glou 3A **26**
Jersey St. GL52: Chelt 2D **4** (5H **11**)
Jesse Mary Chambers Almshouses
GL51: Chelt 6C **10**
Jesson Rd. GL52: Bish C 2F **9**
Jessop Av. GL50: Chelt 3A **4** (6F **11**)
Jessop Ct. GL2: Qued 1E **39**
Jewson Cl. GL4: Tuff 3G **33**
Jeynes Bldgs. *GL20: Tewk 3C 6*
(off Jeynes Row)
Jeynes Row GL20: Tewk 3C **6**
Joan Hawley M. GL52: Charl K 2B **22**
Jobbins Ct GL7: Ciren 1D **54**
John Bevan Cl. GL5: Stro 2E **43**
John Buck Ho. GL52: Chelt 2D **4**
John Daniels Way GL3: Chu 5A **18**
John Lamb Ho. GL51: Shurd 1A **30**
John Moore Countryside Mus. 4B **6**
John Moore Gdns. GL50: Chelt 3E **21**
John St. GL5: Stro 3D **42**
John Wood's All.
GL1: Glou 1H **5** (6A **16**)
Joiners' La. GL6: Bis 2F **45**
Jordans Way GL2: Longf 3A **16**
Joyner Rd. GL51: Chelt 3C **10**
Jubilee Ct. GL50: Chelt 2G **21**
Jubilee Flats GL7: Sidd 5F **55**
Jubilee Grn. GL7: Ciren 2E **55**
Jubilee Rd. GL6: For G 1B **50**
Julian Cl. GL4: Barn 3E **27**
Juniper Av. GL4: Mats 1C **34**
Juniper Ct. GL51: Chelt 5A **10**
Juniper Way GL10: Stone 2C **40**
Jupiter Way GL4: A'md 5G **27**
Justicia Way GL51: Up H 4C **20**

K

Kaskelot Way GL2: Glou 5F **25**
Katherine Cl. GL3: Chu 1G **17**
Katherine Ct. GL51: Chelt 4D **20**
Kaybourne Cres. GL3: Chu 4C **18**
Kayte Cl. GL52: Bish C 3E **9**
Kayte La. GL52: Bish C, South 3F **9**
Keats Av. GL2: Glou 1F **33**
Keats Gdns. GL5: Stro 1B **42**
Keble Cl. GL7: Ciren 4C **54**
Keble Rd. GL6: Fran L 1F **49**
Keepers Ga. GL7: Ciren 1C **54**
Keepers Mill GL52: Woodm 2G **9**
Keirle Wlk. GL51: Chelt 2C **10**
Kemble Cl. GL4: Tuff 3G **33**
Kemble Dr. GL7: Ciren 3C **54**
Kemble Gro. GL51: Chelt 2G **19**
Kemble Rd. GL4: Tuff 3H **33**
Kemerton Rd. GL50: Chelt 3E **21**
Kempsford Acre GL52: Woodm 2G **9**
Kemps La. GL6: Pains 6H **37**
Kempton Gro. GL51: Chelt 5A **10**
Kencourt Cl. GL2: Glou 1C **26**
Kendal Rd. GL2: Longl 6D **16**
Kendrick La. GL5: Stro 3D **42**
Kendrick St. GL5: Stro 3D **42**
Kenelm Dr. GL53: Chelt 3F **21**
Kenelm Gdns. GL53: Chelt 3E **21**
Kenelm Ri. GL54: Winch 3B **56**
Kenilworth Av. GL2: Glou 1C **26**
Kenilworth Ho. GL51: Chelt 4B **10**
Kennedy Cl. GL3: Hucc 2G **27**
Kennel La. GL3: Brock 1D **36**
Kennet Cl. GL20: Tewk 2F **7**
Kenneth Cl. GL53: Chelt 5H **21**
Kennett Gdns. GL4: A'md 1F **35**
Kensington Av. GL50: Chelt 1D **20**
Kent Cl. GL3: Chu 5C **18**
Kentmere Cl. GL51: Chelt 2B **20**
Kenton Dr. GL2: Longl 4D **16**
Kenulf Rd. GL54: Winch 4C **56**
Keriston Av. GL3: Chu 4H **17**
Kerria Ct. GL3: Chu 2H **17**
Kerstin Cl. GL50: Chelt 2F **11**
Kestrel Cl. GL53: Chelt 4F **21**
Kestrel Ct. GL10: Stone 2C **40**
Kestrel Gdns. GL2: Qued 2C **32**
Kestrel Pde. GL3: Inns 3E **17**
Kestrel Way GL20: North 1G **7**
Keswick Cl. GL2: Longl 6C **16**
Keswick Rd. GL51: Chelt 2B **20**
Kevin Cl. GL4: Barn 3E **27**
Kew Pl. GL2: Longl 4E **17**
GL53: Chelt 2G **21**
Keynsham Bank GL52: Chelt 1A **22**
Keynshambury Rd.
GL52: Chelt 6D **4** (1H **21**)
Keynsham Rd.
GL53: Chelt 6C **4** (2H **21**)
Keynsham St. GL52: Chelt 1A **22**
Kidnappers La. GL53: Leck 4E **21**
Kilminster Ct. GL3: Chu 3H **17**
Kimberland Way GL4: A'md 5F **27**
Kimberley Cl. GL2: Glou 5E **17**
Kimberley Wlk. GL52: Chelt 5C **12**
Kimbrose GL1: Glou 4F **5** (2H **25**)
Kimbrose Way
GL1: Glou 4F **5** (2G **25**)
Kimmins Rd. GL10: Stone 2D **40**
Kinder Ho. GL52: P'bury 3C **12**
King Alfred Way GL52: Chelt 1A **22**
King Arthur Cl. GL53: Chelt 2A **22**
King Edward's Av. GL1: Glou 5H **25**
Kingfisher Bus. Pk. GL5: Thru 2F **47**
Kingfisher Dr. GL51: Chelt 2A **10**
Kingfisher Ri. GL2: Qued 4A **32**
King George Cl. GL53: Chelt 3A **22**
King Henry Cl. GL53: Chelt 3A **22**
King Johns Ct. GL20: Tewk 3B **6**
Kingley Rd. GL5: Cash G 3H **41**
Kings Barton St.
GL1: Glou 5H **5** (2H **25**)

66 A-Z Cheltenham & Gloucester

Kingsbridge M. GL51: Chelt 4A 10
Kingsclere Dr. GL52: Bish C 2D 8
Kingscote Av. GL51: Chelt. 2A 20
Kingscote Cl. GL3: Chu 5C 18
GL51: Chelt 2A 20
Kingscote Dr. GL4: A'md 6F 27
Kingscote Gro. GL51: Chelt. 2A 20
Kingscote Rd. E. GL51: Chelt 2A 20
Kingscote Rd. W. GL51: Chelt . . 3A 20
KINGSCOURT 6C 42
Kingscourt La.
GL5: Kings, Rodb 5B 42
Kingscroft Rd. GL3: Hucc 4G 27
KINGSDITCH. 2D 10
Kingsditch La. GL51: Chelt. 3D 10
Kingsditch Retail Pk.
GL51: Chelt 2D 10
Kings Ga. GL20: Tewk 4E 7
KINGSHILL 1G 55
Kingshill Gl7: Preston 3G 55
Kingshill La. GL7: Preston 3G 55
KINGSHOLM 1H 5 (6A 16)
Kingsholm 1H 5 (6H 15)
Kingsholm Ct. GL1: Glou 5H 15
Kingsholm Rd.
GL1: Glou 1H 5 (6H 15)
Kingsholm Sq. GL1: Glou 5H 15
Kingsley Gdns. GL51: Chelt 6B 10
Kingsley Rd. GL4: Glou 6B 10
Kingsmead GL4: A'md 1F 35
GL6: Pains 5G 37
GL7: Ciren 3E 55
Kingsmead Av. GL51: Chelt 3C 10
Kingsmead Cl. GL51: Chelt 3C 10
Kingsmead Ind. Est.
GL51: Chelt 3D 10
Kingsmead Rd. GL51: Chelt 3C 10
King's Mill La. GL6: Pains 6G 37
King's Rd. GL5: Rodb 4C 42
GL10: Stone 1C 40
GL52: Chelt 6A 12
Kings Sq. GL1: Glou 3H 5 (1H 25)
KING'S STANLEY. 6D 40
Kings Theatre 5H 5 (2A 26)
Kingston Dr. GL51: Chelt 1H 19
Kingstone Av. GL3: Hucc 2G 27
Kingston Rd. GL20: North. 2G 7
King St. GL5: Stro. 3D 42
GL6: Minch 6H 47
GL7: Ciren 2E 55
GL50: Chelt 1A 4 (5G 11)
Kingsville Rd. GL51: Chelt 2D 10
King's Wlk. GL1: Glou 4H 5 (3H 25)
GL7: Ciren 1D 54
(off North Way)
Kings Wlk. Shop. Cen.
GL1: Glou 3H 5 (1H 25)
Kingsway GL7: Preston 3H 55
Kingswood Cl. GL52: Bish C 2E 9
King William Dr. GL53: Chelt 3A 22
Kinmoor GL4: A'dle 2E 35
Kipling Cl. GL2: Glou. 1F 33
Kipling Rd. GL51: Chelt 6B 10
Kitchener Av. GL1: Glou 6H 25
Kitesnest La. GL5: Light 6B 42
Knap La. GL6: Pains 6H 37
Knapp, The GL6: Brim, Minch. . . . 5A 48
GL53: Charl K 3C 22
Knapp La. GL6: Brim. 3A 48
GL6: Stro 3A 44
GL50: Chelt. 2A 4 (5F 11)
Knapp Rd. GL50: Chelt. . . 2A 4 (5F 11)
Knightsbridge Cres.
GL53: Chelt 2A 22
Knights Way GL20: Tewk 4D 6
Knoll, The GL4: Cranh. 6E 37
GL5: Stro 3E 43
Knollys End GL2: Qued 5C 32
Knowles Rd. GL1: Glou. 4A 26
Kyderminster Rd.
GL54: Winch 3B 56

L

Laburnum Ct. GL51: Chelt. 5A 10
Laburnum Cres. GL6: Rusc. 1A 42
Laburnum Gdns. GL2: Qued 4C 32
Laburnum M. GL10: Stone 3B 40
Laburnum Rd. GL1: Glou 6G 25
GL10: Stone 3B 40
Laburnum Wlk. GL10: Stone. 3B 40
Lacca Cl. GL2: Longl 4E 17
Lacy Cl. GL2: Longl 3D 16

Ladder, The GL6: Nails 2D 50
Ladybellgate St.
GL1: Glou 4F 5 (2G 25)
Ladychapel Rd. GL4: A'md 5F 27
Lady Downe Rd. GL4: Up L 2F 35
Ladysmith Rd. GL51: Chelt 5H 25
GL52: Chelt. 5C 12
Ladysmith Wlk. GL52: Chelt. 5C 12
(off Ladysmith Rd.)
Ladywell Cl. GL2: Glou 4E 25
LA Fitness Health Club 2B 10
Lagger, The GL6: Rand. 1G 41
Lagger La. GL5: Woodc 3A 46
Lakehouse Pk. GL2: Bish C 1D 8
Lake St. GL52: P'bury 2C 12
Lambert Av. GL51: Shurd 2A 30
Lambert Cl. GL51: Shurd 2A 30
Lambert Dr. GL51: Shurd 2A 30
Lambert Gdns. GL51: Shurd 2A 30
Lambert Ter. GL51: Shurd. 1A 30
Lambourn Cl. GL2: Longl 6F 17
Lampreys, The GL4: Glou. 5C 26
Lancaster Rd. GL20: Tewk 6C 6
Landor Gdns. GL52: Chelt. 5A 12
Lane, The GL6: Rand 1H 41
Lanes, The GL53: Leck 5D 20
Lanes Ct. GL20: Tewk 5B 6
Lanescourt GL20: Tewk. 5C 6
Langdale Gdns. GL2: Longl 4D 16
Langdale Rd. GL51: Chelt. 2C 20
Langdon Rd. GL53: Chelt 3G 21
Langdon Rd. La. GL53: Chelt . . 3G 21
Langley Cl. GL54: Winch 5A 56
Langley Rd. GL4: Mats 6C 26
GL54: Winch 5A 56
Langtoft Rd. GL5: Stro 3F 43
Langton Cl. GL3: Hucc 3F 27
Langton Gro. Rd.
GL52: Charl K 2B 22
Langton Pl. GL53: Charl K 2B 22
Lanham Gdns. GL2: Qued 6C 32
Lannett Rd. GL51: Chelt 5H 25
LANSDOWN 1E 21
Lansdown Castle Dr.
GL51: Chelt 1C 20
Lansdown Cl. GL51: Chelt 1D 20
Lansdown Ct. GL51: Chelt 1F 21
Lansdown Cres. GL50: Chelt. . . . 1E 21
Lansdown Cres. La.
GL50: Chelt 1E 21
Lansdown Ind. Est.
GL51: Chelt 6D 10
Lansdown Lodge Dr.
GL51: Chelt 1D 20
Lansdown Pde. GL50: Chelt 1E 21
Lansdown Pl. GL51: Chelt 1F 21
Lansdown Pl. La. GL51: Chelt . . 1E 21
Lansdown Rd. GL1: Glou 6A 16
GL50: Chelt 1E 21
GL51: Chelt 1C 20
Lansdown Ter. GL50: Chelt. 6F 11
Lansdown Ter. La. GL50: Chelt. . 6F 11
Lansdown Wlk. GL50: Chelt. 6F 11
Lapwing Cl. GL20: North 1G 7
Larch Cl. GL53: Charl K 4C 22
Larches, The GL4: A'md 4F 27
Larchmere Gro. GL51: Up H 4B 20
Larch Ri. GL53: Leck. 5E 21
Larchwood Dr. GL4: Tuff 2H 33
Larkham Cl. GL4: Mats 2C 34
Larkham Pl. GL4: Mats 2C 34
Larkhay Rd. GL3: Hucc. 3H 27
Lark Ri. GL6: Buss 1D 48
Larksfield Rd. GL5: Kings 6B 42
Larkspear Cl. GL1: Glou 6H 25
Larput Pl. GL50: Chelt 4G 11
Larsen Way GL2: Glou. 5F 25
Lasne Cres. GL3: Brock 1E 37
LASSINGTON 2A 14
Lassington Gro. GL2: High 4A 14
Lassington La. GL2: High 4A 14
GL2: Over. 2A 14
Lassington Wood Nature Reserve
. . . . 4B 14
Latimer Rd. GL10: Stone 1A 40
Latymer Cft. GL3: Chu 4A 18
Laura Cl. GL2: Longl 5C 16
Laurel Av. GL20: Wal C 6D 6
Laurel Dr. GL52: P'bury 3C 12
Laurel Farm Ct. GL2: Glou 1A 34
Laurel Ga. GL4: A'md 1G 35
Laurels, The GL1: Glou 4A 26
Laurence Cl. GL51: Shurd 1A 30

Lauriston Pk. GL50: Chelt 3E 21
GL51: Chelt 3E 21
Lavender Av. GL52: P'bury 2B 12
Lavender La. GL7: Ciren 2D 54
Lavender M. GL52: Bish C 2D 8
Lavender Vw. GL4: A'md 1G 35
Lavington Dr. GL2: Longl 5F 17
Lawn, The GL4: Barn. 2E 27
Lawn Cres. GL51: Shurd. 1B 30
Lawns, The GL4: A'dle. 2E 35
GL10: Stone 2B 40
Lawnside GL6: For G. 2A 50
Lawns Pk. GL5: Woodc. 2A 46
Lawn, The 2A 50
Lawrence Cl. GL51: Charl K 3C 22
Lawrence Rd. GL7: Ciren 2C 54
GL8: Aven 5H 51
Lawrence Way Nth. GL2: Glou . . . 5G 15
Lawson Glade GL53: Charl K . . . 5B 22
Laxton Rd. GL4: A'md. 5H 27
GL51: Chelt 5B 10
Laxton Wlk. GL51: Chelt 5B 10
Laynes Rd. GL3: Hucc 4H 27
Leacey Cl. GL3: Chu 2H 17
Leacey M. GL3: Chu. 2H 17
Lea Cres. GL2: Longl 4D 16
Leadon Cl. GL3: Brock 6E 29
Leaholme Ct. GL7: Ciren. 1E 55
Lea Rd. GL3: Brock. 6E 29
Lears Dr. GL52: Bish C 2F 9
Lechmere Rd. GL51: Chelt 4B 10
LECKHAMPTON. 5G 21
Leckhampton Farm Ct.
GL51: Leck 6E 21
Leckhampton Ga. GL51: Up H . . 5D 20
Leckhampton Hill
GL53: Leck H, Leck 4F 31
Leckhampton La. GL51: Shurd . . 1B 30
Leckhampton Pl. GL53: Charl K . 4G 21
Leckhampton Rd.
GL53: Chelt, Leck 3G 21
Leckhampton Vw. GL51: Shurd . . 1C 30
Ledmore Rd. GL53: Charl K 3C 22
Lee Cl. GL51: Chelt. 4C 10
Lee Rd. GL20: North 2H 7
Lee Wlk. GL20: North 2H 7
Lefroy Ct. GL51: Chelt 1D 20
Leighton Rd. GL52: Chelt 6A 12
Leinster Cl. GL3: Chu 3A 10
Leonard Rd. GL1: Glou 5A 26
LEONARD STANLEY 6B 40
Lesanne Ct. GL1: Glou 5G 5
Le Spa GL5: Stro 5E 43
Le Spa at Stratton Place 4C 52
Leven Cl. GL2: Longl. 5E 17
Lewis Av. GL2: Longf 3A 16
Lewisham Rd. GL1: Glou 6H 25
Lewis La. GL7: Ciren 1D 54
Lewis Rd. GL51: Chelt 5A 10
Lewiston Rd. GL51: Chelt 3H 47
Lexington Cl. GL20: Wal C 6D 6
Lexington Sq. GL52: Chelt 2A 12
Ley Ct. GL4: Barn 2G 27
Leyson Rd. GL51: Chelt 3H 19
Libby's Dr. GL5: Stro 2E 43
Libertus Cl. GL51: Chelt 6D 10
Libertus Rd. GL51: Chelt 6C 10
Lichfield Dr. GL51: Chelt 4D 20
Liddington Cl. GL53: Leck 5G 21
Liddington Pk. GL53: Chelt. 4G 21
Liddington Rd. GL2: Longl 6F 17
GL53: Leck 5G 21
LIGHTPILL 6B 42
Lightpill Trad. Est. GL5: Rodb . . 4B 42
Lilac Cl. GL51: Up H 4D 20
Lilac Way GL2: Qued 4B 32
Lilley's All. GL20: Tewk. 4B 6
Lilliesfield Av. GL3: Hucc 3F 27
Limber Hill GL50: Chelt 2F 11
Lime Cl. GL52: P'bury. 2B 12
Lime Gro. GL5: Stro. 3D 42
Lime Rd. GL20: Wal C 6H 7
Limes, The GL2: Longf 4H 15
GL4: Barn 2D 26
Lime Tree Ct. GL1: Glou 6H 25
Linacre Cres. GL7: Ciren. 4C 54
Lincoln Av. GL51: Chelt 4D 20
Lincoln Cl. GL20: Tewk 6A 6

Lincoln Grn. La. GL20: Tewk 6A 6
LINDEN 5G 25
Linden Av. GL52: P'bury 2B 12
Linden Cl. GL52: P'bury 2B 12
Linden Rd. GL1: Glou 4G 25
Lineover Wood Nature Reserve
. . . . 6G 23
Link Rd. GL20: Tewk 5C 6
Links Vw. GL7: Strat 2C 52
Linnet Cl. GL4: A'dle 6D 26
Linsley Way GL4: Tuff 4G 33
Linton Cl. GL53: Chelt. 2H 21
Linwell Cl. GL50: Chelt 2E 11
Linworth Rd. GL52: Bish C 2F 9
Lion Cl. GL2: Qued 3C 32
Lipson Rd. GL51: Chelt 3B 10
Lit. Acorns GL52: Bish C 1D 8
Lit. Awefield GL4: A'dle 1D 34
Lit. Bayshill Ter.
GL50: Chelt 3A 4 (6F 11)
Lit. Cheyne GL10: Stone 2B 40
Lit. Cleevemount GL52: Chelt. . . 4A 12
Littlecote Cl. GL52: Bish C 2D 8
Littledown Rd. GL53: Chelt. 5H 21
Lit. Elmbridge GL2: Glou. 5F 17
Little Fld. GL4: A'md 4E 27
Littlefield GL2: Qued 3B 32
Lit. Fishers GL5: Kings 6B 42
LITTLE HERBERT'S 4C 22
Lit. Herbert's Cl.
GL53: Charl K 4C 22
Lit. Herbert's Rd.
GL53: Chelt 4C 22
Lit. Lancarridge GL2: High 4A 14
Lit. Meadow GL7: Strat 4C 52
Little Mus., The 5B 6
Lit. Normans GL2: Longl 4D 16
Lit. Orchard GL52: Bish C 1D 8
Lit. Pheasants GL53: Charl K . . . 4B 22
LITTLE SHURDINGTON 3A 30
Little Wlk. GL2: Longl. 4D 16
LITTLE WITCOMBE 1F 37
LITTLEWORTH
GL5 . . . . 4C 46
GL54 . . . . 1B 56
Littleworth GL54: Greet. 1B 56
Llandilo St. GL1: Glou 4A 26
Llanthony Ind. Est. GL2: Glou. . . 2F 25
Llanthony Priory (remains of) . . . 3F 25
Llanthony Rd.
GL2: Glou 5E 5 (2F 25)
Lloyd Baker Ct. GL2: Hardw 6B 32
Lloyd Cl. GL51: Chelt 5A 10
Lobleys Dr. GL3: Hucc 6G 27
GL4: A'md, Hucc 6G 27
Locking Hill GL5: Stro 3D 42
Lodgemore Cl. GL5: Stro 3B 42
Lodgemore La. GL5: Stro 3B 42
London Rd. GL1: Glou . . 2H 5 (1A 26)
GL2: Glou 1A 26
GL5: Stro, Thru. 3D 42
GL6: Brim, Chalf 1F 47
GL7: Ciren, Norc 1E 55
GL52: Charl K, Chelt
. . . . 5D 4 (1H 21)
GL54: Charl K 2B 22
Longborough Dr. GL4: A'md 6F 27
Long Eights GL20: North. 1G 7
Long Fld. GL2: High 3A 14
Longfield GL2: Qued 3B 32
LONGFORD 3A 16
Longford La.
GL2: Longf, Longl 3A 16
Longford M. GL2: Longf 3A 16
Longhope Cl. GL4: A'md 6F 27
Longland Ct. GL2: Longl. 4C 16
Longland Gdns. GL2: Longl 5C 16
Longlands Cl. GL52: Bish C 1G 9
Longlands Rd. GL52: Bish C 1G 9
Longleat GL53: Charl K 4B 22
Longleat Av. GL4: Tuff 4F 33
Longlength La. GL6: Hors 6C 50
LONGLEVENS 4D 16
Long Mynd Av. GL51: Up H 3B 20
Longney Rd. GL4: Tuff 2G 33
Longsmith St.
GL1: Glou 3F 5 (1G 25)
Longtown Rd. GL20: Wal C 6D 6
Longville Cl. GL4: A'md. 6G 27
Longway Av. GL53: Charl K 5A 22
Longwood Ct. GL7: Ciren 3E 55
Lonsdale Rd. GL2: Glou 1D 26
Lords Grn. GL52: Woodm. 2H 9
Loriners Cl. GL2: Qued 3C 32

Lovage Cl.—Milton Gro.

Lovage Cl. GL3: Chu 3G 17
Lovedays Mead GL5: Stro 2D 42
Love La. GL7: Ciren 3E 55
Love La. Ind. Est. GL7: Ciren 3E 55
LOWER BARTON END 5C 50
Lwr. Churchfield Rd. GL5: Stro 4E 43
Lwr. Dorrington Ter. *GL5: Stro* *4E 43* *(off Spring La.)*
Lwr. Leazes GL5: Stro 3E 43
LOWER LITTLEWORTH 3C 46
Lwr. Lode La. GL20: Tewk 6A 6
Lwr. Market Rd. GL6: Nails 2A 50
Lwr. Meadow GL2: Qued 6C 32
Lwr. Mill St. GL51: Chelt 5E 11
Lwr. Quay St. GL1: Glou 3F 5 (1G 25)
Lwr. Spillman's GL5: Rodb 4B 42
Lower St. GL5: Stro 4E 43
LOWER TUFFLEY 3F 33
Lwr. Tuffley La. GL2: Glou 1E 33 (not continuous)
Lwr. Washwell La. GL6: Pains 5H 37
Lwr. Wharf Ind. Est. GL5: Stro 3C 42
Loweswater Cl. GL51: Chelt 2C 20
Loweswater Rd. GL51: Chelt 2C 20
Lucinia M. GL51: Chelt 4C 10
Luke La. GL3: Inns 3F 17
Lyefield Cl. GL53: Charl K 3B 22
Lyefield Rd. E. GL53: Charl K 3B 22
Lyefield Rd. W. GL53: Charl K 3B 22
Lygon Wlk. GL51: Chelt 4C 10
Lynch Rd. GL6: Fran L 1F 49
Lyndale Ter. GL51: Chelt 5D 10
Lyndhurst Cl. GL52: Woodm 2G 9
Lyndley Chase GL52: Bish C 1C 8
Lyng Cl. GL4: Barn 3F 27
Lynmouth Rd. GL3: Hucc 5G 27
Lynton Rd. GL3: Hucc 4G 27
LYNWORTH 4B 12
Lynworth Ct. GL52: Chelt 4B 12
Lynworth Exchange GL52: Chelt 4B 12
Lynworth Pl. GL52: Chelt 4B 12
Lypiatt Dr. GL50: Chelt 1F 21
Lypiatt Hill Farm GL6: Lypiatt 3H 43
Lypiatt La. GL50: Chelt 1F 21
Lypiatt M. GL50: Chelt 1F 21
Lypiatt Rd. GL50: Chelt 1F 21
Lypiatt St. GL50: Chelt 2F 21
Lypiatt Ter. GL50: Chelt 1F 21
Lypiatt Vw. GL6: Buss 6B 44
Lysander Ct. GL3: Chu 4B 18
Lyson's Av. GL1: Glou 4G 25

M

Mackenzie Way GL51: Swin V 2D 10
Madia Va. Bus. Cen. GL53: Chelt 3G 21
Madleaze Ind. Est. GL1: Glou 3F 25
Madleaze Rd. GL1: Glou 3F 25
Mafles, The GL7: Ciren 4C 54
Magdala Rd. GL1: Glou 2B 26
Magnolia Ct. GL51: Chelt 5A 10
Magnolia Wlk. GL2: Qued 4B 32
Magpie Ct. GL10: Stone 2C 40
Maida Va. Rd. GL53: Chelt 3G 21
MAIDENHALL 4A 14
Maidenhall GL2: High 4A 14
Maidenhill Recreation Cen. 1C 40
Mainard Sq. GL2: Longl 4D 16
Main Rd. GL51: Shurd 4H 29
MAISEMORE 2D 14
Maisemore Rd. GL2: Maise 3E 15
Malden Rd. GL52: Chelt 1D 4 (5H 11)
Maldon Gdns. GL1: Glou 4A 26
Malet Cl. GL2: Longl 4D 16
Mallard Cl. GL2: Qued 4A 32
GL51: Chelt 2B 10
Malmesbury Rd. GL4: Glou 4C 26
GL51: Chelt 2D 10
Malmsey Cl. GL20: Tewk 6G 7
Malthouse La. GL50: Chelt 4G 11
GL54: Winch 5A 56
Maltings, The GL20: Tewk 4C 6
Malvern Gdns. GL5: Cash G 3H 41
Malvern Pl. GL50: Chelt 1F 21
Malvern Rd. GL1: Glou 5A 16
GL50: Chelt 6E 11
Malverns, The GL4: A'dle 5E 27
Malvern St. GL51: Chelt 3E 11 (not continuous)
Malvern Vw. Bus. Pk. GL52: Bish C 1B 8
Manchester Pk. GL51: Chelt 3E 11
Manchester Way GL51: Chelt 4F 11
Mandara Gro. GL4: A'dle 1E 35
Mandarin Way GL50: Chelt 2E 11
Mandeville Cl. GL2: Longl 4D 16
Mankley Rd. GL10: Leo S 6C 40
Manley Gdns. GL2: Longl 4D 16
Manor, The GL3: Chu 5B 18
Manor Cl. GL6: Minch 6G 47
GL7: Strat 2C 52
Manor Ct. GL51: Swin V 1D 10
Manor Dr. GL5: Woodc 3B 46
Manor Gdns. GL4: Barn 3F 27
GL5: Woodc 2B 46
Manor Pk. GL2: Longl 5F 17
GL20: Tewk 2D 6
GL51: Up H 4A 20
Manor Pk. Bus. Cen. GL51: Swin V 2D 10
Manor Pl. GL20: Tewk 6C 6
Manor Rd. GL51: Chelt, Swin V 2D 10
Manor St. GL6: Bis 1F 45
Manor Vw. GL5: Sels 6H 41
Manse Gdns. GL51: Chelt 2C 20
Mansell Cl. GL2: Glou 6F 25
Manser St. GL50: Chelt 4G 11
Mansfield M. GL2: Qued 6C 32
Maple Cl. GL2: Hardw 5A 32
Maple Ct. GL2: Longl 5F 17
Maple Dr. GL3: Brock 4C 28
GL5: Stro 1B 42
GL53: Charl K 4C 22
Maples, The GL4: A'md 4F 27
Marchant Cl. GL51: Chelt 4C 10
Marconi Dr. GL2: Qued 2E 39
Marefield Cl. GL4: Barn 4F 27
Margaret Rd. GL20: Tewk 6C 6
Margrett Rd. GL50: Chelt 4G 11
Marian Ct. GL1: Glou 2F 5 (1G 25)
Marjoram Cl. GL4: A'md 6G 27
Market Ho. GL6: Minch 6H 47
Market La. GL54: Greet 1C 56
Market Pde. GL1: Glou 3H 5 (1H 25)
Market Pl. GL7: Ciren 6D 52
Market Sq. GL6: Minch 6H 47
Market St. GL6: Nails 3C 50
GL50: Chelt 5F 11
Market Way GL1: Glou 4G 5 (2H 25)
GL51: Shurd 1B 30
Marlborough Cl. GL52: Bish C 2D 8
GL53: Charl K 3A 22
Marlborough Cres. GL4: Glou 4B 26
Marlborough Rd. GL4: Glou 4B 26
MARLE HILL 3G 11
Marle Hill GL6: Chalf 2E 49
Marle Hill Pde. GL50: Chelt 1B 4 (4G 11)
Marle Hill Rd. GL50: Chelt 4G 11
Marleyfield Cl. GL3: Chu 2H 17
Marleyfield Way GL3: Chu 2H 17
Marley La. GL6: Chalf 3F 49
Marling Cl. GL5: Amb 4C 46
Marling Cres. GL5: Stro 3A 42
Marram Cl. GL4: A'md 6G 27
Marshalla Pde. GL50: Chelt 1B 4 (5G 11)
Marsh Cl. GL51: Chelt 4F 11
Marsh Dr. GL51: Chelt 3F 11
Marsh Gdns. GL51: Chelt 4F 11
Marsh La. GL51: Chelt 4F 11
Marsh M. GL10: Leo S 6C 40
Marsh Rd. GL10: Leo S 6B 40
Marsh Ter. GL51: Shurd 1A 30
Marsland Rd. GL51: Chelt 5A 10
Marston Rd. GL52: Chelt 3A 12
Marten Cl. GL4: A'md 6H 27
Martin Cl. GL7: Ciren 2D 54
Martindale Rd. GL3: Chu 3A 18
Martins, The GL5: Cash G 2G 41
Mary Gro. GL2: High 4A 14
Marylone GL1: Glou 4G 5
Mary Rose Av. GL3: Chu 2G 17
Masefield Av. GL2: Glou 1F 33
Masefield Rd. GL7: Ciren 3C 54
Mason Rd. GL5: Stro 3G 43
Massey Pde. GL1: Glou 4A 26
Massey Rd. GL1: Glou 4B 26
Mathews Way GL5: Stro 2A 42
MATSON 2C 34
Matson Av. GL4: Mats 1D 34
Matson House 2C 34
Matson La. GL4: Mats 1C 34
Matson Pl. GL1: Glou 4B 26
MAUD'S ELM 3E 11
Maverdine Ct. GL1: Glou 2F 5
Maxstone Cl. GL20: Wal C 6D 6
Mayall Ct. GL4: Mats 2D 34
Mayfair Cl. GL2: Glou 3F 25
Mayfield Cl. GL52: Bish C 3E 9
Mayfield Dr. GL3: Hucc 3G 27
Mayfield Ho. *GL50: Chelt* *1E 21* *(off Lansdown Rd.)*
Mayhill Way GL1: Glou 1B 26
Mays La. GL8: Aven 6H 51
Maythorn Dr. GL51: Chelt 3A 10
May Tree Sq. GL4: Glou 4D 26
Mead, The GL7: Ciren 6C 52
Mead Cl. GL53: Chelt 4H 21
Meade-King Gro. GL52: Woodm 2G 9
Meadoway GL52: Bish C 3D 8
Meadowbank Ho. GL7: Ciren 2D 54
Meadow Cl. GL7: Ciren 2D 54
GL20: Tewk 2D 6
GL51: Chelt 1H 19
Meadow Ct. GL10: Stone 2C 40
Meadowcroft GL4: A'md 6F 27
Meadow La. GL51: Up H 4B 20
Meadow La. (West) GL5: Dudb 4H 41
Meadow Lea GL52: Bish C 3D 8
Meadowleaze GL2: Glou 6D 16
Meadow Rd. GL7: Ciren 2D 54
GL10: Stone 2C 40
Meadowsweet Wlk. GL2: Qued 4D 32
Meadow Vw. GL7: Baun 1D 52
Meadow Way GL3: Chu 2A 18
GL5: Dudb 4H 41
Mead Pk. Ind. Est. GL53: Chelt 3G 21
Mead Rd. GL4: A'md 5F 27
GL53: Chelt 3G 21
Meads Cl. GL52: Bish C 2F 9
Meadvale Cl. GL2: Longf 3A 16
Meadway Rd. GL10: Stone 4B 40
Medoc Cl. GL50: Chelt 2E 11
Medway Ct. *GL52: Chelt* *5B 12* *(off Whaddon Rd.)*
Medway Cres. GL3: Brock 6E 29
Meerbrook Way GL2: Qued 6C 32
Meerstone Way GL4: A'dle 2E 35
Megabowl Gloucester 1F 27
Melbourne Cl. GL10: Stone 1C 40
GL53: Chelt 3F 21
Melbourne Dr. GL10: Stone 1B 40
Melbourne St. E. GL1: Glou 4A 26
Melbourne St. W. GL1: Glou 4A 26
Meldon Ter. GL5: Stro 3C 42
Melick Cl. GL4: Glou 6B 26
Mellersh Ho. *GL50: Chelt* *2F 21* *(off Painswick Rd.)*
Melmore Gdns. GL7: Ciren 3F 55
Melody Way GL2: Longl 4E 17
Melville Rd. GL3: Chu 4A 18
Mendip Cl. GL2: Qued 5B 32
GL52: Chelt 4B 12
Mendip Ho. GL52: Chelt 4B 12
Mendip Rd. GL52: Chelt 4B 12
Merchants Mead GL2: Qued 4A 32
Merchants Quay Shop. Cen. GL1: Glou 4E 5 (2G 25)
Merchant's Rd. GL2: Glou 6E 5 (3G 25)
Mercian Cl. GL7: Ciren 2E 55
Mercian Ct. GL50: Chelt 2F 21
Mercia Rd. GL1: Glou 1G 5 (6H 15)
GL54: Winch 4A 56
Mercury Way GL4: A'md 5G 27
Meredith Cotts. GL4: Glou 4C 26
Merestones Cl. GL50: Chelt 3E 21
Merestones Dr. GL50: Chelt 3E 21
Merestones Rd. GL50: Chelt 3E 21
Merevale Rd. GL2: Glou 6C 16
Merlin Cl. GL53: Chelt 4F 21
Merlin Dr. GL2: Qued 3B 32
Merlin Way GL53: Chelt 4F 21
Merretts Mills Ind. Cen. GL5: Woodc 5B 46
Merrivale Gdns. GL51: Chelt 4D 10
Merrivale Rd. GL51: Chelt 4C 10
Merryfields, The GL10: Hares 6E 39
Merrywalks GL5: Stro 3C 42
Merrywalks Shop. Cen. *GL5: Stro* *3D 42* *(off Merrywalks)*
Mersey Rd. GL52: Chelt 5B 12
Merton Cl. GL10: Ryef 4E 41
Meteor Bus. Pk. GL2: Chu 1B 18
Meteor Ct. GL4: Barn 1E 27
Meteor Way GL3: Brock 6D 28
Metz Way GL1: Glou 2A 26
GL4: Glou 3D 26
Mews, The GL20: Tewk 4B 6
Michaelmas Ct. GL1: Glou 6B 16
Michaels Mead GL7: Ciren 3C 54
Mickle Mead GL2: High 4A 14
GL4: A'md 5F 27
Middle Cft. GL4: A'md 4E 27
Middlehay Ct. GL52: Bish C 2D 8
Middle Hill GL5: Stro 3E 43
GL6: Chalf H 6D 44
Middle Hill Cres. GL6: Chalf H 1E 49
Middle Leazes GL5: Stro 3E 43
MIDDLE LYPIATT 4A 44
Middle Rd. GL5: Thru 1F 47
Middle Spillman's GL5: Rodb 4B 42
Middle St. GL5: Stro 2D 42 (Badbrook)
GL5: Stro 3D 42 (Mount Pleasant)
Middleton Lawn GL3: Inns 3F 17
Middle Tynings GL6: For G 2B 50
Middle Wharf GL5: Stro 3C 42
Mid Gloucestershire Indoor Bowling Cen. 6C 28
Midland Ct. *GL7: Ciren* *2E 55* *(off School La.)*
Midland Rd. GL1: Glou 6H 5 (3H 25)
GL10: Stone 2B 40
Mid Lane Rd. GL7: Ciren 3E 55
Midsummer Wlk. GL2: Glou 5F 25
Midwinter Av. GL51: Chelt 4F 11
Midwinter Cl. GL50: Chelt 3F 11
Milford Cl. GL2: Longl 4C 16
Mill Avon Holiday Pk. GL20: Tewk 5A 6
Mill Bank GL20: Tewk 4A 6
MILLBOTTOM 3C 50
Millbridge Rd. GL3: Hucc 4H 27
Millbrook GL5: Brim 2A 48
Millbrook Cl. GL1: Glou 2B 26
Millbrook Ct. *GL50: Chelt* *5F 11* *(off Millbrook St.)*
Millbrook Gdns. GL50: Chelt 5E 11
Millbrook Pl. *GL5: Stro* *3D 42* *(off Lansdown)*
Millbrook St. GL1: Glou 3A 26
GL50: Chelt 5E 11
Millbrook Wlk. GL5: Inch 6A 46
Mill Cl. GL5: Brim 2G 47
Mill Cnr. GL3: Witc 1F 37
Millennium Cl. GL20: Wal C 6D 6
Millennium Way GL7: Ciren 6G 53
Miller Cl. GL2: Longl 4E 17
Millers Dyke GL2: Qued 4A 32
Millers Grn. GL1: Glou 2G 5 (1H 25)
Mill Farm Dr. GL5: Stro 2H 41
Millfields GL3: Hucc 3H 27
Mill Gro. GL2: Qued 4A 32
Millham Rd. GL52: Bish C 1F 9
Millhouse Dr. GL50: Chelt 2F 11
Millin Av. GL4: Tuff 2G 33
Mill La. GL3: Brock 5D 28
GL3: Witc 1G 37
GL6: Cranh 6B 36
GL8: Aven 6G 51
GL52: P'bury 3D 12
GL54: Charl K 6E 13
GL54: Greet 1C 56
GL54: Winch 5B 56
Mill Pde. GL52: Bish C 1E 9
Mill Pl. GL1: Glou 4B 26
GL7: Ciren 6C 52
Millpond End GL5: Woodc 2B 46
Mill St. GL1: Glou 2B 26
GL20: Tewk 4A 6
GL52: P'bury 2C 12
Mill Vw. GL7: Baun 1D 52
Mill Way GL51: Chelt 2C 10
Milne Pastures GL20: Tewk 3F 7
Milne Wlk. GL51: Chelt 3B 10
Milo Pl. GL1: Glou 5H 25
Milsom St. GL50: Chelt 1A 4 (5G 11)
Milton Av. GL2: Glou 6F 25
GL51: Chelt 1C 20
Milton Gro. GL5: Stro 3F 43

68 A-Z Cheltenham & Gloucester

Milton Rd. GL51: Chelt 6B 10
Mimosa Av. GL51: Up H 5D 20
Mimosa Ct. GL3: Chu 2H 17
(off Wisteria Way)
MINCHINHAMPTON 6H 47
Minchinhampton Bulwarks, The
. . . . 6E 47
Minchinhampton Common 4D 46
Minchinhampton Market House
. . . . 6H 47
(off Parsons Ct.)
Minerva Cl. GL4: A'md 5G 27
Minerva Cl. GL7: Ciren 1E 55
Minetts Av. GL2: Bish C 2F 9
Minster Cl. GL52: Bish C 1D 8
Minster Gdns. GL4: A'md 5G 27
Minstrel Way GL3: Chu 1G 17
Miserden Rd. GL51: Chelt 1A 20
Mistletoe M. GL3: Chu 3G 17
Mitre Gdns. GL51: Shurd 1B 30
Mitre St. GL53: Chelt 5C 4 (1H 21)
MITTON 2D 6
Mitton Ct. GL20: Tewk 2D 6
Mitton Way GL20: Tewk 2D 6
Moat, The GL2: Qued 4C 32
Moat La. GL51: Uck 1A 10
Moffatt Rd. GL6: For G 2B 50
Mogridge Cl. GL3: Hucc 4H 27
Monarch Cl. GL4: A'md 1F 35
Monica Dr. GL50: Chelt 3H 11
Monkey Mdw. GL20: North 1H 7
Monkey Puzzle Cl. GL5: Ebley . . . 4H 41
Monk Mdw. Dock GL2: Glou 3F 25
Monk Mdw. Trad. Est.
GL2: Glou 4F 25
Monks Cft. GL51: Chelt 6B 10
Monson Av. GL50: Chelt . . 1B 4 (5G 11)
Montery Rd. GL20: Wal C 6H 7
Montfort Rd. GL2: Longl 4C 16
Montgomery Cl. GL3: Hucc 5A 28
Montgomery Rd. GL51: Up H 3A 20
MONTPELLIER 5A 4 (1F 21)
Montpellier Cl. GL1: Glou . . . 5G 5 (2H 25)
Montpellier Arc. GL50: Chelt 5A 4
Montpellier Av. GL50: Chelt 5A 4
Montpellier Ct. GL50: Chelt 1F 21
Montpellier Dr.
GL50: Chelt 5B 4 (1G 21)
Montpellier Exchange
GL50: Chelt 5A 4
Montpellier Gro.
GL50: Chelt 6A 4 (2G 21)
Montpellier Ho.
GL50: Chelt 6A 4 (2F 21)
Montpellier M.
GL1: Glou 5G 5 (2H 25)
Montpellier Pde.
GL50: Chelt 6A 4 (1G 21)
Montpellier Retreat
GL50: Chelt 6A 4 (2G 21)
Montpellier Spa Rd.
GL50: Chelt 5A 4 (1G 21)
Montpellier St.
GL50: Chelt 5A 4 (1F 21)
Montpellier Ter.
GL50: Chelt 6A 4 (1F 21)
Montpellier Vs.
GL50: Chelt 6A 4 (2G 21)
Montpellier Wlk.
GL50: Chelt 5A 4 (1F 21)
Montreal Dr. GL51: Chelt 4B 10
Montserrat Cl. GL51: Rodb C 1E 47
Moon's La. GL6: Bour G 5G 45
Moor Cl. GL5: Rodb C 3D 46
Moor Ct. Dr. GL52: Chelt 5A 12
MOOR END 4A 22
MOOREND 5G 35
Moorend Cres. GL53: Chelt 3F 21
Moorend Glade GL53: Charl K . . . 3A 22
Moorend Gro. GL53: Chelt 4F 21
Moorend Pk. Rd. GL53: Chelt 4F 21
Moorend Rd. GL53: Charl K 4A 22
GL53: Chelt 4G 21
Moorend St. GL53: Chelt 3F 21
Moorfield Rd. GL3: Brock 5D 28
Moor Hall Pl. GL5: Cash G 2H 41
Moorhen Ct. GL2: Qued 4A 32
Moors Av. GL51: Chelt 3D 10
Moor St. GL1: Glou 4B 26
More Hall Pl. GL5: Cash G 2G 41
Morelands Gro. GL1: Glou 6H 25
Morelands Trad. Est.
GL1: Glou 3G 25
Moreton Cl. GL52: Bish C 3F 9

Moreton St. GL1: Glou 4A 26
Morgans Dr. GL50: Chelt 2F 21
Morlands Dr. GL53: Charl K 5C 22
Morley Av. GL3: Chu 3H 17
Morningside Cl. GL52: P'bury 3D 12
Morningside Courtyard
GL52: P'bury 3D 12
Mornington Dr. GL53: Chelt 3G 21
Morpeth St. GL1: Glou 4A 26
Morris Ct. GL51: Chelt 2C 20
Morris Hill Cl. GL51: Swin V 1E 11
Morsetail Dr. GL7: Ciren 3C 54
Mortimer Rd. GL2: Longl 4D 16
Morwent Cl. GL4: A'md 5F 27
Moselle Dr. GL3: Chu 3H 17
Mosley Cres. GL5: Cash G 3H 41
Mosley Rd. GL5: Cash G 2H 41
Mostham Pl. GL3: Brock 5C 28
Mottershead Dr. GL3: Inns 2F 17
Moulder Rd. GL20: Tewk 4D 6
Mount La. GL10: Hares 5B 38
MOUNT PLEASANT 3E 43
Mt. Pleasant GL5: Stro 3F 43
GL6: Bis 2G 45
Mt. Pleasant Rd. GL20: Tewk 4C 6
Mount St. GL1: Glou 2F 5 (6G 15)
GL7: Ciren 2D 54
Mowberry Cl. GL2: Longl 4D 16
Mowbray Av. GL20: Tewk 6G 7
Mulberry Cl. GL2: Hardw 5B 32
Mulberry Ct. GL51: Chelt 5A 10
Mulberry Gdns. GL4: Mats 1C 34
Mullings Cl. GL7: Ciren 6D 52
Munday Cl. GL6: Buss 6C 44
Munsley Gro. GL4: Mats 2D 34
Murray Cl. GL52: Bish C 1D 8
Murvagh GL53: Chelt 6D 4 (2H 21)
Murvagh Cl.
GL53: Chelt 6D 4 (2H 21)
Muscroft Rd. GL52: P'bury 3E 13
Mus. in the Pk. 2C 42
Musket Cl. GL20: Wal C 6D 6
Mutsilver M. GL2: Longl 4F 17
Myers Rd. GL1: Glou 2B 26
Myrtle Cl. GL4: Glou 6B 26
MYTHE, THE 1B 6
Mythe Railway Nature Reserve
. . . . 1A 6
Mythe Rd. GL20: Tewk 2B 6

N

Naas La. GL2: Qued 6C 32
GL4: Brook 1F 39
NAG'S HEAD 5H 51
Nag's Head La. GL8: Aven 5H 51
Nailors Ct. GL20: Tewk 4B 6
NAILSWORTH 2C 50
NAILSWORTH HILL 2E 51
Nailsworth Mills Est.
GL6: Nails 2D 50
Nailsworth Recreation Cen.
GL6: For G 1A 50
Nailsworth Ter. GL50: Chelt 1A 4
Napier St. GL1: Glou 2A 26
Narrowcut La. GL6: Hors 5A 50
Naseby Ho. GL52: Chelt 4B 12
NASHEND 3E 45
National Waterways Mus.
. . . . 5E 5 (2G 25)
NATTON 4H 7
Natton Cotts. GL52: Charl K 2E 23
Nature Cl. GL3: Brock 6D 28
Naunton Cres. GL53: Chelt 3G 21
Naunton La. GL53: Chelt 3G 21
Naunton Pde. GL53: Chelt 2G 21
Naunton Pk. Cl. GL53: Chelt 3H 21
Naunton Pk. Rd. GL53: Chelt 3H 21
Naunton Rd. GL4: Glou 4E 27
Naunton Ter. GL53: Chelt 2G 21
Naunton Way GL53: Chelt 3G 21
Neatafarm GL54: Greet 1B 56
Needham Av. GL2: Qued 6E 33
Nelmes Row GL52: Charl K 3D 22
Nelson St. GL1: Glou 5A 26
GL5: Stro 3D 42
Nene Cl. GL2: Qued 3B 32
Neptune Cl. GL4: A'md 5B 28
Netheridge Cl. GL2: Glou 1D 32
Netherwood Cl. GL51: Chelt 4D 10
Netherwood Gdns.
GL51: Chelt 4D 10

Nettleton Rd. GL1: Glou . . 4H 5 (2A 26)
GL7: Ciren 2A 20
Neville Rd. GL20: Tewk 5C 6
Newark Rd. GL1: Glou 5F 25
New Barn Av. GL52: P'bury 3B 12
New Barn Cl. GL52: P'bury 3B 12
New Barn La. GL52: P'bury 2H 11
New Barn Pk. GL52: P'bury 3C 12
Newcombe Cl. GL7: Ciren 1E 55
Newcourt Pk. GL53: Charl K 3B 22
Newcourt Rd. GL53: Charl K 4B 22
Newent Rd. GL2: High 4A 14
Newick Ho. GL53: Chelt 2H 21
New Inn La. GL1: Glou 3G 5 (1H 25)
Newland St. GL1: Glou 1A 26
Newland Vw. GL51: Chelt 2C 10
NEWMARKET 2A 50
Newmarket Rd. GL6: Nails 2B 50
NEW MILLS 1G 55
New Mills Trad. Est. GL5: Stro . . . 2F 43
New Olympus Theatre 3A 26
New Rd. GL5: Sels 5H 41
GL6: Minch 6G 47
GL52: Woodm, South 3H 9
New Rutland Ct.
GL50: Chelt 1A 4 (5G 11)
New St. GL1: Glou 3G 25
GL6: Pains 5H 37
GL10: King S 6D 40
GL50: Chelt 2A 4 (5H 11)
GL53: Charl K 4B 22
Newton Av. GL4: Glou 4D 26
Newton Cl. GL51: Chelt 5B 10
Newton Rd. GL51: Chelt 5B 10
Newton La. GL20: Tewk 3E 7
Newton's Way GL5: Stro 4C 42
NEWTOWN 4E 7
Newtown Trad. Est. GL20: Tewk . . 3F 7
New Zealand Ho. GL51: Chelt . . . 4C 10
Nickleby Bungs. GL4: Glou 6A 26
Nicolson Cl. GL1: Glou 3F 17
Nightingale Cft. GL3: Inns 3E 17
Nightingale Ho. GL4: A'dle 1E 35
Nine Elms Rd. GL2: Longl 5F 17
Noake Rd. GL3: Hucc 3H 27
Norbury Av. GL4: Mats 2D 34
NORCOTE 5H 53
Norfolk Av. GL51: Chelt 6C 10
Norfolk M. GL1: Glou 5F 5 (2G 25)
GL50: Chelt 5C 10
Norfolk St. GL1: Glou 5F 5 (2G 25)
Normal Ter.
GL50: Chelt 1A 4 (5G 11)
Norman Arch 6D 52
Norman Ball Way GL1: Glou 2C 26
Nortenham Cl. GL52: Bish C 1C 8
Northbank Cl. GL51: Chelt 2G 19
Northbrook Rd. GL4: Glou 2D 26
Northcroft GL50: Chelt 2E 21
North E. Ter. GL20: Tewk 4B 6
Northfield Pas.
GL50: Chelt 1B 4 (5H 11)
Northfield Rd. GL4: Glou 6A 26
Northfields GL5: Stro 2E 43
Northfield Sq. GL4: Glou 6A 26
Northfield Ter.
GL50: Chelt 1B 4 (5H 11)
Northgate St. GL1: Glou . . 3G 5 (1H 25)
Nth. Hall M. GL52: Chelt 5A 12
Nth. Hill Rd. GL7: Ciren 3F 55
North Home Rd. GL7: Ciren 2F 55
North Pl. GL50: Chelt 2C 4 (5H 11)
North Point GL1: Glou 4E 5 (2G 25)
North Rd. GL1: Glou 5A 16
North Rd. E. GL51: Chelt 2G 19
North Rd. W. GL51: Chelt 2F 19
North St. GL50: Chelt . . . 2B 4 (5G 11)
GL54: Winch 4B 56
North Ter. GL7: Ciren 6A 52
Nth. Upton La. GL4: Barn 4F 27
NORTHWAY 3D 6
North Way GL7: Ciren 1D 54
Northway Cl. GL20: Ashc 3H 7
Northway La. GL20: Ashc, Tewk . . 3D 6
Northway Trad. Est. GL20: Ashc . . 3H 7
NORTH WOODCHESTER 2A 46
Norton Cl. GL54: Winch 3B 56
Norton Ct. GL6: For G 1A 50
Norton Ridge GL6: For G 1B 50
Nortonwood GL6: For G 1A 50
Norwich Dr. GL51: Chelt 3D 20
Norwood Rd. GL50: Chelt 2F 21

Notgrove Cl. GL4: Tuff 3F 33
Notley Cl. GL51: Chelt 1B 20
Notley Pl. GL3: Hucc 4H 27
Nottingham Rd. GL52: Bish C 1E 9
Nouncells Cross GL5: Stro 3E 43
Nourse Cl. GL53: Leck 5E 21
NOVERTON 3E 13
Noverton Av. GL52: P'bury 3E 13
Noverton La. GL52: P'bury 3D 12
Nunney Cl. GL51: Chelt 1H 19
NUPEND 5A 50
Nurseries, The GL52: Bish C 3D 8
Nursery, The GL10: King S 6D 40
Nursery Cl. GL5: Stro 4E 43
GL7: Ciren 3F 55
Nursery Cotts. GL7: Ciren 2E 55
Nursery Dr. GL5: Brim 3H 47
Nursery Rd. GL7: Ciren 3E 55
Nursery Ter. GL10: Stone 4C 40
Nursery Vw. GL7: Sidd 6F 55
Nutcroft GL4: Glou 4C 26
Nuthill GL3: Brock 3G 35
GL4: Brock, Up L 3G 35
Nutley Av. GL4: Tuff 3F 33
Nutmeg Cl. GL4: A'dle 1E 35
Nympsfield Rd. GL4: Tuff 2G 33
GL6: For G, Nails 1A 50

O

Oak Av. GL52: Charl K 2B 22
Oakbank GL4: Tuff 1H 33
(not continuous)
Oakbrook Dr. GL51: Chelt 2H 19
Oak Cotts. GL4: Up L 3F 35
Oak Ct. GL52: Chelt 6B 12
(off Oak Mnr. Dr.)
Oakcroft Cl. GL4: Mats 2E 35
Oakdene GL51: Chelt 1E 21
GL52: Chelt 6B 12
Oak Dr. GL3: Brock 5C 28
GL5: Rodb 4C 42
GL20: North 2G 7
Oakfield Rd. GL52: Bish C 2F 9
Oakfield St. GL50: Chelt 2E 21
Oak Ho. GL3: Brock 5C 28
Oakhurst Cl. GL3: Chu 4H 17
Oakhurst Ri. GL52: Charl K 1B 22
Oakland Av. GL52: Charl K 3A 12
Oaklands GL7: Ciren 3D 54
Oakland St. GL53: Charl K 2B 22
Oakleaze GL2: Glou 6E 17
Oakley Rd. GL7: Ciren 3C 54
GL52: Charl K 1B 22
Oak Mnr. Dr. GL52: Chelt 6B 12
Oakridge Cl. GL3: High 4A 14
Oakridge Cl. GL4: A'md 1F 35
(off Cotteswold Rd.)
OAKRIDGE LYNCH 6H 45
Oakridge Village Mus. 6H 45
Oaks, The GL4: A'md 4F 27
GL51: Up H 3A 20
Oak Tree Cl. GL2: Hardw 6B 32
Oaktree Gdn. GL4: Mats 2D 34
Oak Tree Vw. GL4: Mats 2D 34
Oak Way GL10: Stone 3C 40
Oatfield GL2: Qued 3B 32
O'Brien Rd. GL51: Chelt 3D 10
Oddfellows Ter. GL54: Winch 5B 56
Odeon Cinema
Cheltenham 2C 4 (6H 11)
Ogbourne Cl. GL2: Longl 6F 17
Okus Rd. GL53: Charl K 4B 22
Old Acre Cl. GL52: Bish C 1F 9
Old All Saints School
GL51: Chelt 2D 4
Old Baptist Chapel Ct.
GL20: Tewk 4B 6
(off Church St.)
Old Bath Rd. GL53: Chelt 6G 21
Old Bristol Rd. GL6: Nails 3C 50
Oldbury Bldg. Bus. Pk.
GL20: Tewk 3E 7
Oldbury Cl. GL51: Chelt 4A 10
Oldbury Ho. GL20: Tewk 3C 6
(off Cotteswold Rd.)
Oldbury Orchard GL3: Chu 5C 18
Oldbury Rd. GL20: Tewk 4B 6
GL51: Chelt 4B 10
Old Cheltenham Rd.
GL2: Longl 5E 17
Old Comn. GL6: Minch 5A 48
Old Common, The GL6: Buss 6C 44

Old Elmore Rd.—Pirton Cres.

Old Elmore Rd. GL2: Qued 3C 32
OLDENDS 1A 40
Oldends Ind. Est. GL10: Stone 2A 40
Oldends La. GL10: Stone 3A 40
Oldfield GL20: Tewk 4C 6
Oldfield Cres. GL51: Chelt 1C 20
Old Gloucester Rd.
GL51: Stav, Chelt. 2A 10
Old Hill GL8: Aven 6H 51
Old Horsley Rd. GL6: Nails 3C 50
Old Hospital La. GL20: Tewk 3C 6
Old Lodge Ct. GL50: Chelt 1C 4
Old Manor La. GL20: Tewk 2D 6
Old Mkt. GL6: Nails 2C 50
Old Millbrook Ter. GL50: Chelt 5E 11
Old Neighbourhood GL6: Chalf 2D 48
Old Painswick Cl. GL4: Glou 5C 26
Old Painswick Rd. GL4: Glou 5C 26
Old Post Office All. *GL20: Tewk 4B 6*
(off Trinity St.)
Old Rectory Cl. GL5: Rodb 5B 42
Old Reddings Cl. GL51: Chelt 2H 19
Old Reddings Rd. GL51: Chelt 2H 19
Old Rd. GL2: Maise 1D 14
GL52: South 5H 9
Old Row GL1: Glou 3A 26
Old School Cl. GL6: For G 2C 50
Old School Ct. *GL50: Chelt 2G 21*
(off Gt. Norwood St.)
Old School Ho. GL50: Chelt 2A 4
Old School M., The
GL53: Charl K 3C 22
Old Station Dr. GL53: Chelt 3G 21
Old Tewkesbury Rd.
GL2: Longf 4A 16
Old Town, The GL6: Nails 2C 50
Old Tram Rd. GL1: Glou 5F 5 (2G 25)
Oldway GL4: Up L 3F 35
Olio La. GL53: Chelt 6B 4 (1G 21)
Oliver Cl. GL4: Tuff 3G 33
Ollney Rd. GL6: Minch 6G 47
Olympus Pk. GL2: Qued 2D 32
Olympus Pk. Bus. Cen.
GL2: Qued 3D 32
Orangery, The GL4: Barn 4F 27
Orchard, The GL20: Tewk 3C 6
Orchard Av. GL51: Chelt 4B 10
Orchard Cvn. Pk. GL2: Twig 1C 16
Orchard Cl. GL2: Hardw 6A 32
GL2: Longf 4H 15
Orchard Cotts. GL52: Charl K 2E 23
Orchard Ct. GL10: Stone 3B 40
GL20: Tewk 4C 6
Orchard Dr. GL3: Chu 5C 18
Orchard Gro., The
GL51: Shurd 2A 30
Orchard Hill GL8: Aven 6G 51
Orchard Ho. GL7: Ciren 6E 53
GL52: Bish C 2E 9
Orchard La. GL5: Brim 3G 47
Orchard Mead GL6: Nails 2C 50
GL6: Pains 6H 37
Orchard Pk. GL3: Hucc 5H 27
GL51: Chelt 2C 10
Orchard Pl. GL10: Stone 3B 40
Orchard Rd. GL2: Longl 5F 17
GL5: Ebley 4F 41
GL52: Bish C 2E 9
GL54: Winch 5A 56
Orchards, The GL3: Hucc 5H 27
Orchard Springs GL6: Nails 2B 50
Orchard Vw. GL5: Light 6B 42
Orchard Way GL2: Maise 2D 14
GL3: Chu 2A 18
GL51: Chelt 4C 10
Organ's All. GL1: Glou 4H 5 (2H 25)
Oriel Rd. GL50: Chelt 4B 4 (6G 11)
Oriel School Dr. GL52: South 6H 9
Oriel Ter. GL50: Chelt 4B 4 (6G 11)
Oriel Vs. GL50: Chelt 4B 4
Oriole Way GL4: A'dle 5D 26
Ormond Pl. GL50: Chelt 3B 4 (6G 11)
Ormond Ter.
GL50: Chelt 4B 4 (6G 11)
Orrisdale Ter.
GL53: Chelt 5C 4 (1H 21)
Osborne Av. GL4: Tuff 4F 33
Osborne Ho. GL50: Chelt 1E 21
Osborne Ter. GL5: Thru 1F 47
Osbourne Gdns. *GL20: Tewk 4B 6*
(off East St.)
Osier Cl. GL4: Glou 1B 34
Osprey Cl. GL4: A'dle 6E 27
Osprey Dr. GL10: Stone 2C 40
Osprey Rd. GL53: Chelt 4F 21
Osric Rd. GL1: Glou 5A 26
Othello Cl. GL51: Chelt 5B 10
Otter Rd. GL4: A'md 6G 27
Otters Fld. GL54: Greet 2C 56
Oval, The GL1: Glou 5G 25
OVER 5C 14
Over Bridge 5E 15
Overbrook Cl. GL4: Glou 2D 26
Overbrook Dr. GL52: Chelt 4A 12
Overbrook Rd. GL2: Hardw 5B 32
Overbury Rd. GL1: Glou 3B 26
Overbury St. GL53: Charl K. 2B 22
Over Butterrow GL5: Rodb C 1D 46
Over C'way. GL1: Glou 6E 15
Overhill Rd. GL7: Strat 3B 52
Over Ponds Nature Reserve 4F 15
Overton Ct. GL50: Chelt 6F 11
OVERTON PARK 6F 11
Overton Pk. Rd. GL50: Chelt 6F 11
Overton Rd. GL50: Chelt 6F 11
Owl Cl. GL4: A'dle 6E 27
Owls End Rd. GL52: Bish C 1F 9
Oxbode, The GL1: Glou 3G 5 (1H 25)
Oxbutts Cvn. Pk.
GL52: Woodm 1G 9
Oxbutts Ind. Est.
GL52: Woodm 1G 9
Oxford Cl. GL52: Chelt 1A 22
Oxford Ho. GL7: Ciren 6E 53
Oxford Pde. GL52: Chelt 1A 22
Oxford Pas.
GL50: Chelt 2B 4 (5G 11)
Oxford Rd. GL1: Glou 1A 26
Oxford St. GL1: Glou 1A 26
GL52: Chelt 5D 4 (1A 22)
Oxford Ter. GL1: Glou 1A 26
GL5: Stro 2D 42
(off Middle St.)
Oxford Wlk. GL52: Chelt 1A 22
Oxford Way GL51: Chelt 4D 20
Oxmead Cl. GL52: Bish C 1G 9
Oxmoor GL4: A'dle 2E 35
Oxstalls Dr. GL2: Longl 4B 16
Oxstalls Indoor Tennis Cen. 5B 16
Oxstalls La. GL2: Longl 6C 16
Oxstalls Way GL2: Longl 5C 16

P

Paddock Gdns. GL2: Longl 4E 17
Paddock Ri. GL10: Stone 3C 40
Paddocks, The GL2: Glou 5D 24
GL7: Baun 2D 52
GL7: Ciren 1F 55
Paddocks La. GL50: Chelt 3G 11
Padin Cl. GL6: Buss 6D 44
Pady Ct. GL7: Ciren 1D 54
PAGANHILL 2B 42
Paganhill Est. GL5: Stro 2A 42
Paganhill La. GL5: Stro 3A 42
Paget Ho. GL7: Ciren 6E 53
Paget's La. GL20: Tewk 1A 6
Pagets Rd. GL52: Bish C 3F 9
PAINSWICK 5H 37
Painswick Old Rd. GL6: Stro 2C 42
Painswick Rd. GL3: Brock 3C 36
GL4: Cranh 6B 36
GL4: Glou, Mats 4B 26
GL6: Stro 1C 42
GL50: Chelt 3F 21
Painswick Rococo Garden 4G 37
Pakistan Ho. GL51: Chelt 5A 10
Palestra Lodge GL7: Ciren 6D 52
Palmer Av. GL4: A'md 6G 27
Palmers Ct. GL10: Stone 3C 40
Palm Rd. GL20: Wal C 6D 6
Pampas Ct. GL2: Qued 3D 32
Parabola Cl.
GL50: Chelt 4A 4 (6F 11)
Parabola La.
GL50: Chelt 4A 4 (6F 11)
Parabola Rd.
GL50: Chelt 4A 4 (6F 11)
Parade, The GL2: Longl 5F 17
Paragon Ter.
GL53: Chelt 6B 4 (1G 21)
Parish & Oldhills Woods
Nature Reserve 2G 49
PARK, THE 3E 21
Park, The GL6: Minch 5H 47
GL20: North 1G 7
GL50: Chelt 3E 21
Park & Ride
Arle Court 1H 19
Barnwood 2F 27
Javelin 1F 5 (6G 15)
Racecourse, The 2H 11
Severnsider 6C 32
Park Av. GL2: Longl 4D 16
Park Brake GL2: High 5A 14
Parkbury Cl. GL51: Chelt 5D 10
Park Cl. GL20: North 1G 7
Park Ct. GL5: Stro 4E 43
Park Dr. GL2: Qued 4C 32
PARK END 2A 42
Parkend Rd. GL1: Glou 4H 25
Park Farm Ct. GL6: Minch 6H 47
Park Ga. GL50: Chelt 2F 21
Park Ho. GL1: Glou 4H 25
GL50: Chelt 2F 21
PARK HOUSE DAY HOSPITAL 4E 43
Parkland Rd. GL53: Chelt 5A 22
Parklands GL2: Qued 4B 32
GL3: Chu 3H 17
Parklands Sq. GL7: Ciren 3C 54
Park La. GL5: Inch 6A 46
GL7: Ciren 1D 54
GL52: P'bury 1C 12
Park M. GL53: Chelt 3F 21
Park Pde. GL10: Stone 2B 40
Park Pl. GL50: Chelt 2F 21
Park Rd. GL1: Glou 5G 5 (2H 25)
GL5: Stro 4E 43
GL6: Nails 2D 50
(not continuous)
GL10: Stone 3B 40
Park Rd. Cres. GL6: Nails 3D 50
Parkside Cl. GL3: Chu 3G 17
Parkside Dr. GL3: Chu 3G 17
Park St. GL1: Glou 2H 5 (1H 25)
GL7: Ciren 6D 52
GL50: Chelt 5F 11
Park Ter. GL6: Minch 6G 47
Park Vw. GL7: Strat 3C 52
GL51: Chelt 3B 10
Park Vw. Dr. GL5: Cash G 2H 41
Parkway GL7: Sidd 5E 55
Parkwood Cres. GL3: Hucc 5G 27
Parkwood Gro. GL53: Charl K 5B 22
Parliament Cl. GL5: Stro 3D 42
Parliament St.
GL1: Glou 4G 5 (2H 25)
GL5: Stro 3D 42
Parr Cl. GL3: Chu 2G 17
Parr Ho. GL54: Winch 5A 56
Parry Rd. GL1: Glou 5A 26
Parsons Ct. GL6: Minch 6H 47
Parton Dr. GL3: Chu 4B 18
Parton M. GL3: Chu 3A 18
Parton Rd. GL3: Chu 2H 17
Partridge Cl. GL2: Glou 6F 25
GL10: Stone 2C 40
Partridge Way GL7: Ciren 6F 53
Pate Ct. GL50: Chelt 2B 4 (5G 11)
Pates Av. GL51: Chelt 5E 11
Patseamuir M. GL2: Longl 4F 17
Patterdale Cl. GL51: Chelt 2C 10
Patterson Rd. GL7: Ciren 1F 55
Paul's Ri. GL5: Woodc 2B 46
Paul St. GL1: Glou 4A 26
Pavilion Gdns. GL50: Chelt 3F 21
Pavilions, The
GL53: Chelt 6B 4 (1G 21)
Paygrove La. GL2: Longl 5E 17
Paynes Pitch GL3: Chu 5C 18
Paynes Pl. GL5: Rodb 4A 42
Peach Cl. GL20: Wal C 6H 7
Peacock Cl. GL4: A'md 6F 27
GL51: Chelt 5A 10
Peak Fitness
Gloucester 4D 32
Cheltenham 6D 4 (1H 21)
Peakstile Piece GL52: Woodm 2G 9
Pearce Way GL2: Glou 1E 33
Pearcroft Rd. GL10: Stone 3C 40
Pear Orchard, The GL20: North 1H 7
Peart Cl. GL1: Glou 2B 26
Pear Tree Cl. GL2: Hardw 6B 32
GL52: Woodm 2H 9
Pearwood Way GL4: Tuff 3F 33
Pecked La. GL52: Bish C 1F 9
Peel Cen., The
GL1: Glou 6E 5 (3G 25)
Peel Cl. GL53: Charl K 4D 22
Pegasus Ct. GL4: Barn 2F 27
GL51: Chelt 2E 21
Pegasus Gdns. GL2: Qued 3C 32
Peggoty Bungs. *GL4: Glou 4D 26*
(off Stanway Rd.)
Peghouse Cl. GL5: Stro 1E 43
Peghouse Ri. GL5: Stro 1E 43
Pelham Cres. GL3: Chu 3H 17
Pembridge Cl. GL52: Charl K 3D 22
Pembridge Ct. GL50: Chelt 2F 21
Pembroke Rd. GL51: Chelt 3B 20
Pembroke St.
GL1: Glou 6H 5 (3A 26)
Pembury Rd. GL4: Glou 1H 33
Pendil Cl. GL50: Chelt 1E 11
Pendock Cl. GL2: Qued 4B 32
Penharva Cl. GL51: Chelt 4D 10
Penhill Rd. GL4: Mats 1C 34
Pennine Cl. GL2: Qued 5B 32
Pennine Rd.
GL52: Chelt, P'bury 3C 12
Pennington Ct. GL51: Chelt 3B 10
Pennsylvania Av. GL51: Chelt 4C 10
Pennsylvania M. GL51: Chelt 4C 10
Penny Cl. GL2: Longl 5E 17
Penrith Cl. GL51: Chelt 2C 20
Penrith Rd. GL51: Chelt 2C 20
Penrose Rd. GL3: Inns 3E 17
Pensile Rd. GL6: Nails 2D 50
Pentathlon Way GL50: Chelt 2G 11
Percy St. GL1: Glou 4A 26
Peregrine Cl. GL2: Qued 2C 32
Peregrine Rd. GL53: Chelt 4F 21
Perry Cen., The GL2: Qued 1C 38
Perry Cl. GL53: Charl K 4C 22
Perry Hill GL20: Tewk 5B 6
Perry Orchard GL4: Up L 3F 35
GL5: Cash G 2G 41
Persh La. GL2: Maise 2C 14
(not continuous)
Persh Way GL2: Maise 2D 14
Perth GL10: Stone 1B 40
Peter Pennel Cl. GL51: Chelt 3B 10
Peters Fld. GL2: High 4B 14
Pethera Cl. GL7: Ciren 5D 52
Petworth Cl. GL4: Tuff 5F 33
Peveril Ho. GL2: Glou 1F 33
Pheasant La.
GL51: Chelt, Stav 1G 19
Pheasant Mead GL10: Stone 2C 40
Pheasant Way GL7: Ciren 6F 53
Philip St. GL1: Glou 4G 25
Phoenix Pas. GL50: Chelt 1A 4
Phoenix Trad. Est. GL5: Thru 1F 47
Phoenix Way GL7: Ciren 1D 54
Piccadilly St. GL5: Stro 4E 43
Piccadilly Way GL52: P'bury 3E 13
Pickering Cl. GL53: Chelt 3F 21
Pickering Rd. GL53: Chelt 3F 21
Pickwick Cl. GL2: Glou 6E 17
Picton Ho. GL7: Ciren 6E 53
Piece, The GL3: Chu 5B 18
Piggy La. GL4: Tuff 3H 33
Pike Ho. M. GL8: Aven 5F 51
Pike La. GL6: Nails 3C 50
Pilford Av. GL53: Chelt 5H 21
Pilford Cl. GL53: Chelt 5H 21
Pilford Ct. GL53: Chelt 6H 21
Pilford Rd. GL53: Chelt 6H 21
Pilgrim Cl. GL4: A'md 5F 27
Pilgrove Cl. GL51: Chelt 2A 10
Pilgrove Way GL51: Chelt 2A 10
Pillcroft Cl. GL3: Witc 1F 37
Pillcroft Rd. GL3: Witc 1F 37
PILLEY 5H 21
Pilley Cres. GL53: Chelt 5G 21
Pilley La. GL53: Chelt 5G 21
Pillowell Dr. GL1: Glou 1B 26
Pincoate GL2: High 3A 14
Pine Bank GL52: Bish C 2G 9
Pine Cl. GL52: Charl K 1B 22
Pineholt Ga. GL3: Hucc 4A 28
Pine Lawn GL52: Chelt 2D 4
Pinemount Rd. GL3: Hucc 4H 27
Pinery Rd. GL4: Barn 4F 27
Pines, The GL54: Greet 2C 56
Pine Tree Dr. GL4: Barn 3F 27
Pinetrees GL53: Charl K 4A 22
Pineway GL4: A'dle 5C 26
Pinewood Rd. GL2: Qued 5B 32
PINFARTHINGS 6D 46
Pinlocks GL4: Up L 2F 35
Pintail Cl. GL2: Qued 4A 32
Pipers Gro. GL2: High 4A 14
Pippin Cl. GL4: A'md 5H 27
Pirton Cres. GL3: Chu 4A 18

70 A-Z Cheltenham & Gloucester

Pirton La. GL3: Chu 3H **17**
Pirton Mdw. GL3: Chu 4H **17**
Pitch, The GL6: Brown 2B **48**
Pitman Rd. GL51: Chelt 6B **10**
Pitt Mill Gdns. GL3: Hucc. 3H **27**
Pitt St. GL1: Glou 2G **5** (1H **25**)
PITTVILLE 4A **12**
Pittville Cir. GL52: Chelt 5A **12**
Pittville Cir. Rd. GL52: Chelt . . . 5A **12**
Pittville Cres. GL52: Chelt 3A **12**
Pittville Cres. GL52: Chelt 4A **12**
Pittville Cres. La. GL52: Chelt . . 4A **12**
Pittville Lawn
    GL52: Chelt 1D **4** (5H **11**)
Pittville M. GL52: Chelt. . . 1D **4** (5H **11**)
Pittville Pump Room (Spa) 3H **11**
Pittville St.
    GL52: Chelt 3C **4** (6H **11**)
PLAIN, THE 1B **42**
Plain, The GL6: White. 1B **42**
Plantation, The GL2: Hardw 1A **38**
    GL4: A'md 5F **27**
Playhouse GL53: Chelt 4C **4**
Playhouse Theatre, The
    . . . . 4B **4** (6H **11**)
Plock Ct. GL2: Longf. 4A **16**
Plocks, The GL3: Chu 4C **18**
Ploughmans Way GL2: Hardw . . 1B **38**
Plumber's La. GL6: Nails 3A **50**
Plum Tree Cl. GL4: A'md. 1F **35**
Pochard Cl. GL2: Qued 4A **32**
PODSMEAD 1F **33**
Podsmead Ct. GL1: Glou 1G **33**
Podsmead Pl. GL1: Glou 6G **25**
Podsmead Rd. GL1: Glou 6G **25**
    GL2: Glou 5A **12**
Point Rd. GL8: Aven 6G **51**
Polefield Gdns. GL51: Chelt 1E **21**
Poole Ground GL2: High 4A **14**
Pooles La. GL5: Sels 6H **41**
Poole Way GL50: Chelt. 1A **5** (5F **11**)
POOL MEADOW 6F **15**
Pool Mdw. Cvn. Pk. GL1: Glou . . 6F **15**
Popes Cl. GL50: Chelt 1A **4** (4F **11**)
Pope's Ct. GL7: Strat. 3B **52**
Popes Meade GL2: High 4A **14**
Poplar Cl. GL1: Glou 6G **25**
Poplar Cres. GL52: Woodm 1G **9**
Poplar Dr. GL52: Woodm 2H **9**
Poplars, The GL51: Up H 4B **20**
Poplar Way GL2: Hardw 6B **32**
Poppy Fld. GL2: High 3B **14**
Porchester Rd. GL3: Hucc 3G **27**
Portland Pl.
    GL52: Chelt 1D **4** (5H **11**)
Portland Sq.
    GL52: Chelt 2D **4** (5H **11**)
Portland St.
    GL52: Chelt 2C **4** (5H **11**)
Port La. GL5: Brim 3G **47**
Porturet Way GL53: Charl K 3C **22**
Portway GL4: Up L 4G **35**
Postlip Way GL51: Chelt 1A **20**
Post Office La.
    GL50: Chelt 3B **4** (6G **11**)
Post Office Sq. GL7: Sidd 5G **55**
Post Off La. GL20: Tewk 4B **6**
Posy La. GL1: Glou 6B **16**
Potters Fld. Rd. GL52: Woodm . . 2H **9**
Pound Cl. GL3: Brock 1D **36**
    GL7: Sidd. 4F **55**
Pound Farm Courtyard
    GL3: Brock 6D **28**
Pound Hill GL8: Aven 6G **51**
Pound La. GL2: Hardw 2A **38**
Powis La. GL8: Aven. 5H **51**
Prescott Av. GL4: Mats 1C **34**
    (not continuous)
Prescott Wlk. GL52: P'bury. 3C **12**
PRESTBURY 3D **12**
Prestbury Grn. Dr.
    GL52: P'bury 3D **12**
Prestbury Rd.
    GL52: Chelt 1D **4** (5H **11**)
PRESTON 3H **55**
Prices Ground GL4: A'md 5E **27**
Price St. GL1: Glou 4G **25**
Priestley Ct. GL20: Tewk 4B **6**
    (off Lilley's All.)
Primrose Cl. GL4: Glou. 1B **34**
Primrose Way GL7: Sidd 4F **55**
Prince Albert Cl. GL3: Brock. . . . 5B **28**
Prince of Wales Stadium 3G **11**
Princes Ct. GL51: Chelt. 2E **21**

Princes Rd. GL5: Cash G 2H **41**
    GL50: Chelt 2E **21**
Princess Elizabeth Way
    GL51: Chelt 6A **10**
    (not continuous)
Prince's St. GL52: Chelt 6A **12**
Prince St. GL1: Glou 2A **26**
Prinknash Abbey Church 5A **36**
Prinknash Abbey Pottery 5A **36**
Prinknash Bird Pk. 6A **36**
Prinknash Cl. GL4: Mats. 1D **34**
Prinknash Rd. GL4: Mats 1D **34**
    (not continuous)
Priors Ct. GL7: Baun 2D **52**
    GL20: Tewk 4B **6**
    GL52: Chelt 4C **12**
PRIORS PARK. 6C **6**
Priors Rd. GL52: Chelt, P'bury . . 3C **12**
Priory Cl. GL7: Ciren. 6D **52**
Priory Ct. GL3: Chu 4C **18**
Priory Flds. GL6: Hors 6A **50**
Priory La. GL2: Bish C. 1F **9**
Priory M. GL52: Chelt. 4D **4**
Priory Pde. GL52: Chelt. . . . 5D **4** (1H **21**)
Priory Pl. GL1: Glou 4G **5** (2H **25**)
    GL52: Chelt 5D **4** (1H **21**)
Priory Rd. GL1: Glou 2F **5** (1G **25**)
    (not continuous)
Priory St. GL52: Chelt 5D **4** (1H **21**)
Priory Ter. GL52: Chelt 6A **12**
Priory Wlk. GL52: Chelt 6A **12**
Prison Mus. 3F **5** (1G **25**)
Private Rd. GL5: Rodb C. 1C **46**
Promenade GL50: Chelt. . . . 4A **4** (6G **11**)
Prospect Pl. GL7: Ciren. 2E **55**
Prospect Ter. GL52: Chelt 5A **12**
    (off Fairview St.)
Providence Pk. GL51: Chelt 3D **10**
Providence Sq. GL52: Chelt 5A **12**
Puck Pit La. GL54: Winch 4C **56**
    (not continuous)
PUCKSHOLE. 1H **41**
Pullar Cl. GL52: Bish C 1E **9**
Pullar Ct. GL52: Bish C 1E **9**
Pullens Rd. GL6: Pains. 4H **37**
Pullman GL1: Glou 1A **26**
Pumphrey's Rd. GL53: Charl K . . 4B **22**
Purbeck Way GL52: P'bury 4D **12**
Purcell Rd. GL3: Chu 1H **17**
Purley Av. GL7: Ciren 1E **55**
Purley Rd. GL7: Ciren 1E **55**
Purslane Cl. GL4: Glou. 1C **34**
Pyghtell, The GL7: Strat 4C **52**
Pyke Rd. GL20: Tewk 3E **7**
Pyrton M. GL51: Up H. 4B **20**

Q

Quad, The GL50: Chelt 3F **21**
Quadrangle, The
    GL50: Chelt 4A **4** (6G **11**)
Quail Cl. GL4: Barn 4F **27**
Quakers Cl. Walkway
    GL6: Nails 2C **50**
    (off Chestnut Cl.)
Quantock Rd. GL2: Qued 5B **32**
QUARHOUSE 2H **47**
Quarhouse La. GL5: Brim 2H **47**
Quarry Cl. GL7: Strat 3C **52**
Quat Goose La. GL51: Swin V . . . 6A **8**
Quay, The GL1: Glou 2E **5** (1G **25**)
Quay St. GL1: Glou 3E **5** (1G **25**)
    GL20: Tewk 4B **6**
Quebec Dr. GL51: Chelt. 4B **10**
QUEDGELEY 4C **32**
Quedgeley Distribution Cen.
    GL2: Hardw 2C **38**
Quedgeley District Cen.
    GL2: Qued 4D **32**
Quedgeley Pk. (Cvn. Site)
    GL2: Glou 2D **32**
Quedgeley Trad. Est. W.
    GL2: Hardw 2A **38**
Queen Anne's Rd. GL7: Ciren . . . 6F **53**
Queen Elizabeth Rd.
    GL7: Ciren 1F **55**
Queen's Cir.
    GL50: Chelt 4A **4** (6G **11**)
Queens Cl. GL3: Hucc. 2H **27**
Queen's Ct. GL6: Brim 3A **48**
    GL20: Tewk 4B **6**
    GL50: Chelt 1D **20**

Queen's Dr. GL5: Cash G 2H **41**
Queens Hill GL7: Ciren 1D **54**
Queens La. GL7: Ciren 1D **54**
    GL50: Chelt 1F **21**
Queensmead GL6: Pains. 6G **37**
Queens Pde. GL50: Chelt 1F **21**
Queen's Retreat GL51: Chelt. . . . 5E **11**
Queens Rd. GL5: Rodb 4C **42**
    GL7: Ciren. 1D **54**
    GL10: Stone 3C **40**
    GL20: Tewk 6C **6**
    GL50: Chelt 6D **10**
Queens Sq. GL5: Stro 3E **43**
    GL54: Winch 5B **56**
Queen St. GL7: Ciren 2E **55**
    GL51: Chelt 4F **11**
Queen's Wlk.
    GL1: Glou 4H **5** (2H **25**)
Queenwood Gro. GL52: P'bury . . 2E **13**
Quenney's Cl. GL4: Mats 2D **34**
Querns Bus. Cen. GL7: Ciren . . . 2D **54**
    (off Whitworth Rd.)
Quietways GL10: Stone. 2B **40**
Quinton Cl. GL3: Chu 3A **18**

R

Radnor Rd. GL51: Chelt 3B **20**
Raglan St. GL1: Glou 2A **26**
Ragnal La. GL6: Nails 3A **50**
Raikes Rd. GL1: Glou 5G **25**
RAILS MEADOW 1A **34**
Raleigh Cl. GL3: Chu 1G **17**
Ramsdale Rd. GL2: Glou 1E **33**
Rance Pitch GL4: Up L 3F **35**
Randalls Fld. GL6: Pains 6H **37**
    (not continuous)
Randalls Grn. GL6: Chalf H. 1E **49**
Randolph Cl. GL53: Charl K 3A **22**
RANDWICK 1G **41**
Randwick Rd. GL4: Tuff 3G **33**
Range, The GL2: High. 4A **14**
Range La. GL4: Up L 3E **35**
Ranmoor GL4: A'dle. 2E **35**
Ratcliff Lawns GL52: South 5G **9**
Rathmore Cl. GL54: Winch. 4B **56**
Ravensgate Rd. GL53: Charl K . . 5C **22**
Ravis Cl. GL4: Glou. 5C **26**
Reaburn Cl. GL52: Charl K 3C **22**
Read Way GL52: Bish C 3E **9**
Rea La. GL2: Glou. 6C **24**
Rectory Cl. GL4: Up L 3F **35**
Rectory Cl. GL52: Bish C 1F **9**
Rectory La. GL2: Glou 5D **24**
    GL8: Aven 5G **51**
    GL51: Swin V 1E **11**
Rectory Rd. GL4: Mats 1D **34**
Red Admiral Dr. GL4: A'md. 1F **35**
Redding Cl. GL2: Qued 4B **32**
REDDINGS, THE 3F **19**
Reddings, The GL51: Chelt 3F **19**
Reddings Pk. GL51: Chelt 2A **20**
Reddings Rd. GL51: Chelt 2H **19**
Redgrove Pk. GL51: Chelt 3C **10**
Redgrove Rd. GL51: Chelt 3C **10**
Redhouse La. GL5: West 2G **41**
Redland Cl. GL2: Longl. 5C **16**
Red La. GL3: Brock 4B **6**
Redpoll Way GL4: A'dle. 5D **26**
Red Rower Cl. GL50: Chelt 2F **11**
Redstart Way GL4: A'dle. 5D **26**
Redthorne Way GL51: Up H 4B **20**
Red Well Rd. GL4: Mats 3C **34**
Redwind Way GL2: Longl 4E **17**
Redwood Cl. GL1: Glou 6G **25**
Redwood Dr. GL20: North. 1H **7**
    GL51: Chelt 2A **20**
Reeves Cl. GL7: Ciren. 3B **54**
Regency Cl. GL51: Chelt 5F **11**
Regent Arc. GL50: Chelt 3B **4**
Regent Arc. Shop. Cen.
    GL50: Chelt 4B **4** (6G **11**)
Regent Chambers
    GL50: Chelt 3B **4** (6G **11**)
Regent Cl. GL51: Chelt. 1E **21**
Regent Ho. GL50: Chelt. 1F **11**
    (off Lansdown Rd.)
Regent St. GL1: Glou. 6H **5** (3H **25**)
    (not continuous)
    GL10: Stone 4C **40**
    GL50: Chelt 4B **4** (6G **11**)
Regis Cl. GL53: Charl K 4B **22**
Remus Cl. GL4: A'md 5G **27**

Rendcomb Cl. GL4: A'md 1F **35**
Rendcombe Dr. GL7: Ciren. 3B **54**
Reservoir Cl. GL5: Stro 3F **43**
Reservoir Rd. GL4: Glou 1H **33**
    GL5: Stro 3F **43**
Retreat, The GL4: Tuff 3G **33**
    GL5: Sels 6H **41**
Rhodesia Ho. GL51: Chelt. 3C **10**
Ribble Cl. GL3: Brock 6E **29**
Ribston M. GL1: Glou 6H **25**
Richard Pl. GL20: Tewk 6G **7**
Richard Rd. GL6: Minch 6G **47**
Richards Rd. GL51: Chelt 3E **11**
Richmond Av. GL4: Glou 5D **26**
Richmond Dr. GL52: Chelt 6B **12**
Richmond Gdns. GL2: Longl. . . . 4D **16**
Richmond Ho. GL1: Glou 1B **26**
Richmond Rd. GL20: Wal C 6H **7**
Richmonds, The GL4: A'dle. 1E **35**
Ridge, The GL6: Buss. 6B **44**
    (not continuous)
Ridgemont Rd. GL5: Stro 4F **43**
Ridgemount Cl. GL3: Brock 6D **28**
Ridgeway, The GL6: Buss. 1B **48**
Ridings, The GL2: Maise 2D **14**
    GL6: Nails 3D **50**
Ringfield Cl. GL6: Nails 3D **50**
Rippledale Cl. GL51: Chelt 2B **20**
Rissington Cl. GL51: Chelt 1B **20**
Rissington Rd. GL4: Tuff 3H **33**
Rivelands Rd. GL51: Swin V. 6A **8**
River Leys GL51: Chelt 2C **10**
Rivermead Cl. GL2: Glou 5H **15**
Riverside GL54: Winch 4C **56**
Riverside Cl. GL52: Charl K 3C **22**
Riverside Ct. GL20: Tewk 3B **6**
Riverside Ho. GL53: Chelt 6D **4**
Riverside Sports & Leisure Club
    . . . . 1E **5** (6G **15**)
Riverside Wlk. GL20: Tewk. 4B **6**
Riversley Rd. GL2: Glou. 1C **26**
Riversmeet GL3: Brock 6E **29**
Riverview Way GL51: Chelt 3D **10**
Robbers Rd. GL6: Rand. 1F **41**
Robbins Cl. GL5: Ebley 4F **41**
Robert Burns Av. GL51: Chelt . . . 2A **20**
Robert Harvey Ho. GL52: Chelt . . 1D **4**
Robert Raikes Av. GL4: Tuff 3G **33**
Roberts Cl. GL7: Strat. 4C **52**
    GL52: Bish C 1E **9**
Robertson Rd. GL51: Shurd 1A **30**
Roberts Rd. GL3: Inns 2F **17**
    GL52: P'bury 4E **13**
Robin Cl. GL6: Buss 1D **48**
    GL20: North 1G **7**
Robin Ct. GL10: Stone 2C **40**
Robinhood St. GL1: Glou 4G **25**
    (not continuous)
Robins Cl. GL52: Chelt 5B **12**
Robins End GL3: Inns 2E **17**
Robinson Rd. GL1: Glou 4G **25**
ROBINSWOOD 6B **26**
Robinswood Gdns. GL4: Glou. . . 1B **34**
Robinswood Hill Country Pk. . . . 2A **34**
Robins Wood Hill Country Pk.
    Vis. Cen. 1A **34**
Rochester Cl. GL51: Chelt 4D **20**
Rockleigh Cl. GL4: Tuff. 2H **33**
ROCKNESS. 4F **47**
Rockness Hill GL6: Hors, Nails. . . 4B **50**
RODBOROUGH 4B **42**
Rodborough Av. GL5: Rodb 4C **42**
Rodborough Common 1C **46**
Rodborough Hill GL5: Rodb 4C **42**
Rodborough La. GL5: Rodb 5D **42**
Rodney Cl. GL2: Longl 5C **16**
Rodney Rd.
    GL50: Chelt 4B **4** (6G **11**)
Rollers, The GL6: Nails. 2C **50**
Rolleston Way GL51: Chelt. 2C **20**
Roman Amphitheatre. 2D **54**
Roman Hackle Av. GL50: Chelt . . 2F **11**
Roman Hackle Rd. GL50: Chelt. . 2F **11**
Roman Rd. GL4: A'md. 5F **27**
    GL51: Chelt 6D **10**
Roman Way GL3: Brock 5D **28**
    GL6: For G. 1A **50**
Romney Cl. GL1: Glou 6H **25**
Rookery Rd. GL3: Inns 3D **17**
ROOKSMOOR 1B **46**
Rooksmoor Hill
    GL5: Kings, Woodc. 1B **46**
Roosevelt Av. GL52: Charl K 1B **22**
Rope Wlk. GL20: Tewk 4C **6**

Ropewalk GL5: Thru 1F 47
Rose & Crown Ho. GL50: Chelt. . . . 2B 4
Rose & Crown Pas.
GL50: Chelt 2B 4 (5G 11)
Rosebay Gdns. GL51: Chelt 2B 10
Rosebery Av. GL1: Glou 6H 25
Rosedale Av. GL10: Stone 3C 40
Rosedale Cl. GL2: Hardw 5A 32
Rose Fld. Cres. GL20: Tewk 4D 6
Rosehill Ct. GL7: Ciren 4D 52
Rosehill Ri. GL52: Chelt 3H 11
Rosehill St. GL52: Chelt 1A 22
Rosehip Ct. GL51: Up H 5D 20
Rosehip Way GL52: Bish C 1D 8
Rosemary Cl. GL4: A'dle. 1D 34
Rose's Theatre 3B 6
Rose Way GL7: Ciren. 3F 55
Rothermere Cl. GL51: Up H 4C 20
Rothleigh GL51: Up H. 4B 20
Rotunda Ter.
GL50: Chelt. 5A 4 (1F 21)
Roundabout La. GL8: Aven. 6H 51
Roundabouts, The
GL5: Brim, Burl. 3G 47
ROWANFIELD 5D 10
Rowanfield Exchange
GL51: Chelt. 5D 10
Rowanfield Rd. GL51: Chelt 6C 10
Rowan Gdns. GL3: Brock 4C 28
Rowans, The GL52: Woodm 2G 9
Rowan Way GL51: Up H 4B 20
Rowcroft GL5: Stro 3C 42
Rowcroft Retreat GL5: Stro. 3C 42
Rowe Ct. GL50: Chelt 6F 11
Rowena Cade Av. GL50: Chelt . . . 2E 21
Roxton Dr. GL51: Chelt 2H 19
Royal Ct. GL51: Chelt 5A 10
Royal Cres. GL50: Chelt . . 3A 4 (6G 11)
Royal La. GL1: Glou 1A 26
(not continuous)
Royal Oak M.
GL50: Chelt 2A 4 (5G 11)
Royal Oak Rd.
GL1: Glou. 2E 5 (1G 25)
Royal Pde. *GL50: Chelt. 1F 21*
(off Parabola Rd.)
Royal Pde. M.
GL50: Chelt. 5A 4 (1F 21)
Royal Well La.
GL50: Chelt. 3A 4 (6F 11)
Royal Well Pl.
GL50: Chelt 3A 4 (6G 11)
Royal Well Rd.
GL50: Chelt 3A 4 (6G 11)
Rudge, The GL2: Maise. 1E 15
Rudhall Ct. GL1: Glou 2F 5
Rumsey Cl. GL4: A'dle. 1F 35
Runnings, The GL51: Chelt. 1D 10
Runnings Rd. GL51: Chelt 1D 10
Runnymede GL51: Up H 4B 20
Ruscombe Rd. GL6: Rusc. 1H 41
Rushes, The GL2: Qued 3D 32
Rushley La. GL54: Winch 4C 56
Rushworth Cl. GL51: Chelt 5A 10
Rushworth Ho. GL51: Chelt. 5A 10
Rushy Ho. GL52: P'bury 3B 12
Rushy M. GL52: P'bury. 3B 12
Ruskin Mill 3C 50
Ruspidge Cl. GL4: A'md 6F 27
Russell Pl. GL51: Chelt 4F 11
Russell St. GL1: Glou 4H 5 (2H 25)
GL5: Stro 3D 42
GL51: Chelt 4F 11
Russet Cl. GL4: Tuff 2E 33
Russet Rd. GL51: Chelt. 4C 10
Rustic Cl. GL4: Mats. 6D 26
Rutherford Way GL51: Chelt 2D 10
Rutland Ct. GL50: Chelt. 6E 11
Rutland Pl. GL7: Ciren 2D 54
Rydal Rd. GL2: Longl 5C 16
Rydal Wlk. GL51: Chelt. 2B 20
Ryder Row GL3: Inns. 3F 17
Rye Av. GL51: Chelt 2A 10
Ryecroft St. GL1: Glou 3A 26
RYEFORD. 4D 40
Ryeford Ind. Est. GL10: Ryef 4D 40
Ryeford Rd. (North)
GL10: Ryef 4D 40
Ryelands GL4: Tuff 2F 33
Ryelands, The GL6: Rand. 1G 41
Ryelands Cl. GL10: Stone. 2B 40
Ryelands Rd. GL10: Stone 2B 40
Ryeleaze Cl. GL5: Stro 3D 42
Ryeleaze Rd. GL5: Stro 3D 42
RYEWORTH 2C 22
Ryeworth Dr. GL52: Charl K 2C 22
Ryeworth Rd. GL52: Charl K. 2C 22

S

Sabre Cl. GL2: Qued. 2D 32
Sackville App. GL50: Chelt. 3G 11
Saddlers La. GL50: Chelt 2F 21
Saddlers Rd. GL2: Qued 3C 32
Saffron Cl. GL4: Glou 6B 26
Saffron Rd. GL20: Tewk 4B 6
Sage Cl. GL3: Chu 3G 17
St Aidan's Cl. GL51: Chelt. 5B 10
St Alban's Cl. GL51: Chelt 4D 20
St Albans Way GL2: Glou 6F 25
St Aldate St. GL1: Glou . . . 3H 5 (1H 25)
St Aldwyn Rd. GL1: Glou 5A 26
St Andrews Grn. GL3: Chu 4A 18
St Annes Cl. GL3: Brock 5C 28
GL52: Chelt 5A 12
St Anne's Rd.
GL52: Chelt 3D 4 (6H 11)
St Anne's Ter.
GL52: Chelt 3D 4 (6H 11)
St Ann Way GL1: Glou 6E 5 (3G 25)
St Arvans Ct. GL52: Chelt 3H 11
St Barnabas Cl. GL1: Glou 1H 33
St Brendan's Rd. GL5: Stro. 3F 43
SAINTBRIDGE 6C 26
Saintbridge Cl. GL4: Glou. 6C 26
Saintbridge Pl. GL4: Glou. 6C 26
Saintbridge Sports Cen. 6C 26
St Catherine St.
GL1: Glou 1G 5 (6H 15)
ST CHLOE 4C 46
St Chloe Mead GL5: Amb 4C 46
St Clement's Wlk. GL7: Ciren. . . . 6D 52
St Cloes Pitch GL5: Amb. 4B 46
St Cyrils Rd. GL10: Stone. 3C 40
St David's Cl. GL4: Tuff 2F 33
GL51: Chelt 3D 20
St Edward's Wlk.
GL53: Charl K 3B 22
St Francis Way GL3: Inns 3E 17
St George's Av. GL10: King S 6D 40
St Georges Bus. Pk.
GL51: Chelt 5D 10
St George's Cl. GL4: Tuff. 2F 33
GL10: King S. 6D 40
GL51: Chelt 5E 11
St George's Dr. GL51: Chelt 5E 11
St George's Ga. GL51: Chelt 5E 11
St George's Pl.
GL50: Chelt 3A 4 (6G 11)
St George's Rd. GL3: Brock 6D 28
GL50: Chelt 3A 4 (5E 11)
St George's Sq. GL50: Chelt 2A 4
St George's St.
GL50: Chelt 2A 4 (5G 11)
St George's Ter. GL50: Chelt. 3A 4
St Georges Twr. GL50: Chelt. 2A 4
St Giles Ct. GL2: Maise. 2D 14
St James' GL2: Qued 4C 32
St James' Cen., The
GL2: Qued. 4C 32
St James Cl. GL2: Qued 4C 32
St James Ct. GL50: Chelt 2A 4
St James Nth. GL50: Chelt 2A 4
St James Pl. GL50: Chelt 2F 21
St James Sth. GL50: Chelt 2A 4
St James' Sq.
GL50: Chelt 2A 4 (5G 11)
St James St. GL1: Glou. 3A 26
GL52: Chelt 4C 4 (6H 11)
St James' Ter. GL50: Chelt 6A 4
St John's Av. GL3: Chu 3H 17
GL52: Chelt 3D 4 (6H 11)
St John's Cl. GL7: Strat. 4C 52
GL52: Bish C 1E 9
St John's Ct. GL50: Chelt 5E 11
St John's La. GL1: Glou. . . 3G 5 (1H 25)
St John's Rd. GL7: Ciren. 5D 52
St Judes Wlk. GL53: Charl K. 2A 22
St Kilda Pde. GL1: Glou. . . 4H 5 (2A 26)
St Lawrence Cl. GL7: Ciren. 6C 52
St Lawrence Rd. GL4: Glou. 4E 27
St Leonards Cl. GL4: Up L 3F 35
St Lukes Ct. GL53: Chelt 5B 4
St Luke's Pl.
GL53: Chelt 5C 4 (1H 21)
St Luke's Rd.
GL53: Chelt 5B 4 (1G 21)
St Luke St. GL1: Glou. 6F 5 (3G 25)
St Margaret's GL1: Glou 1B 26
St Margaret's Pde. GL50: Chelt . . . 2B 4
St Margarets Rd. GL3: Hucc. 3G 27
GL50: Chelt 1B 4 (5G 11)
St Margaret's Ter.
GL50: Chelt 1C 4 (5G 11)
ST MARK'S 6C 10
St Mark's Ct. GL1: Glou 6A 16
St Mark St. GL1: Glou. 6H 15
St Mary de Crypt Church Schoolroom
. . . . 4G 5
ST MARYS 2C 48
St Mary's Cl. GL1: Glou . . . 2F 5 (1H 25)
St Mary's Hill GL5: Inch 5B 46
ST MARYS HOSPITAL 4A 28
St Mary's La. GL20: Tewk. 4B 6
St Mary's Mead GL6: Pains 6G 37
St Mary's Rd. GL7: Ciren. 1F 55
GL20: Tewk 4A 6
St Mary's Sq. GL1: Glou. . . 2F 5 (1G 25)
St Mary's St. GL1: Glou. . . 2G 5 (1H 25)
GL6: Pains 5H 37
St Michaels Av. GL52: Bish C 2F 9
St Michael's Cl. GL53: Charl K . . . 3B 22
St Michaels' Ct. GL1: Glou. 4G 5
St Michaels Pl. GL5: Cash G 2G 41
St Michaels Rd. GL7: Ciren 2D 54
GL51: Chelt. 4D 20
St Michael's Sq.
GL1: Glou 5G 5 (2H 25)
St Nicholas Ct. GL1: Glou 2F 5
GL2: Hardw 6B 32
St Nicholas Dr. GL50: Chelt 2G 11
St Nicholas Sq.
GL1: Glou. 2F 5 (1G 25)
St Oswalds Pk.
GL1: Glou. 1F 5 (5H 15)
St Oswald's Priory 1F 5 (6G 15)
St Oswald's Rd.
GL1: Glou. 1E 5 (6G 15)
St Patricks Ct. GL3: Brock 6D 28
ST PAUL'S
Cheltenham 4G 11
Gloucester. 6E 5 (3G 25)
St Paul's Ct. GL1: Glou. 3H 25
St Paul's La.
GL50: Chelt 1A 4 (5G 11)
St Paul's Pde.
GL50: Chelt 1B 4 (5G 11)
St Paul's Rd. GL1: Glou 3H 25
GL50: Chelt. 1B 4 (4F 11)
St Paul's St. Nth.
GL50: Chelt 1A 4 (5G 11)
St Paul's St. Sth.
GL50: Chelt 1A 4 (5G 11)
St Paul's Ter. GL50: Chelt 1B 4
ST PETER'S 3F 11
St Peter's Cl. GL51: Chelt. 4D 10
St Peter's Ct. GL7: Ciren. 1D 54
St Peters Rd. GL4: Mats. 2D 34
GL7: Ciren 1D 54
St Peter's Sq. GL51: Chelt 3D 10
St Peters Way GL54: Winch 4B 56
St Philips Ct. GL1: Glou 4G 25
St Phillip's Cl. GL3: Hucc 3H 27
St Phillip's St. GL50: Chelt. 2G 21
St Stephen's Cl. GL51: Chelt. 2E 21
St Stephen's Mnr. GL51: Chelt . . . 2E 21
St Stephen's Rd. GL51: Chelt 2E 21
St Swithin's GL10: Leo S 6B 40
St Swithuns Rd. GL2: Glou. 5D 24
St Vincent Way GL3: Chu 1H 17
Salamanca Rd. GL52: Chelt 5C 12
Salisbury Av. GL51: Chelt. 3C 20
Salisbury Rd. GL1: Glou. 3B 26
Salix Ct. GL51: Up H. 5D 20
Sallis Cl. GL20: North. 1G 7
Salmons Springs Trad. Est.
GL6: Stro. 1C 42
Salterley Grange
GL53: Leck H 4G 31
Salvia Cl. GL3: Chu 3G 17
Sandalwood Dr. GL2: Glou 4E 25
Sandfield, The GL20: North 1H 7
Sandfield Rd. GL3: Chu 5C 18
SANDFIELDS 4D 10
Sandford Leaze GL8: Aven 5G 51
Sandford Mill Cl. GL53: Chelt. . . . 2A 22
Sandford Mill Rd. GL53: Chelt . . . 2A 22
Sandford Pk. Pl.
GL52: Chelt 5D 4 (1H 21)
Sandford Parks Lido 6D 4 (1H 21)
Sandford Pk. Vs. GL50: Chelt 5B 4
Sandford Rd.
GL53: Chelt 6B 4 (1G 21)
Sandford St.
GL53: Chelt 5C 4 (1H 21)
Sandford Way GL4: Tuff 3E 33
Sandhurst La.
GL2: Glou, Sand, Longf 2G 15
Sandhurst Rd. GL1: Glou 5H 15
(not continuous)
GL2: Glou 5H 15
GL52: Charl K 3C 22
Sandown Lawn GL3: Chu 3H 17
Sandown Rd. GL52: Bish C. 1E 9
Sandpiper Cl. GL2: Qued 4A 32
SANDPITS 1F 41
Sandpits La. GL6: West. 1F 41
Sandringham Av. GL4: Tuff 4F 33
Sandringham Ct. GL53: Chelt. . . . 2A 22
Sandstar Cl. GL2: Longl 4E 17
Sandycroft Rd. GL3: Chu 2H 17
(not continuous)
Sandy La. GL53: Charl K. 4A 22
Sandy La. Rd. GL53: Charl K 4A 22
Sandyleaze GL2: Glou. 6E 17
Sandy Pluck La. GL51: Shurd. . . . 3G 29
San Remo GL1: Glou 5H 25
Sappercombe La.
GL53: Charl K 4C 22
Sapperton Rd. GL4: Glou 6A 26
Sapphire Cl. GL4: Tuff. 3E 33
Sarah Siddons Wlk.
GL50: Chelt 3E 21
Saturn Cl. GL4: A'md 5G 27
Savernake Rd. GL4: Glou 4B 26
Saville Cl. GL50: Chelt 3H 11
Saw Mills End GL4: Barn 1E 27
Saxon Cl. GL2: Longl 4D 16
Saxon Rd. GL7: Ciren 6F 53
Saxon Way GL52: Chelt. 1A 22
Sayers Cres. GL3: Brock. 6D 28
Saylittle M. GL2: Longl 4F 17
Scar Hill GL6: Box, Minch 2E 51
Scholars Ct. GL51: Chelt. 5E 11
Scholar's Wlk. GL2: Qued. 4C 32
School Hill GL7: Strat. 3B 52
School Ho. GL50: Chelt. 2B 4
School La. GL2: Hardw, Qued. . . . 5A 32
GL7: Ciren 2E 55
GL51: Shurd 1B 30
GL52: South 5H 9
School Mead GL51: Chelt. 5D 10
School M. GL4: Mats 1C 34
School Rd. GL6: Bis 1F 45
GL6: Minch 6H 47
GL52: Bish C 1F 9
GL53: Charl K 3C 22
School Rd. Flats
GL53: Charl K 3C 22
School Sq. *GL5: Sels 5H 41*
(off Bell La.)
Scott Av. GL2: Glou 1F 33
Scott Ho. GL51: Chelt 4B 10
Seabright Cl. GL51: Chelt. 2B 10
Seabroke Rd. GL1: Glou 6A 16
Seabrook Rd. GL3: Brock. 6D 28
Seacombe Rd. GL51: Chelt. 5A 10
Sebert St. GL1: Glou. 6A 16
Secunda Way GL2: Glou 5E 25
Sedgewick Gdns. GL51: Up H. . . . 3A 20
Sedgley Cl. GL4: Tuff 3F 33
Sedgley Rd. GL52: Bish C. 1E 9
Sefton Wlk. GL51: Up H 3A 20
Selborne Rd. GL52: Bish C 1E 9
Selkirk Cl. GL52: Chelt 5A 12
Selkirk Ct. GL52: Chelt 5A 12
Selkirk Gdns. GL52: Chelt. 5A 12
Selkirk St. GL52: Chelt . . . 1D 4 (5A 12)
Sellars Rd. GL2: Hardw 6A 32
Selsey Rd. GL5: Woodc 2A 46
SELSLEY 5H 41
Selsley Herb Farm 6H 41
Selsley Hill GL5: Dudb 5H 41
GL5: Sels 6H 41
SELSLEY WEST. 6F 41
Selworthy GL51: Up H. 4B 20
Selwyn Cl. GL10: King S. 5D 40
Selwyn Rd. GL4: Glou. 6A 26
Seneca Way GL50: Chelt. 2E 11
Serlo Rd. GL1: Glou 1G 5 (6H 15)
Sevelm GL51: Up H. 4B 20
Seven Acres GL4: A'md. 4E 27
Seven Acres Rd. GL6: Nails 2B 50
Seven Posts All. GL52: P'bury . . . 3C 12
Seventh Av. GL4: Tuff. 3G 33

Seven Waters—Stratford Leisure Cen.

Seven Waters GL10: Leo S. 6A **40**
Severn Cl. GL2: Maise. 2E **15**
Severn Dr. GL20: Tewk 2F **7**
Severn Oaks GL2: Qued 6C **32**
Severn Rd. GL1: Glou 4E **5** (2G **25**)
GL10: Stone 2B **40**
GL52: Chelt 5B **12**
Severnside Trad. Est.
GL2: Glou 2F **25**
Severnvale Dr. GL2: Qued 4B **32**
Seymour Pl. GL20: Tewk. 5B **6**
GL54: Winch 5B **56**
Seymour Rd. GL1: Glou 5G **25**
Sezincote Cl. GL6: Buss 5C **44**
Shackleton Cl. GL3: Chu. 4A **18**
Shaftesbury Hall
GL50: Chelt 2A **4** (5G **11**)
Shaftesbury Ind. Est.
GL51: Chelt 1E **11**
Shaftesbury Pl. GL51: Chelt 5A **10**
Shakespeare Av. GL2: Glou. 2F **33**
Shakespeare Cotts.
GL51: Chelt 2G **19**
Shakespeare Ct. GL20: Tewk 4B **6**
Shakespeare Rd. GL51: Chelt. . . . 5B **10**
Shalford Cl. GL7: Ciren 2C **54**
Shambles, The GL5: Stro 3D **42**
Shamrock Cl. GL3: Chu 3G **17**
Shannon Pl. GL20: Tewk 2F **7**
Shannon Way GL20: Tewk. 3F **7**
Shaw Grn. La. GL52: P'bury 2C **12**
Shears Pitch GL6: Nails 1D **50**
Shearwater Gro. GL3: Inns 3E **17**
Sheepscombe Cl. GL51: Chelt . . . 1B **20**
Sheep St. GL7: Ciren 1D **54**
Sheevaun Cl. GL2: Longl 4E **17**
Shelburne Rd. GL51: Chelt 2C **20**
Sheldons Ct.
GL52: Chelt 2C **4** (5H **11**)
Shelduck Rd. GL2: Qued. 4A **32**
Shelley Av. GL2: Glou 1F **33**
GL51: Chelt 6B **10**
Shelley Rd. GL51: Chelt 6B **10**
Shephard Mead GL20: Tewk 5A **6**
Shepherd Rd. GL2: Glou 2E **33**
Shepherds Cl. GL5: Stro 2E **43**
GL51: Chelt 2A **10**
Shepherds Cft. GL5: Stro 2E **43**
Shepherds Ride GL7: Ciren. 6A **52**
Shepherds Way GL3: Chu. 2G **17**
GL7: Ciren. 5D **52**
Shepherds Well GL5: Rodb C 3E **47**
Sheppard Way GL6: Minch 5F **47**
Sherborne Cl. GL10: Stone. 2C **40**
Sherborne Ho. *GL1: Glou 6A 16*
(off Sherborne St.)
GL10: Stone 2C **40**
Sherborne Pl.
GL52: Chelt 3D **4** (6H **11**)
Sherborne St. GL1: Glou. 1A **26**
GL52: Chelt 2D **4** (5H **11**)
Shergar Cl. GL4: A'dle. 1E **35**
Sherwood Grn. GL2: Longf. 3A **16**
Shipton's Grave La.
GL6: Hors, Nails 5C **50**
Shipway Ct. GL52: Bish C 1E **9**
Shooters End GL5: Stro 2D **42**
Short St. GL53: Chelt. 3F **21**
SHORTWOOD **3A 50**
Shortwood Rd. GL6: Nails. 3A **50**
Shrublands GL53: Charl K. 4A **22**
SHURDINGTON **1A 30**
Shurdington Rd.
GL3: Brock, Shurd. 6E **29**
GL51: Chelt, Up H. 5D **20**
GL53: Chelt. 5D **20**
Sibree Cl. GL6: Buss. 1B **48**
SIDDINGTON. **5F 55**
Siddington Hall GL7: Sidd 5F **55**
Siddington Rd.
GL7: Ciren, Sidd 3F **55**
Sidney St. GL1: Glou. 2B **26**
GL52: Chelt 4D **4** (6H **11**)
Silcock Cl. GL3: Chu. 2G **17**
Silk Mill Ct. GL54: Winch 5C **56**
Silk Mill La. GL54: Winch. 5C **56**
Silver Birch Cl. GL2: Qued 4B **32**
Silver Cl. GL4: Tuff 2F **33**
Silverdale Pde. GL3: Hucc 3G **27**
Silver St. GL6: Chalf H 2D **48**
GL7: Ciren. 6D **52**
Silverthorn Cl. GL53: Chelt 4E **21**
Silvertree Gdns. GL5: Thru 1F **47**
Silverwood Way GL51: Up H 4B **20**
Simmonds Ct. GL6: Minch 6H **47**
Simmonds Rd. GL3: Hucc 4G **27**
Simon Rd. GL2: Longl 4D **16**
Simpson's Orchard GL4: A'dle. . . . 2F **35**
Sims La. GL2: Qued 2C **32**
Sinclair Rd. GL51: Shurd 2A **30**
Sinderberry Dr. GL20: North. 1H **7**
Sinope St. GL1: Glou 2A **26**
Sissinghurst Gro. GL51: Up H . . . 4D **20**
Sisson End GL2: Glou 1E **27**
Sisson Rd. GL2: Glou 1D **26**
Sivell Cl. GL2: Longf. 3B **16**
Six Acres GL4: Up L 2G **35**
Skaiteshill GL6: Brown 2C **48**
Skillicorne M. GL50: Chelt 1D **20**
Skinner St. GL1: Glou 1H **5** (6H **15**)
Skylark Way GL4: A'dle. 6C **26**
Slade Brook GL5: Stro. 2F **43**
Slad La. GL6: Stro 2G **43**
Slad Rd. GL5: Stro 3D **42**
GL6: Stro 2F **43**
Slaney St. GL1: Glou. 4A **26**
Slimbridge Rd. GL4: Tuff 2G **33**
Smiths Ct. GL20: Tewk 4B **6**
Smith's Fld. GL7: Ciren 2B **54**
Smith's La. GL20: Tewk 4B **6**
Smithwood Gro. GL53: Charl K. . . 5B **22**
Smithy, The GL7: Ciren 2F **55**
Smithy La. GL54: Greet. 1B **56**
Smythe Ho. GL7: Ciren 6E **53**
Smythe Mdw. GL6: Brown 2B **48**
Smythe Rd. GL51: Swin V. 1E **11**
Snake's La. GL5: Amb 6C **46**
Snead Pk. GL4: A'md 6G **27**
Sneedhams Rd. GL4: Mats 3C **34**
Snowdon Gdns. GL3: Chu. 2H **17**
Snowdonia Rd. GL20: Wal C 6D **6**
Snowdrop Cl. GL4: A'md 6F **27**
Snowshill Cl. GL4: Barn 4F **27**
Snowshill Dr. GL52: Bish C 2D **8**
Soldiers of Gloucestershire Mus.
. . . . 4F 5 (2G 25)
Soldier's Wlk. GL3: Chu 6A **18**
Solway Rd. GL51: Chelt 4A **10**
Somerford Ct. *GL7: Ciren 2D 54*
(off Somerford Rd.)
Somerford Rd. GL7: Ciren 2D **54**
Somergate Rd. GL51: Chelt 3A **10**
Somerset Av. GL51: Chelt. 5D **10**
Somerset Ho. GL50: Chelt 2A **4**
Somerset Pl. GL1: Glou . . . 6F **5** (3G **25**)
GL20: Tewk. 6G **7**
Somerville Ct. GL7: Ciren. 3C **54**
Somme Rd. GL52: Chelt 5C **12**
Sorrel Cl. GL4: Glou 1B **34**
Sth. Africa Ho. GL51: Chelt. 3C **10**
SOUTHAM **5H 9**
Southam La. GL52: South. 5E **9**
Southam Rd. GL52: P'bury. 1D **12**
Southbank GL5: Woodc. 2A **46**
Southbrook Rd. GL4: Glou 2D **26**
Sth. Cerney Rd. GL7: Sidd 5G **55**
South Cl. GL2: Longl. 5C **16**
Southcourt Cl. GL53: Chelt 4G **21**
Southcourt Dr. GL53: Chelt. 4G **21**
Southern Av. GL4: Tuff 1H **33**
Southern Rd. GL53: Chelt. 5H **21**
Southfield GL6: Minch 6G **47**
Southfield App. GL53: Chelt 5H **21**
Southfield Cl. GL53: Chelt 5H **21**
Southfield Mnr. Pk.
GL53: Charl K 5A **22**
Southfield Ri. GL53: Chelt 5H **21**
Southfield Rd. GL4: Glou 1H **33**
GL5: Woodc 2B **46**
Southgate Cres. GL5: Rodb 5B **42**
Southgate Dr. GL53: Chelt 2A **22**
Southgate Gdns. GL5: Rodb 5B **42**
Southgate M. GL7: Ciren. 2E **55**
Southgate St.
GL1: Glou. 6F **5** (3G **25**)
Southmead GL7: Ciren. 3F **55**
South Point GL1: Glou 4E **5** (2G **25**)
South Ter. GL7: Ciren 6A **52**
South Vw. GL5: Ebley 3G **41**
South Vw. Way GL52: P'bury 3D **12**
South Way GL7: Ciren. 1D **54**
SOUTH WOODCHESTER **3A 46**
Southwood La. GL50: Chelt. 1F **21**
Sovereign Ct. GL1: Glou 1A **26**
Spa, The 6G 5
Spa Gdns. GL20: Tewk 3E **7**
Spa M. GL1: Glou. 5F **5** (2G **25**)
Spa Rd. GL1: Glou. 5F **5** (2G **25**)
Sparrow Cl. GL6: Buss 1D **48**
Spartan Cl. GL4: A'md. 5F **27**
Spartgate La. GL7: Sidd 5D **54**
Spa Vs. GL1: Glou 6G **5** (3H **25**)
Speedwell Cl. GL4: A'md 6F **27**
Spencer Cl. GL3: Hucc 4G **27**
Spenser Av. GL51: Chelt 6B **10**
Spenser Rd. GL51: Chelt. 6B **10**
Speringate GL7: Ciren. 2E **55**
Spey Cl. GL2: Qued. 3C **32**
Spider La. GL5: Stro 4E **43**
Spillman's Pitch GL5: Rodb 4B **42**
Spillman's Rd. GL5: Rodb 4B **42**
Spindles, The GL53: Leck. 5D **20**
Spinnaker Ho. GL2: Glou. 3F **25**
Spinnaker Rd. GL2: Glou. 3F **25**
Spinners Ho. *GL5: Stro. 3D 42*
(off Wesley Ct.)
Spinney, The GL52: Chelt 3H **11**
Spinney Ct. GL5: Brim 4G **47**
Spinney Rd. GL4: Barn 4F **27**
Spinning Wheel Ct.
GL5: Cash G 3H **41**
Spire Way GL4: Barn. 3E **27**
Spitalgate La. GL7: Ciren 6D **52**
Spittlel Leys GL54: Winch 4B **56**
Spoonbill Cl. GL2: Qued. 4A **32**
Sport Connection Fitness Club
. . . . 6G 21
Spread Eagle Ct. GL1: Glou 3H **5**
Spread Eagle Rd.
GL1: Glou 3H **5** (1H **25**)
SPRINGBANK **3A 10**
Springbank Cl. GL51: Chelt. 3A **10**
Springbank Dr. GL51: Chelt 4A **10**
Springbank Gro. GL51: Chelt 4A **10**
Springbank Rd. GL51: Chelt 4A **10**
Springbank Way GL51: Chelt 3A **10**
Springbank Way Shop. Cen.
GL51: Chelt. 2B **10**
SPRING BOTTOM **3C 22**
Springdale Cl. GL2: Hardw. 5A **32**
Springfield GL2: Hardw. 6B **32**
GL20: Tewk 3E **7**
Springfield Bus. Cen.
GL10: Stone 2A **40**
Springfield Cl. GL51: Chelt. 2G **19**
Springfield Ct. GL10: Stone 3C **40**
Springfield Ho. GL51: Chelt 3B **10**
Springfield Rd. GL5: Cash G 2G **41**
GL5: Stro 2D **42**
GL7: Ciren 3C **54**
Springfield Ter. GL5: Ebley. 4G **41**
GL5: Rodb. 4B **42**
Spring Gdns. GL20: Tewk 4C **6**
Spring Hill GL6: Nails 2C **50**
Springhill Cl. GL6: Nails 2C **50**
Springhill Cres. GL6: Nails 2C **50**
Spring La. GL5: Stro. 4D **42**
GL5: Thru 1F **47**
GL52: P'bury. 1C **12**
Spring Mill Ind. Est.
GL6: Nails 3E **51**
Springwater Cl. GL20: North 1H **7**
Springwell Gdns. GL3: Chu 2A **18**
Square, The GL5: Stro 2D **42**
GL10: Stone 2C **40**
Squires Cl. GL6: Buss. 1B **48**
Squirrel Cl. GL2: Qued 6B **32**
Stables, The GL52: P'bury 3D **12**
Staites Orchard
GL4: Up L 2F **35**
Stamages La. GL6: Pains 6G **37**
Stamp's Mdw. GL2: Longf 4A **16**
Stanbury M. GL3: Hucc. 5A **28**
Stancombe Gro. GL51: Up H 4D **20**
Stancombe La. GL54: Winch 4D **56**
Stancombe Vw. GL54: Winch 4B **56**
STANFIELDS **6C 42**
Stanford Rd. GL20: North 2H **7**
Stank La. GL2: Hardw. 2A **38**
Stanleigh Ter. GL2: Maise. 2D **14**
Stanley, The GL4: Up L. 3G **35**
Stanley Cotts. GL1: Glou. 3A **26**
STANLEY DOWNTON **5B 40**
Stanley Pk. GL5: Sels 6H **41**
Stanley Pl. GL51: Chelt. 4A **10**
Stanley Rd. GL1: Glou 5H **25**
GL52: Charl K 1B **22**
Stanley Ter. GL1: Glou 4H **25**
Stanley Vw. GL5: Dudb. 5A **42**
Stanley Wlk. GL4: Up L 4G **35**
Stanmoor GL4: A'dle 2E **35**
Stansby Cres. GL3: Chu 3H **17**
Stansby Ho. Cvn. Pk.
GL51: Chelt. 3G **19**
Stansby Ho. Cvn. Site
GL51: Chelt. 3G **19**
Stansted Ho. GL1: Glou . . . 2F **5** (1G **25**)
Stanton Rd. GL5: Cash G 2H **41**
GL20: Tewk 3C **6**
Stantons Dr. GL51: Swin V 6A **8**
Stanton Way GL51: Chelt 1B **20**
Stanway Rd. GL4: Glou. 4D **26**
GL51: Chelt. 1A **20**
Stanwick Cres. GL51: Chelt. 2E **11**
Stanwick Dr. GL51: Chelt 2E **11**
Stanwick Gdns. GL51: Chelt 3E **11**
Star Ct. GL52: Chelt 5A **12**
Star Hill GL6: For G. 1B **50**
Star La. GL8: Aven 6H **51**
Starling Ct. GL10: Stone. 2C **40**
Station App. GL1: Glou . . . 3H **5** (1A **26**)
Station Cl. GL3: Chu 4C **18**
GL53: Chelt. 4G **21**
Station La. GL20: Tewk. 3C **6**
Station Rd. GL1: Glou 3H **5** (1H **25**)
GL3: Chu 3B **18**
GL5: Stro. 3C **42**
GL5: Woodc 3B **46**
GL6: Nails 2C **50**
GL10: Stone 3A **40**
GL20: Tewk. 4C **6**
GL52: Bish C 1E **9**
Station St. GL20: Tewk 4C **6**
GL50: Chelt. 2A **4** (5F **11**)
Station Vw. GL10: Stone. 2A **40**
Staunton Cl. GL4: A'md. 1F **35**
Staverton Technology Pk.
GL51: Stav 1D **18**
Steadings Bus. Cen., The
GL2: Maise 1D **14**
Steeple Cl. GL4: Barn 3E **27**
Stella Way GL52: Bish C. 1C **8**
Stephenson Dr. GL2: Qued 1E **39**
Stepping Stone La. GL6: Pains. . . 6G **37**
Step's La. GL8: Aven 5G **51**
Stepstairs Ct. GL7: Ciren. 2E **55**
Stepstairs La. GL7: Ciren 2E **55**
Sterling Ct. GL51: Chelt 5E **11**
Stevans Cl. GL2: Longf. 4B **16**
Stevens Way GL6: Hors 5A **50**
Steward Rd. GL20: North 2H **7**
Stewarts Mill La. GL4: A'md. 1F **35**
Sticky La. GL2: Hardw 1B **38**
Stirling Way GL4: Tuff. 3E **33**
Stirrup, The GL5: Cash G 3G **41**
Stirrup Cl. GL2: Glou. 5E **25**
Stockdale Cl. GL2: Hardw. 5A **32**
Stocken Cl. GL3: Hucc 5A **28**
Stockley Way GL4: Pains, Up L. . . 6E **35**
Stockton Cl. GL53: Charl K 5A **22**
Stockwell La. GL52: Woodm 2H **9**
Stoke Pk. Cl. GL52: Bish C. 1D **8**
Stoke Pk. Ct. GL52: Bish C. 1D **8**
Stoke Rd. GL52: Bish C, Stok O . . . 1A **8**
Stokes Ct. *GL20: Tewk 4B 6*
(off Trinity Wlk.)
Stonebrack Piece GL4: A'md. 5F **27**
Stonechat Av. GL4: A'dle. 6D **26**
Stone Cl. GL4: Barn. 4F **27**
Stonecote Ridge GL6: Buss 6C **44**
Stone Cres. GL51: Chelt 5C **10**
Stonecroft Cl. GL52: Bish C 1D **8**
Stonedale Rd. GL10: Stone 2A **40**
Stonehenge Rd. GL4: Glou 4C **26**
STONEHOUSE **3C 40**
Stonehouse Commercial Cen.
GL10: Stone 3A **40**
Stonehouse Station (Rail) **3C 40**
Stoneleigh Cl. GL53: Chelt. 6G **21**
Stone Mnr. Ct. GL5: Stro. 3F **43**
Stoneville St. GL51: Chelt. 5F **11**
Stoney Bri. GL4: A'md. 5F **27**
Stoney Fld. GL2: High. 4B **14**
Stony Riding GL6: Chalf H. 2E **49**
Storrington Pl. GL10: Stone 3C **40**
Storrington Rd. GL10: Stone. 3C **40**
Stow Cl. GL4: Glou 6A **26**
Stow Ct. GL51: Chelt. 6D **10**
Stowell M. GL4: Barn 4E **27**
Stow Rd. GL7: Ciren 1G **53**
Strachans Cl. GL5: Stro 3B **42**
Strand, The GL1: Glou 1B **26**
GL50: Chelt 4C **4** (6H **11**)
Strand Ct. GL53: Chelt 4C **4**
Stratford Cl. GL2: Glou 1F **33**
Stratford Leisure Cen. 2C 42

A-Z Cheltenham & Gloucester 73

Stratford Pk. Swimming Pool . . . 2B 42
Stratford Rd. GL5: Stro 2A 42
STRATTON 4C 52
Stratton Brook GL7: Strat 3B 52
Stratton Cnr. GL1: Glou 3A 26
(off Barton St.)
Stratton Ct. GL20: Tewk 3C 6
Stratton Hgts. GL7: Strat. 3C 52
Stratton Laurels GL7: Strat 4C 52
Stratton Mill GL7: Strat. 4D 52
Stratton Rd. GL1: Glou 3A 26
Streamside GL2: Qued 3D 32
GL5: Stro 3D 42
GL52: Bish C 1E 9
Street, The GL5: Kings 1B 46
GL6: Hors 5A 50
GL10: Leo S 6B 40
Strickland Rd. GL52: Chelt 1A 22
Stringer's Cl. GL5: Rodb. 5B 42
Stringer's Dr. GL5: Rodb. 5B 42
STROUD 3D 42
Stroud Enterprise Cen.
GL5: Sels. 6A 42
STROUD GENERAL HOSPITAL . 4E 43
STROUD HILL 3E 43
Stroud Rd. GL1: Glou, Tuff . . . 3G 25
GL4: Brook, Tuff, Whad. . . 5A 34
GL6: Bis. 1F 45
GL6: Inch, Nails. 6B 46
GL6: Pains 6G 37
GL7: Ciren 2A 54
STROUD MATERNITY HOSPITAL
. . . . 4E 43
Stroud Station (Rail) 3C 42
Stroud Subscription Rooms . . . 3D 42
Stroudwater Bus. Pk.
GL10: Stone 2A 40
Stuart Ct. GL6: Minch 6H 47
Studland Dr. GL52: P'bury 3D 12
Stump La. GL3: Hucc 3A 28
Sturmyes Rd. GL6: Fran L . . . 1F 49
Sudbrook Trad. Est.
GL2: Glou 6E 5 (3G 25)
Sudbrook Way GL4: Glou 6C 26
Sudeley Castle 6D 56
Sudeley Rd. GL54: Winch 5C 56
Sudgrove Pk. GL4: A'md 6F 27
Sudmeadow Rd. GL2: Glou 2E 25
SUE RYDER CARE CENTRE . . . 6F 21
Suffolk Ho. GL50: Chelt . . . 6A 4 (1F 21)
Suffolk Pde.
GL50: Chelt 6A 4 (1G 21)
Suffolk Pl. GL50: Chelt 1F 21
Suffolk Rd. GL50: Chelt . . . 6A 4 (1F 21)
Suffolk Sq. GL50: Chelt . . . 6A 4 (1F 21)
Suffolk St. GL50: Chelt 2G 21
Sugley La. GL6: Hors 4A 50
Sulgrave Cl. GL4: Tuff 4F 33
Summer Cl. GL5: Stro 3F 43
Summer Cres. GL5: Stro 3F 43
Summerland Dr. GL3: Chu 4B 18
Summer Mdw. GL4: Mats. 1C 34
Summersfield Cl. GL6: Minch . . . 6A 48
GL51: Chelt 2C 10
Summersfield Rd.
GL6: Minch 5A 48
Summers Rd. GL54: Winch . . . 4B 56
Summer St. GL5: Stro 3E 43
Sunderland Cl. GL3: Chu 4B 18
Sunground, The GL8: Aven. . . . 5G 51
Sunningend Works
GL51: Chelt 6D 10
Sunnycroft Cl. GL52: Bish C . . . 3F 9
Sunnycroft M. GL5: Stro 6H 25
Sunnyfield La. GL51: Up H . . . 4H 19
Sunnyfield Rd. GL2: Hardw . . . 4A 32
Sunnyhill GL5: Cash G 2G 41
(not continuous)
Sunset La. GL52: South 5H 9
Sun St. GL20: Tewk. 3B 6
GL51: Chelt 4F 11
Surrey Av. GL51: Chelt 5C 10
Surrey M. GL51: Chelt. 5C 10
Sussex Av. GL51: Chelt 5D 10
Sussex Gdns. GL3: Hucc 4A 28
Sutton Gdns. GL5: Stro 3E 43
Swallow Cres. GL3: Inns 2E 17
Swallowtail Cl. GL51: Chelt . . . 5A 10
Swan Ct. GL1: Glou 2F 5 (1G 25)
Swan La. GL5: Stro. 3D 42
Swan Rd. GL1: Glou . . . 1H 5 (6A 16)
Swanscombe Pl.
GL51: Up H 4B 20

Swanswell Dr. GL51: Chelt 1B 20
Swan Yd. GL7: Ciren. 6D 52
(off West Mkt. Pl.)
Sweetbriar Cl. GL52: Bish C 1D 8
Sweetbriar Ho. GL52: Chu 5B 18
Sweetbriar St.
GL1: Glou 1H 5 (6H 15)
SWELLSHILL 3F 47
Swells Hill GL5: Brim 3F 47
Swift Rd. GL4: A'dle 6E 27
Swifts Hill Vw. GL5: Stro. 1F 43
Swilgate Rd. GL20: Tewk. 4B 6
SWINDON 1D 10
Swindon Cl. GL51: Chelt 4F 11
Swindon La. GL50: Chelt. 1E 11
GL51: Swin V 1E 11
Swindon Mnr. GL51: Swin V . . . 1D 10
Swindon Rd.
GL7: Ciren, Preston 1E 55
GL50: Chelt 1A 4 (5G 11)
GL51: Chelt 2E 11
Swindon St. GL51: Chelt 5F 11
(not continuous)
Swordfish Cl. GL3: Chu. 4B 18
Sybil Rd. GL1: Glou 5A 26
Sycamore Cl. GL1: Glou 6G 25
Sycamore Ct. GL51: Chelt. 5A 10
Sycamore Cres. GL52: Woodm . 1G 9
Sycamore Dr. GL5: Stro 2E 43
Sycamore Rd. GL20: North. . . . 2H 7
Sydenham Rd. Nth.
GL52: Chelt 6A 12
Sydenham Rd. Sth.
GL52: Chelt 1A 22
Sydenham Ter. GL1: Glou. 4H 25
Sydenham Vs. Rd.
GL52: Chelt 1A 22
Sydney GL10: Stone 1B 40
Syon Rd. GL6: Minch 6A 48

T

Tabernacle Wlk. GL5: Rodb . . . 6B 42
Tabrams Pitch GL6: Nails 2D 50
Taena Pottery 3A 36
Tainmor Cl. GL2: Longl 4F 17
Talbot M. GL1: Glou 5G 25
Talbot Rd. GL51: Chelt 1D 20
Tall Elms Cl. GL3: Chu 4A 18
Tallis Rd. GL3: Chu 1G 17
Tamarisk Cl. GL51: Up H 5D 20
Tamarisk M. GL2: Qued 4B 32
(off Curtis Haywood Dr.)
Tamar Rd. GL3: Brock. 6E 29
GL52: Chelt 5B 12
Tandey Wlk. GL3: Inns 3F 17
Tanglewood Way GL6: Buss . . . 6C 44
Tanners Cl. GL3: Brock. 5D 28
Tanners Ct. GL51: Chelt 4C 10
Tanner's Piece GL6: Nails. 3D 50
Tanner's Rd. GL51: Chelt 4C 10
Tannery Cl. GL10: Leo S 6B 40
Tansy Cl. GL4: A'md 6G 27
Target Cl. GL5: Stro 3G 43
Tarlings Yd. GL52: Bish C 1E 9
Tarlton Cl. GL4: A'md 1F 35
Tarrington Rd. GL1: Glou 4A 26
Tatchley La. GL52: P'bury 3C 12
Taurus Cl. GL2: Longf 4B 16
Tawny Cl. GL20: North 1G 7
Tayberry Gro. GL51: Up H. . . . 5C 20
Taylors End GL50: Chelt 3E 21
Taylors Ground GL2: Qued . . . 3C 32
Teal Cl. GL2: Qued 4A 32
Teasel Cl. GL2: Longf 4A 16
Tebbit M. GL52: Chelt . . . 2C 4 (5H 11)
Teddington Gdns.
GL4: Glou 5C 26
Ted Preston Cl. GL20: Tewk . . . 6C 6
Telford Ho. GL51: Chelt. 4C 10
Telford Way GL2: Qued 1C 38
Telstar Rd. GL51: Chelt 6A 10
Teme Rd. GL51: Chelt 5B 12
Temple Cl. GL4: Barn 3F 27
Tennyson Av. GL2: Glou. 1F 33
Tennyson Rd. GL51: Chelt 6B 10
Tensing Rd. GL53: Chelt. 5H 21
Terhill GL52: Chelt 5A 12
Tern Cl. GL4: A'dle 5B 12
Terrace, The GL10: Hares. 6D 38
Terry Ruck Cl. GL51: Chelt 6A 10
Tetbury Hill GL8: Aven 6G 51
Tetbury La. GL6: Nails 3D 50

Tetbury Rd. GL4: Tuff 4H 33
GL7: Ciren. 3A 54
(not continuous)
Tetbury St. GL6: Minch. 6H 47
TEWKESBURY 4B 6
Tewkesbury Abbey 5B 6
Tewkesbury Abbey Cvn. Club Site
GL20: Tewk. 5B 6
Tewkesbury Bus. Pk.
GL20: Tewk 2F 7
Tewkesbury Cen. GL20: Tewk. . . 3D 6
TEWKESBURY HOSPITAL 4C 6
Tewkesbury Ind. Est.
GL20: Tewk 3E 7
Tewkesbury Rd.
GL2: Longf, Twig. 5A 16
GL20: Tewk 1E 7
GL51: Chelt, Uck 1A 10
Tewkesbury Sports Cen. 4F 7
Tewkesbury Town Mus. 4B 6
Thames Rd. GL52: Chelt. 5B 12
Thatcham Rd. GL4: Wal C . . . 6H 7
Thatcher's End GL52: Woodm . 2G 9
THEESCOMBE 6C 46
Theescombe Hill GL5: Amb . . . 6C 46
Theocs Cl. GL20: Tewk 6B 6
Theresa St. GL1: Glou 4G 25
(not continuous)
Thessaly Rd. GL7: Strat 3C 52
Theyer Cl. GL3: Brock. 6D 28
Thirlestaine Ho. Cotts.
GL53: Chelt 2G 21
Thirlestaine Rd. GL53: Chelt . . 2G 21
Thirlmere Rd. GL51: Chelt 2B 20
Thistlebank GL2: Longl 4C 16
Thistledown Cl. GL51: Chelt . . . 3A 10
Thistledowns GL20: North 1H 7
Thomas Moore Cl. GL3: Chu . . 1H 17
Thomas Stock Gdns.
GL4: A'md 5F 27
Thomas St. GL1: Glou. 3A 26
GL7: Ciren. 6D 52
Thomond Cl. GL50: Chelt 2F 11
Thompson Dr. GL53: Leck 5G 21
Thompson Rd. GL5: Stro. 2E 43
Thompson Way GL3: Inns 3E 17
Thoresby GL52: Chelt 2H 11
Thoresby Av. GL4: Tuff 4F 33
Thornbury Cl. GL51: Chelt. 5E 11
Thorncliffe GL51: Chelt 1E 21
Thorncliffe Dr. GL51: Chelt 1E 21
Thornhaugh M. GL51: Up H . . . 4B 20
Thornhill Cl. GL1: Glou 6F 25
Threadneedle St. GL5: Stro . . . 3D 42
Three Cocks La.
GL1: Glou 2F 5 (1G 25)
Three Groves Wood Nature Reserve
. . . . 1G 49
Three Sisters La.
GL52: P'bury 4E 13
THRUPP. 5F 43
Thrupp La. GL5: Thru 5F 43
Thrush Cl. GL4: A'dle 5D 26
Tibberton Gro. GL51: Chelt. . . . 2G 19
Tibbiwell Gdns. GL6: Pains . . . 5H 37
Tibbiwell La. GL6: Pains 5H 37
Ticklestone La. GL6: Pains. . . . 6H 37
Tidswell Cl. GL2: Qued 5C 32
Tilney Rd. GL50: Chelt 3G 11
Timbercombe La.
GL53: Charl K 6C 22
Timbercombe M.
GL53: Charl K 5C 22
Timmis Cl. GL4: Mats 1D 34
Timperley Way GL51: Up H . . . 4B 20
Tinglesfield GL7: Strat 3C 52
Tintern Rd. GL4: Tuff 2G 33
Tirle Bank Way GL20: Tewk . . . 4E 7
Tirley Cl. GL2: Qued 4B 32
Tiverton Cl. GL51: Chelt 4A 10
TIVOLI 2E 21
Tivoli Cir. GL50: Chelt 2F 21
Tivoli La. GL50: Chelt 2F 21
Tivoli M. GL50: Chelt 2F 21
Tivoli Rd. GL50: Chelt 2F 21
Tivoli St. GL50: Chelt 2F 21
Tivoli Wlk. GL50: Chelt 1E 21
TOADSMOOR 6B 44
Toadsmoor Rd. GL5: Brim 3A 48
Tobacco Cl. GL54: Winch 6A 56
Tobacconist Rd. GL6: Minch. . . 6H 47
Tobyfield Cl. GL52: Bish C 2F 9
Tobyfield La. GL52: Bish C 2E 9

Tobyfield Rd. GL52: Bish C 1F 9
Tolsey Gdns. GL2: Glou. 2E 33
GL4: Tuff 2E 33
Tommy Taylor's La.
GL50: Chelt 3G 11
Tom Price Cl.
GL52: Chelt 3D 4 (6H 11)
Tone Dr. GL3: Brock 6E 29
Tooke Rd. GL6: Minch. 5F 47
Tourist Info. Cen.
Cheltenham. 3A 4 (6G 11)
Cirencester 6D 52
Gloucester 4G 5 (2H 25)
Stroud 3D 42
Tewkesbury 4B 6
Winchcombe 5C 56
Tower Cl. GL4: Barn 3E 27
Tower Ho. GL52: Chelt. . . 1D 4 (5H 11)
Tower St. GL7: Ciren 1E 55
TOWNSEND 1G 41
Townsend St. GL51: Chelt 4F 11
Tracey Row GL20: Tewk 3C 6
(off Jeynes Row)
Trafalgar Dr. GL3: Chu 1G 17
Trafalgar Rd. GL7: Ciren. 5D 52
Trafalgar St.
GL50: Chelt 5A 4 (1G 21)
Trajan Cl. GL4: A'md. 5G 27
Transport Mus. 3F 5 (1G 25)
TREDWORTH 4B 26
Tredworth Rd. GL1: Glou 4H 25
GL4: Glou 5B 26
Treelands Cl. GL53: Chelt. 4G 21
Treelands Dr. GL53: Chelt. 4G 21
Trelawn Ct. GL50: Chelt 4B 4
Trenchard Gdns. GL7: Sth C . . 6H 55
Trent Rd. GL3: Brock. 6E 29
Tresmere GL52: Chelt 5A 12
Tretawn Gdns. GL20: Tewk . . . 4E 7
Trevor Rd. GL3: Hucc 5G 27
Triangle, The GL7: Longl 6D 16
Tribune Pl. GL4: A'md 5F 27
Trier Way GL1: Glou 6F 5 (3G 25)
Trinity Dr. GL6: Minch. 6A 48
Trinity La. GL52: Chelt . . . 2C 4 (5H 11)
Trinity Rd. GL4: A'md 5G 27
GL5: Stro 4E 43
GL7: Ciren. 2D 54
Trinity School La.
GL52: Chelt 2D 4 (5H 11)
Trinity M. GL20: Tewk 4B 6
Trinity Wlk. GL20: Tewk 4B 6
Triscombe Way GL51: Chelt . . . 4A 10
Troughton Pl. GL20: Tewk. . . . 4D 6
Trowscoed Av. GL53: Chelt. . . . 3G 21
Trubshaw Ct. GL3: Chu 4B 18
Tryes Rd. GL50: Chelt 3F 21
Trygrove GL4: A'md. 5E 27
Tuckwell Theatre, The 1D 20
Tudor Cl. GL3: Chu 2G 17
Tudor Ct. GL1: Glou. 6B 16
GL10: Leo S 6B 40
Tudor Lodge GL50: Chelt 3F 21
Tudor Lodge M. GL50: Chelt . . . 2F 21
Tudor Lodge Rd. GL50: Chelt . . 3F 21
Tudor Pl. GL20: Tewk 6C 6
Tudor Rd. GL7: Ciren. 6F 53
Tudor St. GL1: Glou 5F 25
TUFFLEY 3H 33
Tuffley Av. GL1: Glou. 5F 25
Tuffley Cres. GL1: Glou 6F 25
Tuffley La. GL4: Tuff 3E 33
Tuffley Pk. GL4: Tuff 1E 33
Tuffley Trad. Est. GL2: Glou . . . 1E 33
Tug Wilson Cl. GL20: North . . . 1H 7
Tulworths, The GL2: Longl 4C 16
Tunacre GL2: High. 3A 14
Turkdean Rd. GL51: Chelt. 1B 20
Turners Cl. GL2: High 5A 14
Turner's Ct. GL20: Tewk 4B 6
(off St Mary's La.)
Turnstone Dr. GL2: Qued. 4A 32
Tweenbrook Av. GL1: Glou . . . 5H 25
Twenties, The GL7: Sidd 5F 55
TWIGWORTH 1C 16
Twixtbears GL20: Tewk. 3B 6
Two Hedges Rd. GL52: Bish C . 2E 9
Twyver Bank GL4: Up L 2G 35
Twyver Cl. GL4: Up L 2G 35
Tylea Cl. GL51: Chelt 2H 19
Tyler Cl. GL51: Chelt. 5B 10
Tylers Way GL6: Chalf H 1E 49
Tyndale Cl. GL3: Hucc 3H 27
Tynings, The GL6: Minch 5A 48

Tynings Ct. GL3: Chu 4C 18
Tynings Rd. GL6: For G 2B 50
Tythe Ct. GL54: Winch 4B 56
Tythe Ter. GL54: Winch 4B 56

U

UCKINGTON 1A 10
ULLENWOOD 4E 31
Ullenwood Ct. Bus. Pk.
  GL53: Ull 4E 31
Ullenwood Rd. GL4: Glou 4E 27
  (not continuous)
Ullswater Rd. GL51: Chelt 2B 20
Undercliff Av. GL53: Chelt 6G 21
Undercliff Rd. GL53: Chelt 6G 21
Underhill Rd. GL4: Mats. 1D 34
Union Pl. GL20: Tewk 4C 6
Union St. GL1: Glou. 1H 5 (6A 16)
  GL5: Stro 3D 42
  GL52: Chelt 2D 4 (5H 11)
University of Gloucestershire
  FCH Campus 4G 11
  Hardwick Campus 4F 11
  Park Campus 2E 21
Unwin Cl. GL51: Chelt. 2H 19
Unwin Rd. GL51: Chelt 2H 19
UP END 5C 22
UP HATHERLEY. 4B 20
Up Hatherley Way GL51: Up H . . 3A 20
Uphill Pl. GL1: Glou 6G 25
UPLANDS 2E 43
Uplands Rd. GL5: Stro 2D 42
Uplands Vw. Ter. GL5: Stro. 3E 43
UPPER BARTON END 6C 50
Up. Bath St. GL50: Chelt. 2G 21
Up. Church Rd. GL5: Cain. 3H 41
Up. Churchside GL7: Ciren 1F 55
Up. Dorrington Ter. GL5: Stro . . 4E 43
Upperfield Rd. GL51: Chelt. 2D 10
Upper Grn. La. GL10: Hares 6E 39
Up. Hayes Rd. GL6: For G 1C 50
UPPER HYDE 5C 48
Upper Leazes GL5: Stro 3E 43
Up. Lynch Rd. GL6: Fran L 1F 49
Up. Mill La. GL52: P'bury 2E 13
Up. Mills Ind. Est.
  GL10: Stone 4C 40
Up. Norwood St. GL53: Chelt . . . 3F 21
Up. Pk. Rd. GL6: Nails 3D 50
Upper Pk. St. GL50: Chelt 1A 22
Up. Quay St. GL1: Glou . . . 3F 5 (1G 25)
Up. Queens Rd. GL10: Stone . . . 3C 40
UPPER SIDDINGTON 5E 55
Up. Springfield Rd. GL5: Stro . . 2D 42
Upper Tynings GL6: For G 2B 50
Upper Tynings, The
  GL5: Cash G 2G 41
Up. Washwell GL6: Pains 4H 37
Upton Cl. GL4: Barn. 4F 27
Upton Hill GL4: Up L 5E 35
Upton La. GL4: A'md, Up L 6G 27
  GL4: Brook 6C 34
UPTON ST LEONARDS 3G 35
Upton St. GL1: Glou 3A 26
Usk Way GL3: Brock 6E 29

V

Vaisey Rd. GL7: Strat 2C 52
Valerian Cl. GL4: A'md 4F 27
Vale Rd. GL7: Strat 3C 52
Valiant Way GL3: Brock, Hucc . . 5B 28
Valley, The GL6: Chalf. 2F 49
Valley Cl. GL6: Brim 3A 48
VALLEY CORNER 2F 49
Valley Cotts. GL4: Up L 4H 35
Valley La. GL4: Up L 4H 35
Valley Vw. Rd. GL5: Stro 4F 43
Van Der Breen St. GL6: Bis 1G 45
Varley Av. GL3: Hucc 5A 28
VATCH, THE 1H 43
Vatch La. GL6: Buss 6B 44
Vatch Vw. GL5: Stro 1F 43
Vauxhall Rd. GL1: Glou 3A 26
Vauxhall Ter. GL1: Glou 3A 26
Velhurst Dr. GL6: Brown 1C 48
Vensfield Rd. GL2: Qued 3B 32
Venture Bus. Cen. GL1: Glou . . . 3G 25
Verbena Cl. GL4: A'md 4F 27
Vernal Cl. GL4: A'md 6G 27
Verney Cl. GL53: Chelt 3H 21

Verney Rd. GL10: Stone 3C 40
Verneys, The GL53: Chelt 3H 21
Vernon Ct. GL53: Chelt 4C 4
Vernon Pl. GL53: Chelt . . 4C 4 (6H 11)
Vertican Rd. GL3: Inns 3E 17
Vervain Cl. GL3: Chu 2H 17
Vestry Gdns. GL4: Glou 4D 26
Vetch Cl. GL4: Glou. 1B 34
Viburnum Cl. GL50: Chelt 3E 21
Viburnum Vw. GL4: A'md 6G 27
Vicarage Cl. GL3: Chu 5B 18
  GL51: Shurd 1B 30
Vicarage Ct. GL3: Brock 6D 28
Vicarage La. GL3: Brock 6D 28
Vicarage Rd. GL1: Glou 4B 26
Vicarage St. GL6: Pains 5H 37
Viceroy Cnr. GL50: Chelt. 5F 11
Victoria Cl. GL2: Longf 3A 16
Victoria Pl. GL52: Chelt 6A 12
Victoria Retreat GL50: Chelt. . . 2G 21
Victoria Rd. GL2: Longf 3A 16
  GL5: Brim 3G 47
  GL7: Ciren 1E 55
Victoria St. GL1: Glou 3A 26
  GL6: Pains 5H 37
  GL50: Chelt. 4G 11
Victoria Ter. GL52: Chelt 6A 12
Victory Cl. GL3: Chu 1H 17
Victory Rd. GL1: Glou 4A 26
Village Farm GL7: Preston 3H 55
Village M. GL51: Chelt 3C 10
Village Rd. GL51: Chelt 4C 10
Vilverie Mead GL52: Bish C 1C 8
Vincent Av. GL4: Tuff 4F 33
Vine Ct. GL50: Chelt 4F 11
Vine Ter. GL1: Glou. 6A 16
Vine Way GL20: Tewk 6G 7
Vineyard Cl. GL1: Glou 4G 5
Vineyard La. GL51: Chelt 6E 11
VINEYARDS, THE 6D 10
Vineyards, The GL51: Chelt 6D 10
Vineyards Cl. GL53: Charl K 5C 22
Vineyard St. GL54: Winch. 5B 56
Vinings Warehouse GL1: Glou . . 4E 5
Virginia Cl. GL20: North 2H 7
Virginia Rd. GL20: North 2H 7
Vittoria Wlk.
  GL50: Chelt 5B 4 (1G 21)
Voxwell La. GL52: Bish C 2D 8
Voyce Cl. GL4: Tuff. 3G 33
Vulcan Way GL4: A'md 5G 27
Vyners Cl. GL7: Ciren 3D 54
Vyvian Ct. GL1: Glou 5G 5

W

Wade Cl. GL51: Chelt 2H 19
Wagtail Dr. GL20: North 1G 7
Wakeman Cl. GL20: Wal C 6D 6
Waldrist Cl. GL51: Chelt 2C 10
WALHAM 5G 15
WALHAM GREEN 4G 15
Walham La. GL2: Glou 5G 15
Walkley Hill GL5: Rodb 5B 42
Walkley Rd. GL20: Tewk 3C 6
WALKLEYWOOD 3B 50
Wallace Apartments
  GL52: Chelt 2D 4
Wallace Ho. GL51: Chelt. 3C 20
Wallbank Ho. GL1: Glou 6B 16
Wallbridge GL5: Stro 4C 42
  (not continuous)
Wallbridge Ind. Est. GL5: Stro . . 4C 42
WALLOW GREEN 4A 50
Walnut Cl. GL4: A'dle 2E 35
  GL52: Chelt 3H 11
Walter Preston Ct.
  GL5: Cash G 3H 41
WALTON CARDIFF 5D 6
Walton Cl. GL4: Up L 2F 35
  GL20: Tewk 3E 7
Walton Dr. GL20: Tewk 3E 7
Walton Gdns. GL20: Tewk. 4E 7
Walton Ho. GL51: Chelt 6B 10
Ward Av. GL3: Inns 3F 17
Ward Cl. GL52: Bish C 1F 9
WARDEN HILL 3C 20
Warden Hill Cl. GL51: Chelt 3C 20
Warden Hill Rd. GL51: Chelt . . . 3C 20
Warder's All. GL20: Tewk 4B 6
  (off Eagles All.)

Wards Rd. GL51: Chelt 3A 20
Warehouse, The
  (Climbing and Leisure Cen.)
  . . . . 4G 5 (2H 25)
Warren, The GL2: Qued 3D 32
Warren Cl. GL3: Chu. 2H 17
  GL51: Chelt 3C 20
Warren Rd. GL20: North. 2G 7
Warwick Av. GL4: Tuff 4F 33
Warwick Cl. GL5: Rodb. 6B 42
Warwick Cres. GL52: Charl K . . . 3C 22
Warwick Pl. GL20: Tewk 6C 6
  GL52: Chelt 2C 4 (5H 11)
WASHPOOL 5B 50
Wasley Rd. GL50: Chelt 6B 10
Waterdale Cl. GL2: Hardw 5A 32
Waterfield Cl. GL53: Chelt 2G 21
Waterford Cl. GL53: Chelt 3F 21
Water La. GL5: Brim 3F 47
  GL5: Sels, Woodc 6H 41
  GL52: Charl K 3C 22
Water La. Hill GL5: Brim. 4F 47
Waterloo, The GL7: Ciren. 6D 52
Waterloo Cl. GL53: Chelt 4E 11
Waterloo St. GL51: Chelt 4E 11
Watermans Ct. GL2: Qued 4A 32
Watermead La. GL3: Brock 1D 36
Water Mdw. GL2: Qued 4A 32
Watermint Dr. GL2: Qued 4D 32
WATERMOOR 2E 55
Watermoor Cl. GL51: Chelt. 3A 10
Watermoor Ho. GL7: Ciren 1E 55
Watermoor Rd. GL7: Ciren 1D 54
Watermoor Way GL7: Ciren. 2E 55
Watershoot Cl. GL52: P'bury . . . 2B 12
Waterside Cl. GL2: Qued 4A 32
  GL52: Charl K 4D 22
Waterside Works GL5: Brim 3G 47
Waters Reach GL2: Glou. 5E 25
Waterton Cl. GL3: Hucc 5A 28
Waterwells Bus. Pk.
  GL2: Quod 1D 38
Water Wells Dr. GL2: Qued. 1D 38
Water Wheel Cl. GL2: Qued 4A 32
Watery La. GL4: Up L 5G 35
WATLEDGE 1C 50
Watledge Bk. GL6: Nails 1C 50
Watledge Cl. GL20: Tewk 4C 6
Watledge Rd. GL5: Amb, Nails . . 6C 46
Watling Cl. GL6: Nails 6C 46
Watson Gro. GL4: A'md 6G 27
Watson Ho. GL52: Chelt 2D 4
Watts Cl. GL3: Hucc 4A 28
Waverley Rd. GL51: Chelt 1D 26
Wayridge, The GL4: A'dle 1E 35
Weald Cl. GL4: Mats. 6C 26
Weatherleigh Dr. GL2: High 4A 14
Weavers, The GL6: Chalf H. 1E 49
Weavers Cft. GL5: Stro 4E 43
WEAVERS CROFT (HOSPITAL) . 4E 43
Weavers Ho. GL5: Stro 3D 42
Weavers Rd. GL2: Qued 3C 32
  GL7: Ciren 1F 55
Webber Ho. GL20: Tewk 5A 6
Wedgwood Dr. GL2: Longl 5D 16
Weir Bri. Cl. GL4: Barn 3F 27
Welches Farm Camping &
  Caravanning Club Site
  GL5: Stand 1D 40
Welch Ho. GL51: Shurd 1A 30
  (off Atherton Cl.)
Welch Rd. GL51: Chelt 3B 10
Welland Cl. GL52: Chelt 3B 12
Welland Dr. GL52: Chelt 3B 12
Welland Lodge Rd.
  GL52: Chelt 3A 12
Welland Rd. GL2: Qued 3C 32
Wellbrook Rd. GL52: Bish C 1E 9
Well Cl. GL20: North 1H 7
Well Cross Rd. GL4: Glou. 1A 34
Well End GL5: Stro 1F 43
Weller Bungs. GL2: Glou. 1F 43
Wellesley Rd.
  GL50: Chelt 1B 4 (4G 11)
  (not continuous)
Wellesley St. GL1: Glou 5A 26
Wellfield Cl. GL20: Tewk 3E 7
Well Hill GL6: Minch 1H 51
Wellington Cl. GL20: Tewk 4H 5
Wellington Ho. GL7: Ciren 6E 53
Wellington La.
  GL52: Chelt 1C 4 (5H 11)
Wellington Pde. GL1: Glou 1A 26

Wellington Pl.
  GL52: Chelt. 4D 4 (6H 11)
Wellington Rd.
  GL52: Chelt 1C 4 (4H 11)
  GL50: Chelt 4B 4 (6G 11)
Wellington Sq. GL50: Chelt 4H 11
Wellington St.
  GL1: Glou 5H 5 (2H 25)
  GL50: Chelt 4B 4 (6G 11)
Well Pl. GL50: Chelt 6E 11
Wells Cl. GL51: Chelt 4C 20
Wellsprings Rd. GL52: Glou. . . . 6D 16
Wellsprings Rd. GL2: Longl 6D 16
Wells Rd. GL4: Glou 2D 26
Well Wlk. GL50: Chelt 2B 4 (5G 11)
Welveland La. GL4: Barn 2F 27
Welwyn M. GL51: Up H 4B 20
Wendover Gdns. GL50: Chelt . . . 6E 11
Wenlock Rd. GL20: Tewk 5C 6
Wentworth Cl. GL2: Longl. 4C 16
  GL51: Chelt 4A 10
Wentworth Rd. GL51: Chelt 4A 10
Wesley Cl. GL1: Glou 3A 26
  GL5: Stro 3D 42
Wesley Rd. GL10: Leo S 6B 40
Wessex Dr. GL52: Chelt 6C 12
Westal Grn. GL50: Chelt 1E 21
Westal Pk. GL51: Chelt 2E 21
West App. Dr. GL52: Chelt 3H 11
Westbourne Dr. GL2: Hardw . . . 6B 32
  GL52: Chelt 5A 12
Westbourne Ho. GL52: Chelt . . . 5A 12
Westbury Rd. GL4: Tuff 2G 33
  GL53: Chelt 4H 21
Westcote Rd. GL4: Tuff. 4H 33
Westdown Gdns. GL52: Chelt . . 6A 12
West Dr. GL50: Chelt 4H 11
WEST END 6F 51
West End GL6: Minch 6H 47
West End La. GL3: Hucc 5A 28
Westend Pde. GL1: Glou 6F 15
Westend Ter. GL1: Glou 6F 15
Western Cl. GL50: Chelt 4E 11
Western Ga. GL51: Chelt 4E 11
Western Rd. GL50: Chelt 4E 11
West Fld. GL2: High 4A 14
Westfield Av. GL3: Brock 5C 28
  GL20: North 2H 7
Westfield Rd. GL3: Brock 5C 28
Westfield Ter. GL2: Longf. 4H 15
Westgate Galleria, The
  GL1: Glou 1E 5 (6G 15)
Westgate Leisure Area . . 1E 5 (6G 15)
Westgate St. GL1: Glou . . 2E 5 (1G 25)
West Grange Cl. GL5: Stro 2C 42
Westland Rd. GL2: Hardw 6A 32
W. Lodge Dr. GL4: Glou 4E 27
West Mkt. Pl. GL7: Ciren 6D 52
Westmead Rd. GL2: Longl 4E 17
Westminster Cl. GL53: Chelt . . . 2A 22
Westminster Ct. GL2: Glou 5A 26
Weston Rd. GL1: Glou 6F 5 (3G 25)
Westover Cl. GL3: Chu 2A 18
West Quay GL1: Glou 5E 5 (2G 25)
WESTRIP 2F 41
Westrip Cl. GL5: Cash G 1G 41
Westrip La. GL5: Cash G 2G 41
Westrip Pl. GL5: Cash G 2G 41
West Tynings GL6: For G 2B 50
Westward Cl. GL5: Ebley 4G 41
Westward Rd. GL5: Cain, Ebley. . 4F 41
West Way GL7: Ciren 1D 54
Westwood La. GL2: P'bury 4E 13
Weyhouse Cl. GL5: Stro 5E 43
WHADDON
  GL4 . . . . 5H 33
  GL52 . . . . 5B 12
Whaddon Av. GL52: Chelt 5B 12
Whaddon Dr. GL52: Chelt 5A 12
Whaddon Road 4A 12
Whaddon Rd. GL52: Chelt. 5A 12
Whaddon Way GL4: Tuff 4G 33
Whardale Sq. GL51: Chelt 4C 10
Whardale Way GL2: Hardw 5A 32
  GL10: Stone 4B 40
Wheatland Dr. GL51: Chelt 3A 10
WHEATRIDGE 2D 34
Wheatridge, The GL4: A'dle 1D 34
Wheatridge Cl. GL4: A'dle 6E 27
Wheatridge E., The GL4: A'dle . . 1F 35
Wheatsheaf Cl. GL52: Bish C . . . 1C 8
Wheatstone Cl. GL20: North. . . . 1H 7
WHEATSTONE DAY HOSPICE . . 3F 27
Wheatstone Rd. GL1: Glou 4H 25
Wheatway GL4: A'dle. 2E 35

Wheelers Wlk. GL5: Stro 2A 42
Whimbrel Rd. GL2: Qued 4A 32
Whips La. GL6: Amb, Nails. . . . 1C 50
Whitcomb Cl. GL4: Up L 3F 35
Whitebeam Cl. GL2: Longl 4C 16
Whitecroft GL6: For G 2C 50
Whitecross Sq. GL53: Chelt . . . 2H 21
Whitefield Cl. GL10: Stone. . . . 4C 40
Whitefields Rd. GL52: Bish C. . . 1C 8
Whitehall GL5: Stro. 3E 43
Whitehart Ho. GL51: Chelt . . . 4F 11
Whitehart St. GL51: Chelt 4F 11
Whitehorse La. GL6: Pains. . . . 5H 37
Whitehouse Pk. GL5: Cain 3H 41
Whitehouse Way GL52: Woodm. . . 2G 9
Whitelands La. GL51: Shurd . . 3H 29
Whitelands Rd. GL7: Ciren . . . 6F 53
Whitemarsh Cl. GL51: Chelt. . . 3A 10
Whitethorn Dr. GL52: P'bury. . . 4C 12
WHITEWAY 5B 50
White Way GL7: Baun, Ciren. . . 1E 53
White Way, The GL7: Ciren . . . 5D 52
Whiteway Bank GL6: Hors 5B 50
Whiteway Ct. GL7: Ciren 5E 53
Whiteway Rd. GL4: Mats 6C 26
Whiteway Vw. GL7: Strat 4C 52
Whitewell Cl. GL4: Barn 4F 27
Whitfield St. GL1: Glou . . . 4H 5 (2H 25)
Whitfield's Tump Long Barrow
. . . . 4D 46
Whitmore Rd. GL54: Winch . . . 3B 56
Whittington Rd. GL51: Chelt. . . 1A 20
Whittle Av. GL4: Tuff. 3G 33
Whittle Cl. GL51: Chelt. 1H 19
Whitworth M. GL3: Hucc. 5B 28
Whitworth Rd. GL7: Ciren. . . . 2D 54
Whornes Orchard GL4: Up L . . . 2G 35
Wickridge Cl. GL5: Stro 2E 43
Wicliffe Ind. Cen. GL5: Stro . . . 4A 42
Widden St. GL1: Glou 2A 26
Wigeon La. GL20: Wal C 5D 6
WIGGOLD 1H 53
Wigmore Cl. GL4: A'md. 5F 27
Wildlife Wlk. GL3: Brock 1D 36
Wildwood Res. Cvn. Pk.
GL7: Sidd 3G 55
Wilkes' All. GL20: Tewk 4B 6
(off Hanover Ct.)
Wilkes Av. GL3: Hucc. 3H 27
Wilkinson Rd. GL7: Ciren 4D 54
Willersey Rd. GL51: Chelt . . . 1B 20
William Gough Cl.
GL51: Chelt 2A 10
Williams Orchard GL2: High. . . 4A 14
Willis Wlk. GL20: North 1H 7
Willow Av. GL4: Glou 4C 26
Willowbrook Dr. GL51: Chelt . . 3A 10
Willow Cl. GL52: Woodm. 2G 9
Willowcroft Cl. GL4: Mats. . . . 2E 35
Willow Dr. GL52: Woodm. 1G 9
Willowherb Cl. GL52: P'bury . . 4D 12
Willowleaze GL2: Glou 6E 17
Willow Pk. Dr. GL52: Bish C . . . 1E 9

Willow Rd. GL10: King S 6D 40
GL10: Stone 3B 40
GL53: Charl K 4D 22
Willows, The GL1: Glou 6A 16
GL2: Qued 4B 32
Willow Way GL4: Glou 4C 26
Wilson Rd. GL51: Shurd. 2A 30
Wilton Cl. GL1: Glou. 5G 25
Wilton Rd. GL1: Glou 5G 25
Wimberley Mills GL6: Brim . . . 3A 48
Wimborne Cl. GL51: Up H . . . 3B 20
Wincel Rd. GL54: Winch. 4C 56
WINCHCOMBE 5C 56
Winchcombe GL54: Winch . . . 5B 56
Winchcombe Abbey. 5B 56
(off Cowl La.)
WINCHCOMBE COMMUNITY HOSPITAL
. . . . 6A 56
Winchcombe Folk & Police Mus.
. . . . 5B 56
Winchcombe Pottery 2D 56
Winchcombe Railway Mus. . . . 5B 56
Winchcombe Rd. GL4: Tuff. . . 3H 33
Winchcombe St Peter's Church
. . . . 4B 56
Winchcombe Sports Hall 4B 56
Winchcombe Station (Rail). . . 2C 56
Winchcombe St.
GL52: Chelt 3C 4 (6H 11)
Winchester Ct. GL50: Chelt. . . 6E 11
Winchester Dr. GL4: Tuff 2H 33
Winchester Way GL51: Chelt . . 3C 20
Windermere Cl. GL51: Chelt. . . 2B 20
Windermere Rd. GL2: Longl. . . 5D 16
GL51: Chelt 2B 20
Windfall Way GL2: Glou 1D 26
Windmill Fld. GL4: A'md. 4E 27
Windmill Pde. GL1: Glou 2B 26
Windmill Rd. GL5: Minch 5E 47
GL6: Minch 5E 47
Windrush Rd. GL4: Tuff 3G 33
(not continuous)
GL52: Chelt 5B 12
Windsor Dr. GL4: Tuff 3F 33
WINDSOREDGE 1A 50
Windsoredge La. GL6: For G . . . 6A 46
Windsor Pl. GL6: Bis 1C 42
Windsor St. GL52: Chelt 4A 12
Windsor Ter. GL7: Ciren 1F 55
(off Queen Elizabeth Rd.)
Windsor Wlk. GL7: Ciren 6B 52
Windyridge GL6: Bis 1F 45
Windyridge Gdns. GL50: Chelt . 2F 11
Windyridge Rd. GL50: Chelt . . 3E 11
WINFIELD CAPIO HOSPITAL . . 4H 15
Winniecroft Cotts. GL4: Mats . . 3E 35
Winnycroft La. GL4: Mats. . . . 5C 34
Winsley Rd. GL4: Mats. 1D 34
(not continuous)
Winslow Pl. GL3: Chu. 3A 18
Winstan Cl. GL51: Chelt 1A 20
Winstonian Rd. GL52: Chelt . . 5A 12
Winston Rd. GL3: Chu 4A 18
Winterbotham Rd. GL51: Chelt. . 4A 10

Winton Cl. GL51: Chelt 2C 20
Winton Rd. GL51: Chelt 2D 20
Wishford Cl. GL2: Longl 5F 17
Wisteria Ct. GL51: Up H 5D 20
Wisteria Way GL3: Chu 3H 17
Wistley Rd. GL53: Charl K 5C 22
WITCOMBE 1H 37
Witcombe Pl.
GL52: Chelt 4D 4 (6H 11)
Witcombe Reservoirs Nature Reserve
. . . . 2F 37
Withers, The GL52: Bish C . . . 1E 9
Withyfield Rd. GL52: Bish C . . . 1F 9
Withyholt Ct. GL53: Charl K . . . 4A 22
Withyholt Pk. GL53: Charl K . . . 4A 22
Withy M. GL4: Glou. 6C 26
Withypool GL51: Up H 4B 20
Witley Lodge Cl. GL51: Up H . . 3A 20
Woburn Av. GL4: Tuff. 4F 33
Woefuldane Bottom
GL6: Minch 6A 48
Wolseley Rd. GL2: Glou 1D 26
Wolseley Ter.
GL50: Chelt 4B 4 (1G 21)
Woodbine Cl. GL4: A'md. 6F 27
Woodbines Cvn.
Pk. GL51: Up H. 3A 20
Woodborough Cl. GL6: Pains . . 6H 37
WOODCHESTER 2B 46
Woodcock Cl. GL4: A'dle. 6D 26
GL10: Stone. 1C 40
Woodcock La. GL10: Stone. . . . 2C 40
Woodcote GL2: Longl 4C 16
Woodend Cl. GL4: Barn. 3F 27
Wood End La. GL6: Nails 2A 50
Woodford Ct. GL4: Glou 4C 26
Woodgate Cl. GL4: Barn 3F 27
GL52: Charl K 4D 22
Woodhouse Cl. GL7: Ciren . . . 2C 54
Woodhouse Dr. GL5: Rodb . . . 4C 42
Woodland Grn. GL4: Up L . . . 2F 35
Woodlands, The GL5: Stro . . . 2E 43
GL10: Leo S 6B 40
Woodlands Dr. GL5: Stro. . . . 2F 43
Woodlands Pk. Cvn. Pk.
GL50: Chelt 2G 11
Woodlands Pk. (Mobile Homes)
GL2: Qued 5A 32
Woodlands Rd. GL7: Ciren . . . 3C 54
GL51: Chelt 4E 21
Wood La. GL6: Nails 2D 50
Woodleigh Fld. GL2: High 3B 14
WOODMANCOTE 2H 9
Woodmancote Pk. Homes
GL52: Woodm. 1G 9
Woodmancote Va.
GL52: Woodm. 1G 9
Woodmans Way GL52: Bish C. . 2E 9
Woodmeade Cl. GL52: Charl K. . 3D 22
Wood M. GL2: Over 5D 14
Woodpecker Rd. GL2: Glou. . . 6F 25
Woodpecker Wlk. GL6: For G . . 1A 50
Woodrow Way GL2: Glou 2D 32
Woodruff Cl. GL4: Glou. 1C 34

Woodrush Rd. GL20: Wal C . . . 6D 6
Woods Ct. GL20: Tewk 4B 6
Woodside GL5: Stro 2G 43
Woods Orchard GL4: Tuff 3A 34
Woods Orchard Rd. GL4: Tuff. . 3H 33
Wood Stanway Dr.
. . . . 1D 8
Woodstock Cl. GL8: Aven 5F 51
Woodstock La. GL8: Aven 5F 51
Woodville Rd. GL20: Tewk 6G 7
Woolmarket, The GL7: Ciren. . . 6E 53
Woolstrop Ho. GL2: Qued 4C 32
Woolstrop Way GL2: Qued 2D 32
Worcester Pde.
GL1: Glou 1H 5 (6H 15)
Worcester St.
GL1: Glou 3H 5 (1H 25)
Wordens, The GL5: Cash G . . . 2G 41
Wordsworth Av. GL51: Chelt. . . 6B 10
WORLEY 2B 50
Worley Ridge GL6: Nails. 2B 50
Wormwood Hill GL6: Hors 5B 50
WOTTON 1B 26
Wotton Ct. GL4: Barn 2E 27
Wotton Elms Ct. GL2: Glou. . . 1C 26
Wotton Hill GL1: Glou. 1B 26
WOTTON LAWN HOSPITAL . . 1B 26
Wren Cl. GL4: A'dle. 5C 26
Wren Ter. GL3: Inns 3E 17
Wychbury Cl. GL53: Chelt. . . . 4G 21
Wye Rd. GL3: Brock 6E 29
Wymans Cl. GL50: Chelt 2F 11
Wymans Ct. GL50: Chelt 2F 11
Wyman's La. GL51: Swin V. . . . 2E 11
Wyman's Rd. GL52: Chelt. . . . 4B 12
Wynyards Cl. GL20: Tewk. . . . 4C 6

Y

Yalta Cl. GL51: Chelt. 5B 10
Yarlington Cl. GL52: Bish C . . . 1D 8
Yarnell's All. GL20: Tewk 4B 6
(off Barton La.)
Yarnolds GL51: Shurd. 2A 30
Yarnold Ter. GL51: Chelt. 3D 10
Yarrow Cl. GL4: Glou 1B 34
Yeend Cl. GL51: Chelt. 2C 10
Yeldham M. GL52: Chelt 3A 12
Yew Tree Cl. GL50: Chelt. . . . 2F 11
Yew Tree Way GL3: Chu 4G 17
GL5: Thru 1F 47
York Rd. GL4: Glou 3D 26
GL20: Tewk 6B 6
York Row GL52: P'bury. 3B 12
York St. GL52: Chelt 2D 4 (5H 11)
Youngs Orchard GL4: A'md. . . 5E 27
GL5: Brim 3A 48

Z

Zinnia Cl. GL3: Chu 2G 17
ZOONS COURT RDBT. 2H 27
Zoons Rd. GL3: Hucc 3H 27